CORPORATE BIGAMY

*How to Resolve the
Conflict between Career and Family*

CORPORATE BIGAMY

*How to Resolve the
Conflict between Career and Family*

by Mortimer R. Feinberg, Ph.D.
with Richard F. Dempewolff

WILLIAM MORROW AND COMPANY, INC.
New York   1980

Library of Congress Cataloging in Publication Data

Feinberg, Mortimer R
    Corporate bigamy.

    Bibliography: p.
    Includes index.
    1. Married people—Employment—United States—Case studies. I. Dempewolff, Richard F., 1914- joint author. II. Title.
HQ734.F37   301.42   79-26322
ISBN 0-688-03534-5

Book Design by Michael Mauceri

Printed in the United States of America

First Edition

1 2 3 4 5 6 7 8 9 10

To Gloria and Rita

Acknowledgments

The authors wish to express their thanks to the many people who provided much valuable data and advice that helped to make this book possible.

Special appreciation goes to Mr. J. C. Seabrook of Auckland, New Zealand, for his thought-provoking letter that provided the initial impetus for the research that resulted in the volume. We also are especially grateful to longtime friends and associates Joseph N. Bell of Corona del Mar, California, and Saul Pett of the Associated Press in New York, the former for the use of his interesting material on Alan Alda, the latter for permission to use his warm, insightful observations regarding President Jimmy Carter.

Thanks go as well to Ms. Joanna Bendheim for allowing us to use her excellent material on Westchester County (New York) tycoons; to Dr. Nelson Bradley, Medical Director of Gillian's Manor in Sidney, B.C., Canada, for permission to reprint his "workaholic" checklist; to Ms. Ruth Burger, Editorial Director of the Research Institute of America, and to Ms. G. G. Michelson, Vice-President for Labor Relations of the R. H. Macy Company of New York, for the time they gave to interviews and thoughtful observations regarding women executives; to Dr. Gene Gordon of Children's Hospital, National Medical Center, in Washington, D.C., for the use of his fascinating material on "maternal" instincts in male executives; to Barbara Keiser, director of the Monroe County Public Library in Stroudsburg, Pennsylvania, for her help in procuring from other libraries hard-to-find books needed by the authors; to Marylynn Machlowitz for the use of her astute observations on workaholism; to Jacqui Lee Schiff for use of her extensive work—cited in a paper on marriage problems by Denver psychologist Abe Wagner—on "discounting"; to Ms. Edie Stevens for providing useful information on outside activities for wives of executives.

Grateful thanks also are rendered to Gloria Feinberg and Rita Dempewolff, the authors' respective wives, Gloria for her many insightful observations during the progress of the book, and Rita for her informative interviews with woman executives that appear in these pages, as well as her patient help with the actual production of the manuscript. Thanks, too, to Howard Cady, Senior Editor of William Morrow & Company, and William Quigley, his able assistant, for their sound editorial advice and suggestions that served to improve the quality of the text.

The authors also wish to acknowledge the assistance of the following individuals who enriched the book by sharing their experience and knowledge with us; their patience with our questions, and willingness to share private events bearing on the relationship between job and family, provided a significant bridge between theory and reality:

Valentine Appel, Ph.D., Executive Vice-President SMRB, W. R. Simmons & Associates

Benjamin Balunsky, Ph.D., Professor Emeritus, Baruch College

Mr. George C. Barber, Chairman of the Board, Anchor Hocking Corp.

Mr. David Binder, Chairman of the Board, Huk-A-Poo Sportswear, Inc.

Mr. Charles R. Bronfman, President, The Seagram Co., Ltd.

Mr. William P. Cleaver, President, American Sugar Division, Amstar Corp.

Mr. Robert A. M. Coppenrath, President, Agfa-Gevaert Corp.

Mr. John F. Dealy, President, Fairchild Industries

Mr. James L. Dutt, Chairman of the Board and CEO, Beatrice Foods Co.

Mr. Donald P. Eckrich, President and COO, Beatrice Foods Co.

Ms. Gloria Feinberg, President, BFS Psychological Associates, Inc.

Mr. John W. Field, Jr., Chairman of the Board, Warnaco, Inc.

Mr. Howard Haas, President, Sealy, Inc.

Mr. Jerold C. Hoffberger, Chairman, Diversified Resource Management, Ltd.

Mr. Richard H. Hughes, Chairman of the Board, Florafax International, Inc.

Mr. Michael Kievman, Vice-President, Cox Broadcasting Co.

Mr. Scott C. Lea, President, Rexham Corp.

Governor George M. Leader, Former Governor of Pennsylvania and President, Commonwealth Industries, Inc.

Aaron Levenstein, J.D., Editor, *Interaction*, Professor at Baruch College

Mr. Monroe R. Meyerson, President, Central Rigging and Contracting Corp.

Mr. Robert O. Nagle, President, California & Hawaiian Sugar Co.

Mr. Ralph A. Powers, Jr., President, Robertson Paper Box Co., Inc.

Mr. Robert T. Quittmeyer, President, Amstar Corp.

Mr. Louis T. Rader, Chairman, Electric Engineering, University of Virginia

Mr. Wallace N. Rasmussen, Director and Chairman Executive Committee, Beatrice Foods Co.

Mr. Meshulam Riklis, Chairman of the Board, Rapid-American Corp.

Mr. Harvey E. Sampson, Jr., Chairman of the Board and President of The Harvey Group, Inc.

Dean Emanuel Saxe, Professor Emeritus, Baruch College

Mr. George T. Scharffenberger, Chairman and CEO, City Investing Co.

Mr. William A. Schwartz, President, Broadcast Division, Cox Broadcasting Corp.

Mr. Mahlon M. Scott, Vice-President, Morey LaRue Laundry Co.

Mr. Joel E. Smilow, President, International Playtex Corp.

Dean Paul M. Steinberg, Hebrew Union College

Dr. Alfred Steiner, Professor, Columbia University Medical School

Mr. John J. Tarrant, author and consultant

Mr. J. Ray Topper, President, Anchor Hocking Corp.

Mr. Thomas Turner, Falcon Jet Corp.

Mr. Edward G. Uhl, Chairman of the Board, Fairchild Industries

Mr. Gus G. Van Sant, President, Huk-A-Poo Sportswear, Inc.

Mr. Richard A. Voell, President and COO, The Penn Central Corporation

Mr. R. Lyman Wood, Corporate Group Vice-President, Lenox, Inc.

Contents

Introduction

☞ About a dozen years ago, I wrote an article for a national magazine in which I discussed the relentless drive and aggressive work habits of high achievement-oriented men striving for success in business or professions. I deplored the fact that, in too many cases, their families were sacrificed to the cause. I had an abundance of case history to back my contentions, along with suggestions for easing the strain on the home front.

In response I received a thoughtful letter from a young New Zealand businessman who said: "You could say I fall roughly into the category of the young businessmen depicted. Your suggestions are good and I'm keeping them for reference and reminders from time to time. I would be most interested, now, to see you balance off the other half of the problem.

"Why can't the young wives of young men with a drive to achieve more than others—and are prepared to undergo the rigors of business to do so—become effective members of the family team? Why can't they help to achieve mutual goals, providing the many things for a family that business can never provide?

"New experience can help women as well as men. Many women feel they have to compete with business rather than offset it in such a way that the family and business fall into their true and proper perspectives for both wife and husband. At thirty-four, in a top executive position for a company employing nearly 600 people, I am interested in both sides of this problem—not only for myself but also for others."

In a way, this book should be dedicated to that young businessman because he stimulated me to write, lecture, and gather material to "balance out the picture" as he had suggested.

The subject of high achievers, and leadership in industry, was not a new one to me even then. For the past quarter of a century, I have functioned as an industrial psychologist, advising corporations large and small. I have also served as an Assistant Dean and as a Professor of Psychology and Management at Baruch College of the City University of New York, the training ground for many captains of industry. During these years I have been collecting data and gathering my own thoughts on the problem of job and family.

As some wag once put it, industrial psychology is like sex among the elephants—it is practiced at very high levels amid much noise and confusion. The organization of which I am Chairman of the Board works with the problem of executive training and executive selection. So we are very familiar with the kind of mind that spells leadership, and the kind of dedication that leadership demands. I have also served as a principal lecturer for the American Management Association as well as the Young Presidents' Association, and am frequently called upon to expound on my ideas relative to leadership, management, the acquisition and use of power, as well as the potential hazard that all these factors bring to bear on the domestic front.

We've known for a long time, for instance, that the road to the top—whether in a corporation, a demanding profession, or other endeavor—calls for intensely concentrated effort; also that the challenge it presents attracts people with highly competitive personalities—and "tunnel vision," so that distracting elements such as marriage and family can be kept conveniently in second place and not interfere.

My New Zealand correspondent prompted the thought that this kind of one-way street might not be essential to big success in business; that through the application of compromise and understanding on all sides—including the corporation or organization itself—the "balance" suggested by my New Zealander may indeed be achieved.

What it boils down to, really, in transactional analysis terms, is behavior on an adult rather than a child level. The level of the child is sullen, hostile, angry—"Mine is bigger than yours!" The level of the adult is to listen, to try to relate, to synthesize and integrate experiences.

I have a homey little illustration that I like to use in some of my talks. If I come home tonight for a dinner party that we've been invited to, and I say to my wife, "Dear, where are my cuff links?" she may respond in one of two ways. She may say:

"If you were better organized you'd know where they are."

That might prompt a sharp reply from me: (Her parent is talking to my child and I react.) "Don't talk to me that way. I've had a rough day and don't need any smart cracks from you."

That would fire her up to something like: "Don't talk to me the way you talk to your mother."

And we're off to the races child to child—both schussing all the way down the hill to the bunny slope.

But suppose she had responded to my initial question with: "I knew it was likely to be a hard day, dear, so I polished your links and put them in your top drawer with a little note saying 'I love you.'"

That would really get to me, and I'd say, "Gee, honey, you're marvelous," and give her a warm kiss. She strokes me and I stroke her and we never get to the party. That's functioning as adult to adult.

In any case, this is a book on marriage and people; on corporate life, company life, professional life. The identical problems face administrators in industry, universities, and art colonies. The book applies to doctors, lawyers, authors, archaeologists, and explorers who have achieved the top level in their field—people who don't work at a nine-to-five clerical or other traditional job situation.

The reason for the catchy title is that the corporation in America is the kind of place that most typifies the problem of corporate bigamy. Corporate life is the laboratory in which the extremes among corporate bigamists are found. It is typically their number-one bailiwick. The kind of guy who aspires to become—or is—a top dog in his business or profession, along with his family, comprises the audience toward which this book is aimed. Hopefully, it will provide guidance in achieving a more balanced approach to life along the rugged road.

—*M. R. Feinberg, Ph.D.*

1

What Is *Corporate Bigamy?*

☞ A friend of mine lives in one of those exurban communities where everyone except the real estate agents, local tradesmen, and groundkeepers is a commuting corporate chairman, president, upwardly mobile VP, lawyer, doctor, or other successful career professional. He told me recently how he was heading from the bar with a fresh drink at a neighborhood soiree, when his route took him toward a couple he knew. As he stepped up, the lady was introducing her escort to a newcomer—as follows: ". . . and I'd like you to meet my husband—ahh, what's-his-name."

Whether a Freudian slip or deliberate dig at her company-oriented mate, the remark packs in a tidy nutshell the most poignant elements of this volume's main thrust. "What's-his-name" had to be one of the industrial or professional top brass that I have dubbed "corporate bigamists." The term was by no means invented in an attempt to be whimsical or cute; it is grimly appropriate.

The corporate bigamist is not (necessarily) an industrial pirate who moves in on two or three businesses, milks them white, and

17

goes on to the next without benefit of Title C; nor is he a "Re-markable Mr. Pennypacker" type, with separate businesses *and* families in Boston, Philadelphia, New York, and so on. He may be all those things—but only symptomatically. Our bigamist (he or she these days) usually is a top-echelon professional or business person who is married to both a job and—often incidentally—a human mate. And the corporate bigamist of most interest here is the one for whom the number-one mate in the company-home-stead harem is the job.

Obviously, the dichotomy between job and family spells stress. The corporate bigamist, at best, is devoted to one and dedicated to the other. At worst, he has completely abdicated the family role for the more (to him) stimulating and challenging excitement of the business battlefield—where he is the unquestioned "Field Marshal." At home when he makes demands or issues edicts he is apt to be told by his precocious teenagers where to head in. And mom usually is hardly afraid to talk back.

I can't imagine any father getting away with handling his wife or college-age daughter the way that a corporate chairman, whom I knew well, handled a young lady employee. The chief executive wanted a confidential file that was being used by a newly hired receptionist to type envelopes. He marched out to the reception room and demanded the list.

"I'm sorry," the young lady told him with a pleasant smile, "but I was ordered not to give this list to anyone, on pain of death."

"Well, you can give it to me," he snapped.

"I'm sorry, sir, but I can't give it to *anyone*."

"Do you know who I am?" he asked ominously.

"No, sir, I don't," replied the girl.

"Well," said our hero, "ask them when you pick up your final paycheck this afternoon."

For such an administrator, the business turf provides an arena where he can satisfy his ego, power, and authoritarianism. The domestic scene ranks a poor second.

Not all corporate bigamists are quite that top-heavy, of course, and we'll get to the types and the degrees of their affliction a little later. But, although drives, psychological needs, and modus operandi may differ from one to another, nearly all exhibit a compulsive dedication to the job first. The corporate bigamist doesn't have to be a chief executive, or dedicated professional wheel, for that matter. His affliction is a built-in frame of mind, discernible in climbers at lower levels as well. The picture of a typical junior corporate bigamist was summed up recently by his *domestic* wife, in a poignant essay in the *Pacific Citizen*, a West Coast Japanese-American newspaper.

"I have been married to a bigamist [her own term] for twenty-five years," she wrote. "We had only been married a year when he acquired his second wife. My emotions regarding this situation have ranged from jealousy to acquiescence. I have always known that she came first.

"It was proven this month when they observed their silver anniversary. I can remember ours which occurred last year. To begin with, he had the wrong date. He came home bearing a bunch of red roses, the least favorite of my flowers.

"I can't remember all the gifts we have exchanged during the span of years. But I do recall the watch I bought him for one anniversary. It was during our early years and I had carefully hoarded the money to buy it. He never did wear it much. I haven't seen it around for years so he probably gave it to some panhandler.

"He has a new watch now. She gave it to him together with a substantial check and other tokens. Later there was a cake and punch with more friends. Congratulatory letters and phone calls came from across the country.

"He came home that night with the watch. He showed me where it was engraved with his name and a crest and the date. . . . He has worn it every day since he has received it. It means a lot to him, much more than the watch I gave him. It should.

"My husband's other wife has been the company he works for. They just observed a milestone. He was welcomed into their Quarter Century Club. Even for a man who ordinarily dislikes ceremonies, asserting they are too pretentious, this day was one of importance.

"For one thing, neither of us seriously thought that he would reach this day. . . . In summarizing this period, he says, 'The first twenty-five years are on-the-job training, so the second quarter century should be easy.'

"I think our son makes the best observation of this marriage between a man and his company when he says, 'I hope I'll be as lucky in my life's work as dad has been.'"

Our mission here will be to deal with the problem of balancing this conflict of pressures that are growing more and more common to contemporary life. Most active, modern families are affected by them to some degree. The problem, exemplified by the cases cited, involves, simply, pressures of the job versus pressures from the demands imposed on working members of busy families by this dichotomy of inputs. And they are draining the vital forces that bind marriages together. Despite some apparently uncompromising factors reflected in today's "life-styles," as younger folk call their bad habits these days, I firmly believe that it is possible to develop what we refer to in psychological terms as a "homeostasis" or, in English, the concept that it is possible to balance these two forces so that families can retain their integrity and raise healthy, productive, and satisfied children. It is not going to be easy because, unfortunately, the pressures of business in America today can easily accumulate to create a time bomb at the family fireside. But what we can do is try to define the problems, outline the challenges, and explore avenues to meet and dominate them.

I want to emphasize that we are not just referring to men. Women now are becoming a vital part of this whole scene. Quite literally they are swarming into the job market. Today 42 million women hold 42 percent of the jobs in this country. One-fifth of the nation's salaried income is earned by women—60 percent of whom are married, and 40 percent of those have school-aged kids. While women so far account for only 2.3 percent of the executives earning $25,000 a year or more, they have more than doubled their ranks in that category since 1975. These women already are proving to be just as prone to corporate bigamy as men. They are having the same kind of problems that the "man of the family" has enjoyed (or endured) for some centuries. Many of them are finding themselves drained by their jobs, without sufficient energy or time to maintain the marital relationship. And, just to be "psychological" about it, that is often precisely what they want.

Problems at the home hearthside may be even more magnified when both parties to the marriage are highly motivated achievers in business or professions. The wife of a prominent physician I know became a practicing psychologist after the last of her four sons reached school age. She now spends more and more time flying around the country, lecturing and delivering papers at conventions. "When she returns," says her husband, "there is a backlog of messages and appointments . . . she isn't even home when she's here. I feel as though she merely squeezes us in."

So far, those two still are married because the husband is a remarkably self-sufficient and understanding fellow. In far more instances the route leads to violent altercation: "Where in hell have you been three nights this week? Who gives a damn about your promotions and responsibilities to the goddamn company; what about responsibilities to your family?" etc., etc. One or both begin to hit the bottle; the violence may get physical, and the final upshot is divorce.

So, it's easy to see that Cinderella doesn't live here anymore. As women continue to move into executive and professional careers—which they most assuredly will—the problem of corporate bigamy increasingly goes both ways. This must bring to bear on an already stress-ridden institution of holy matrimony, a pretty *un*holy deluge of additional strain. Can even "good" marriages stand up under it? No one can guarantee it, but it is my firm belief that, given these intelligent people who are gifted enough to organize vast empires, application of the same aptitudes to the domestic scene should have a highly positive effect.

To understand marriage today, one has to understand the nature of change. We are living in a world in which our minds are deluged with intolerable pressures due to volatile cultural changes, brought on by specific factors in modern life-style. I have a list of nine of those factors. Not ten. When I was a young psychologist, I used to run around lecturing on what amounted to "The Ten Commandments for Child-Rearing Practices." When I got married, I changed the title to "Ten *Guides* for Child-Rearing Practices." When my second son arrived on the scene, I decided not to lecture anywhere in the United States where my children could be observed. Everything I pontificate about now is limited to nine rather than ten items.

So, here are nine of the factors contributing to the dramatic changes of that life-style in our culture:

1. The trend to instant gratification. This factor is affecting marriages as well as the economy. People today are anxious to avoid what I call "sweating the smallies of life." Everything must be done conveniently in every area of life. You know, have it now, enjoy it now.

2. Avoidance of food that requires preparation. This involves a phenomenon that manifests itself in a craze for convenience foods—TV dinners and other inedible stuff. Mothers don't want to shop and peel and clean. They want to be like a mother whale that feeds her young once a week. The little belly swells and you shove the kid out the back door so that you can go out and fulfill yourself, swimming. It's 180 compass degrees from the phenomenon I remember. My mother was always scrubbing, shopping, and cleaning. Coupled with food-preparation avoidance is the need to avoid housework. My first memories are of paper on the floor on a Friday afternoon after she scrubbed the floor. In fact, I got my first job from an ad that I read on the floor where my mother had put the paper. She even put paper under the cuckoo clock. Women don't do that today. They're not sweating the smallies.

3. A deep-seated yearning to have fun and color in every phase of modern life. It is even supposed to be fun to blow your nose. You are supposed to have different-colored toilet paper to go with the decor of your bathroom, and built-in music boxes in the toilet paper roller. A best-selling item in a Philadelphia souvenir shop near Independence Square during the US Bicentennial was a toilet seat that played the "Star Spangled Banner" when you sat on it. However, people would be wise not to extend themselves or go into debt to get that kind of color or superficial knowledge in their life. This is a generation of eclectic *noshers,* a well-worn Jewish word for dilettantes. They want to sample wines but not know them in depth. At Baruch College, we offered a series of adult education courses. Those most often selected had to do with superficial subjects which could buy cheap entertainment for one evening—such as "Belly Dancing."

4. The need for pleasures of an entirely different sort. Today, as you know, the drug of choice of the aging generation is alcohol. The drug of choice of my son's generation is marijuana. If you *don't* know, then you are like Lady Godiva's husband who grabbed her and said, "Where have you been? The horse has been back for an hour and a half."

I asked my physician son the other day: "If my generation is hooked on alcohol and yours is on pot, what do you think my grandson will be on?" He replied, "I'll probably come home some night and find him hooked into the electrical circuitry getting weird stimulation through his rectum." Then he added, deadpan, "You ought to try it, Dad."

It's not all just nonsense, either. There are fifteen pleasure centers in the brain that can be stimulated electrically. I can just see people a few years from now, hooked into a printed circuit "breadboard" and punching "stimulus buttons" on a control console. The conversation at a neighborhood "stimulus tickle center" might go like this:

GIRL: How do you get so out?

BOY: It's a gas. Try it! Two and seven.

GIRL: Sexy?

BOY: You gotta believe it!

GIRL: I'm not allowed to punch my own buttons.

BOY: Oh, a virgin? Don't feel bad. Let me hook you up to my console. Try three, five, and six.

GIRL: Is that a good trick?

BOY: Far out.

GIRL: Well, I am only doing what you said—here goes!

BOY: Oh, no!

Actually, I'm square enough to think there is something immoral about playing your own console. There should be two consenting adults playing each other's console.

5. Then, of course, we have an important factor in the areas of sexual repression and sexual possibilities. We are living in an era where we are adrift in a sea of sexual possibilities—aswim in an unending neurotic sizzle. My generation was raised in an aura of sexual repression that people like Sigmund Freud and Bertrand Russell once worried about. Now the pendulum has swung the entire distance from repression to total freedom. It has reached the point where I don't know what the girls that my sons go with represent in the long range. I refer to them as my "friends-in-law." Most of the young people to me look like robots in heat. Sexual freedom without responsibility may have benefits but it

also has produced the highest-ever rate of gonorrhea, which now is almost at epidemic proportions.

Linked with this whole phenomenon is the delayed, if at all, marriage, and the epidemic divorce rate. I have composed three wedding announcements to cover the new trend. They underscore this point.

Selection A

Mr. & Mrs. John Anderson are relieved to announce the marriage of their daughter, Joan, who is no longer living in sin with Dr. Alvin Goodgold. This happy event took place on the eighth of June, 1980.

Selection B

Mrs. Constance DeWitt announces her divorce from . . . [expletive deleted] . . . Please celebrate at 10 Homer Lane—the Fourth of October.

Selection C

Mr. and Mrs. J. Hayes are delighted to announce the marriage of their spinster daughter, Carol, to our lovable senior citizen Mr. Vince Harper. Conception immediately following.

6. Undoubtedly, one of the most vital factors influencing change in today's scene is the women's liberation movement. It has lifted women's expectations. No longer are they content to stay at home and follow traditional roles. They want careers and they want to be self-fulfilled. They want to make certain that they make a contribution and that they do not just live in the shadow of a successful husband.

7. All of this has resulted in the next factor, which is a de-functionalization of the wife's role. Now she *really* has no place in the home. Convenience foods, and color TV, the search for stimulation of all sorts, foolproof methods of birth control that enhance sexual possibilities and concomitantly weaken family ties, the women's liberation movement—all have eroded the woman's traditional role. She has become my next factor.

8. The de facto wife, exemplified by the Japanese experience.

In Japan the husband keeps his wife at home. But the husbands have geisha girls who kind of fan, feed, and soothe them at the end of the day, and then they go home to their wives who function in their traditional role. It's a pretty cut-and-dried system in which everyone thoroughly understands his or her accepted function and knows how to play the proper role. Our roles have become blurred. We have a loss of the wife's credentials. Due to her education, she has built up anticipations and expectations which lead to conflict.

9. A brand-new era of change in attitudes toward work. Many of the younger people no longer see their whole fulfillment in work. This change has occurred, I would guess, within the last eight to ten years.

My brother is a psychiatrist and he brings home work every night and every weekend, because he is working on a book on child psychiatry. This led to a dialogue between his daughter and her mother.

"Mommy," my small niece asked one day, "why does daddy bring home work every night?"

"I guess he can't finish all his work in the regular work day," her mother replied. "He's got too much to do and can't handle it all."

"I have an idea, mommy," sparkled the little girl. "Let's go see the principal and have them put daddy in a slower group."

The children are saying to their fathers, "Don't work so hard." That's the new generation. I always used to say that I taught my kids the value of work. Well, it really has sunk in. Now they keep saying to me, "Dad, work harder."

These are the changes I see. Some are lasting and some are transitory, and that is a question that plagues the mind. Which of these changes are permanent and which of them are just part of the last decade of our lives?

Here I would like to turn for some guidance to Henry Kissinger. Because he started as a student at Baruch College, we quote him as the "Gospel According to Henry." In a speech before the National Press Club he delivered a perspective about changing attitudes in America, and he said, "Throughout our history we believed that effort was its own reward. Partly because so much has been achieved here in America, we have tended to suppose that every problem must have a solution and that good intentions would guarantee good results. Utopia was not seen as a dream but as our logical destination if only we traveled the right road. Our generation is the first to learn that the road is endless, and that in traveling it we will find not Utopia, but ourselves. . . ."

In short, Americans are slowly coming to learn, as a wise old psychoanalyst friend of mine put it, that "life is not steps forever upward, leading to the top. It is steps out. And some go up, and some go down."

When all the words of controversy have been stilled, all that will matter will be whether what was done made a difference, regardless of whether it marked an episode or an epoch.

2

How to Tell a Corporate Bigamist When You See One
(Even in a Mirror)

🐾 Unfortunately, it isn't possible to run a nice, neat statistical analysis of the "composite corporate bigamist." Besides, you have to watch out for statistics.

There's a story that when Stalin died, Khrushchev had the job of putting him away—as far as possible. So he called Ben-Gurion in Israel and said, "Ben-Gurion, I have decided to bury Stalin's remains in the Negev Desert. I want your official approval for the press, and if you refuse you'll get a skyful of MIGs. How about it?"

Ben-Gurion thought a minute and said, "Okay, Khrushchev. We're a weak little country and can't retaliate. But I should warn you that, statistically, we have the highest percentage of resurrection known to mankind."

There are, however, a number of generalizations that can be made regarding the basic characteristics of the corporate bigamist.

Whether he is chairman of the board, outstanding artist, author, lawyer, doctor, or other top professional, the typical corporate bigamist is totally preoccupied with his job. Away from it even

27

briefly he's like a fish out of water, and his behavior often betrays him.

An informal survey of top trial lawyers recently turned up a fascinating phenomenon. Many of these honorable gentlemen spend much of their working time fighting bitter court battles in an aura of anger. Then they go home, still mad, and re-create the job atmosphere in a classic transference of their adversary role to the family group which (subconsciously) becomes "the enemy." They will take almost any remark made by a member of the family as a thrust to be parried and, if possible, angrily put down. Not surprisingly, intrafamily relationships at such gatherings tend to disintegrate rapidly.

While that sort of behavior is pretty obvious, few corporate bigamists would realize what they were doing even if you pointed it out to them. They wouldn't know what you were talking about. Most are totally unaware of the transference phenomenon —the psychological gymnastics by which a person subconsciously redirects hostility or other feelings toward a different subject than the one at whom it should be aimed.

In the popular press, the corporate bigamist would certainly be tagged as a "workaholic" which, in plain English, is a work addict.

Recently the workaholic has been variously and disparagingly described as the victim of a "social disease presumably responsible for the disintegration of the family"; an "anxious, guilt-ridden, insecure . . . slave to a set schedule, merciless in his demands upon himself for peak performance . . . compulsively overcommitted"; a "person irrationally committed to excessive work . . . driven to behavior that he can't control and that is self-destructive."

While the negative aspects of his compulsions are certainly there in varying degrees, this picture of the workaholic is decidedly lopsided. He has many positive attributes as well, which will become clear as we examine him closer up.

Not all workaholics are necessarily corporate bigamists, but virtually all corporate bigamists are workaholics to some degree.

Habitually, they put in 60 to 100 hours a week at the job. You're apt to find them in the office at five in the morning and unless there's a business dinner or other affair, they seldom leave the desk before eight or nine in the evening. A briefcase goes home with this type of fellow on the few nights a week that he gets there, and he may read, dictate into a machine, or burn up the long-distance phone lines half the night and all weekend. Some chief executives we know have messengers from their office deliver and pick up satchels of work at their suburban homes and town houses whenever they're home—including weekends and holidays.

Amadeo Giannini, late founder and head of the Bank of America and the vast Transamerica Corporation, once told an interviewer: "I work twenty-four hours a day. I think when I'm asleep. I often wake at night with the solution to a problem at hand, and keep a pad at my bedside so I can write it down."

Many such twenty-four-hour-a-day people also expect their troops to reflect the same work addiction they enjoy. The president of a large, well-known publishing company used to give his editors a Christmas present of a pen that had a microflashlight in its tip so that "when you get great ideas for your magazine in the middle of the night you can write them down without waking your spouse. I hope you enjoy using it as much as I enjoy using mine."

For the corporate bigamist, the job is the center of the universe. His great energy produces vast emotional satisfaction for him. If he takes a vacation at all, it's usually under protest and is limited to a few days or a week at the most. The late Fred Lewis, erstwhile executive vice-president and general manager of the Hearst Magazine Division, used to boast about the fact that he had never taken a day's vacation in more than half a century.

When corporate bigamists *do* take a holiday, however, by the end of the first week they are irritated and climbing the walls.

Most such people don't know what to do on a vacation when they take a real one. Isaac Asimov, the prolific author of some 200 books, told us that his then wife had made arrangements for him and their children to spend a two-week vacation at a cottage she'd rented on Cape Cod. "Can you imagine?" he groaned. "*Two weeks!* What in hell does anyone do way out on the Cape for two solid weeks? I'll get sand in my typewriter!"

In a similar vein, one Monday morning when an associate of Ralph Nader mentioned that he'd spent a restful weekend walking, reading the papers, and just lying on the beach, Nader reportedly exclaimed in utter disbelief: "That takes all weekend?"

In 1975, Dr. Marilyn Machlowitz, a Manhattan psychologist, surveyed a group of known workaholics for a master's thesis at Yale. Her first step was to interview half a dozen notorious workaholics in financial and academic positions. By questioning these people she found fifteen distinct characteristics common to all of them. Each had:

1. An extraordinary drive and desire to excel.
2. Intense energy.
3. Ability to work anywhere and under any condition.
4. A specific and distinctive work style.
5. Exceptional initiative.
6. An ongoing sense that "time is running out."
7. A comprehensive view of what the job requires.
8. A dedication to the use of lists, notes, and timesaving tricks and devices.
9. A deeply instilled, long-workday habit.
10. An ability to get by on four to six hours' sleep a night.
11. Little interest in food; an inclination to quick meals.
12. A deep-seated belief in the value of their own work.
13. A low threshold at the line of distinction between work and leisure.
14. An almost total inability to tolerate (let alone enjoy) idleness.
15. A genuine dread of retirement.

For the final survey seventeen interviews were taped with management consultants, a field noted for people with aggressive work habits. Those that proved to have at least ten of the fifteen basic workaholic characteristics became the sample group. A dozen qualified—ten men and two women. The data they produced proved interesting in the extreme.

First, as Dr. Machlowitz explains in her book *Workaholics*, these people should not be confused with "hard workers." Both types work long hours, she points out. But the hard worker may be working overtime to meet mortgage payments or college tuitions, whereas the workaholic puts in long hours automatically—not because he needs extra money, or has a compulsion to satisfy stockholders or a boss, but simply because he enjoys it.

At the root of this type's intense drive lies a work libido. They are oriented entirely to the business goals they set. Meeting a sales quota is far more vital than a son's "A" in math. A successful novelist said, "Writing for me is so richly rewarding that I do not think of it as work. . . . 'Work' seems to have an aura of obligation . . . rather than doing something for the sake of it, for pleasure."

Another told her: "I don't think of work as any different from play . . . I do enjoy it; I'd rather do that than . . . play at anything else. I don't know why anyone has to draw the distinction."

Ralph Nader would agree. The outspoken public advocate reportedly once asked, "Why is it supposed to be so much more pleasurable to watch a movie or a football game or listen to music than to protect the consumer interest?"

For many workaholics, says Dr. Machlowitz, "Monday provides welcome relief from the short-lived but regularly recurring 'Sunday neurosis,' a syndrome characterized by depression and anxiety caused by the weekend's enforced (relative) inactivity." And the three-day weekend, she points out, "is really murder for the workaholic." According to a woman advertising executive, three-day holidays left her bored, depressed, and "turned in on myself." Said another top executive: "If I'm home for four days, she [his wife] wants me to go back to work more than I want to. I go crazy."

This singleness of purpose characterizes the tunnel vision mentioned earlier. As Dr. Machlowitz put it for her workaholics, "The cliché 'TGIF' does not exist [for them] nor are they affected by Monday morning blues." In virtually any situation he may find himself, the workaholic's and the corporate bigamist's focus is pinpointed to his job.

Everything that happens around the workaholic must relate somehow to that pinpoint, or he is uncomfortable and irascible. The late Charles Revson, whose drive and dedication to the Revlon Company he founded and ran with mailed fist, is legend. On one occasion, in the middle of a meeting in Revlon's board room overlooking Fifth Avenue in New York, Pope John XXIII arrived at St. Patrick's Cathedral trailing his large retinue and an endless parade of loyal followers. Several board members rose from the table during a lull and went to the windows overlooking the avenue to catch a glimpse of the Pope and watch the excitement. Revson called them back like an angry schoolteacher scolding naughty boys. "Will you men sit down; we've got business to settle here," he snapped. "How much nail polish does the Vatican buy?"

The compulsive drive to work that these fellows possess may not necessarily surface to a point where a casual observer can spot it—or even where the executive himself can recognize what he's doing to himself. President Lyndon Johnson, for instance, was noted for the frequent nightmares he had that revealed his fears and foibles more eloquently than anything he ever said or did during his waking hours. In one such dream that he described to associates, cited by Doris Kearns in her book *An American Dream*, he was at his desk in the executive office building, hovering a few yards in space. "I had finished signing one stack of letters," he recalled, "and had turned my chair toward the window. The activity on the street below suggested to me that it was just past five o'clock. All of Washington, it seemed, was on the street, leaving work and heading for home. Suddenly, I decided I'd pack up and go home, too. For once, I decided, it would be nice to join all those people on the street and have an early dinner with my family. I started to get up from my chair, but I couldn't move. I looked down at my legs and saw they were manacled to the chair with a heavy chain. I tried to break the chain, but I couldn't. I tried again and failed again. Once more and I gave up; I reached for the second stack of mail. I placed it directly in front of me, and got back to work."

For most corporate bigamists there is little if any time for diversions of any kind—particularly recreation or exercise unless it can be tied into business, like golf.

Arthur Carlsberg, a West Coast real estate investment tycoon who became a millionaire in his twenties, and chairman of Rammco Investment Corporation at thirty-one, takes pride in setting aside fifteen minutes every morning when he gets out of bed, for push-ups, sit-ups, and bends "while I listen to stock market reports on the radio."

Contrary to popular belief, the corporate chief's motivation is seldom just materialistic, much less is it a Midas-like drive for the accumulation of money for money's sake. Carlsberg says that for him "Accumulating money is a hobby, a game, a drive. I enjoy it."

Most top executives would agree with Robert K. Lifton who heads up the Transcontinental Investing Corporation in New York. "This is our form of creating," he told *Time* magazine a few years ago. "If artists give up the world's pleasures to pursue their calling, people understand it. What they don't understand is that many businessmen have the same creative drives, and derive the same satisfactions as artists—but what they are doing is translated into dollars and cents. When I come up with a good deal, that's creative. Successfully merchandizing a product is creative. Taking a business idea and making it work is creative."

For anyone interested in checking personal workaholic proclivities, Dr. Nelson Bradley, Medical Director of Grillain Manor in Sidney, B.C., Canada, has devised a checklist of what he considers to be the danger signs of potential workaholism, and which he has given us permission to reprint here:

		yes	*no*
1.	When you leave the office at the end of the day do you take your work with you?	□	□
2.	Would your wife or family agree with this statement: "I leave my worries at the office"?	□	□
3.	Do you get restless and irritable on a long weekend?	□	□
4.	Do you take an annual vacation and look forward to it?	□	□
5.	Has your family ever accused you of being more interested in your work than in them?	□	□
6.	Has anyone ever blamed family problems on your work?	□	□
7.	Do you find yourself drinking too much, smoking too much, restless or irritable when you are not working?	□	□
8.	Do you feel time passes too quickly for what you want to do?	□	□

9. Do you compete to win at everything, includ- ☐ ☐
ing playing games with your family?

10. Are you always looking at your watch? Are you ☐ ☐
usually impatient?

If you answered "yes" to 2 and 4 only, you probably will not become a workaholic. If you answered "yes" to one of the other questions, you should begin to examine your work habits. If you answered "yes" to two of the other questions, you may be on your way to work addiction. If you said "yes" to three or more of the others, you are a workaholic, and should evaluate your motives.

For most of us, the platitude that "people need people" would be relatively true. It is not true for corporate bigamists. They have a remarkably limited need for genuine emotional relationships with *any* person—in sharp contrast to the image projected by public relations offices, which tend to paint the boss as an all-American, small-town-type fella who loves to visit the folks back home on the farm every summer, and worships his family. Nothing could be further from the truth.

For most corporate bigamists, a close emotional tie is frightening, a thing to be avoided at any cost. Emotional reactions abandon logic and reason—something that a leader in business seldom permits himself in any facet of his life. Most would never admit it, however. One top executive accused of having no long-term emotional attachments in his life was highly incensed. "What the hell do you mean," he roared. "I've had the same mistress for three years."

Frequently, they will re-create the family in their office environment—a family they can control and with which they can be coldly objective. One corporate president I knew took a promising young company lad under his wing and treated him far better than his own son. The youth was the only person he would visit or with whom he would celebrate holidays. When the president moved on, the new president fired the youth.

A kid in the office is grateful for favoritism flung his way, naturally, and often will call his boss "Dad." The inherent danger is that some of these fair-haired favorites count on the boss for their future and can wind up destroyed.

The term "office wife" is no joke, either. Sometimes the boss's secretary becomes so much "the lady" of his office family that no one dares say anything about her that they don't want to get back to him. It's like a royal court. Only a few are appointed to the court by the king, and those are the ones invited out on the yacht. They are the "adopted family"; usually younger, nonthreatening people to whom "Dad" can be generous without feeling any obligation, legally or emotionally. Avoidance of deep emotional attachments also reflects the corporate bigamist's real fear of dependency—or even a show of dependency—on any person other than himself.

What makes the office family safe to deal with, of course, is that the office is the officially accepted battlefield. Most successful executives are desensitized to the sensuous aspects of that turf. The corporate bigamist doesn't blanch at the sight of blood, whether spilled by friend or foe. It's all part of the game and has little if anything to do with people as living, breathing human beings. His peers in the industry understand this, so he's not considered an ogre if he finds it necessary to sever a relationship with unfeeling dispatch.

The president of a large food wholesaler once complained: "Everyone calls me a butcher because I fired 500 incompetent executives. No one asks me about the 500 people I hired to replace them."

When another empire builder was asked how many people he had fired in an organizational shake-up, he replied, "I don't usually do that. I have a hatchet man who does it for me. But I did fire a secretary I'd had for a long time. She cried," he added gratuitously, "so I laid her. Then I financed her in her own business and she's much better off today than she would have been here."

A graphic example of this kind of cold objectivity was Harry Truman's historic decision to use the A-bomb on Nagasaki and Hiroshima. He gave the order after lengthy weighing of alternatives—then went to bed and to sleep.

For these people, tension is a totally unwanted personal response over which they have no control, and they must have control at all times—over people, time, their families. Any show of anxiety or depression is considered serious weakness, and they want no part of it, whether it applies to impersonal corporate events or to individual people.

The fact is that the corporate bigamist never sees people as an end in themselves. He's like the fellow who asked, "How did Michelangelo know that the Pietà was in that rock?" This is particularly true when he's dealing with his own employees. They are a means to accomplish his own ends; little more.

At a recent annual dinner for the saleswomen of a large national dry cleaning chain, at which I was speaker, the chairman gave a brief talk praising them and thanking them for their splendid work and their charm. He was delightful.

It was all pure sham. Later, when I asked him if he enjoyed being surrounded by all that pulchritude, he sneered and made grossly demeaning remarks about the women. "But," he added through clenched teeth, "goddamnit, I need them."

Generally speaking, unless she's a company administrator, or happens to suggest potentials that will satisfy a need or purpose (not necessarily sexual), most chief executives hate to sit next to any woman at official company functions. They do it only when necessary—if the woman is the wife of a valued executive, for example. But they practically go bananas trying to make and listen to what they consider to be "small talk"—defined as anything at all outside the area of business.

Another characteristic of these fellows is that they tend to be slightly paranoid, not always without reason. Henry Kissinger once pointed out that "even paranoids have real enemies." There are power struggles in any organization, so that paranoia can be legitimate. Most top executives don't overreact, but they have to be wary. As one corporate president put it: "I trust everybody, but with reservations." They recognize that there are power blocs, always throwing rocks at the guy on top, but they can't afford to spend their time throwing the rocks back down at them. They have to accept that, and also recognize that the power seekers are not working out a master plot to overthrow them every day. You don't *always* try to "get even," even though you are always aware that the knives are out.

In one of Lyndon Johnson's recurring dreams, he was paralyzed from the neck down—an affliction of his grandmother and also, curiously, of Woodrow Wilson. During his Presidency, the dream occurred, placing him in bed in the White House Red Room. In the adjoining room, he could hear his aides fighting among themselves to divide up his power between them. Joe Califano claimed the legislative program; Walt Rostow wanted to be foreign policy boss; Arthur Okun wanted budget; and George Christian public relations. In the dream, Johnson couldn't move or talk but he could hear every word. Though he was helpless, not one assistant tried to protect his interest. Johnson woke, terrified, and walked through the halls to Wilson's portrait. Touching it somehow restored his confidence. He was alive and well; it was Wilson who had been paralyzed and died.

A few chief executives do go overboard, of course. Richard Nixon, for instance, with his tapes and personal vendettas, carried his suspicions to unhealthy extremes. And some of the shrewd members of his coterie—like Colson—played to his paranoia.

Usually, however, these men possess the self-confidence to know they can handle the job and the opposition. When you are on top you are checking all the time, and when the apparent paranoia seems justified, you do something about it.

The successful business types we're talking about hate to waste time beating around the bush. They have a natural talent for striking at the core of any problem and solving it by direct confrontation.

Meshulam Riklis, when he was the bright young president of Rapid American, needed a million-dollar loan at one point, and had chosen a particular bank that, he found out later, had a board of directors reputed to be unanimously anti-Semitic. Rik's advisors warned him that he didn't stand a chance of getting a loan; that the only Jewish firms they dealt with were a few old and established ones, heavy with capital assets. Ricklis refused to cancel and try elsewhere. Instead, he marched into the conference room at the appointed time, greeted the tight-lipped group facing him, and sat down. According to an aide who was with him, before anyone uttered a word Rik said in a loud voice: "I hear you boys are anti-Semitic." It was, recalls the aide, "like a punch in the mouth." Upshot? The bankers, completely shaken by the frontal attack on their prejudices, were so intent on their heated denials of the charge that the loan became a secondary issue and, when they got around to it, was granted hands down.

3

Dreamers, Schemer-Reamers, and Healers

Not all high-powered executives operate the same way, of course. Each has his own approaches, techniques, and characteristics. Among them are fellows for whom I have my own labels. I see them classified as the "dreamer," the "schemer-reamer," or the "healer."

The dreamer comes in several models—with high drive, low drive, and a range of IQs. The high-IQ, high-drive dreamer approaches every project with a "why not?" attitude. "I have a dream," he says, and he burns in the night with it. "I am going to be the biggest retailer, the biggest manufacturer of turbines, the largest perfume producer in the world." Nothing matters to him but that dream; not his family, not his children, nothing but that all-consuming dream. And he can make that product. He can make things happen that nobody else can make happen. He is smarter than anyone else—too intelligent, too bright, too aggressive—and he's a discounter of people. He's always pointing out what's wrong with you, never what's right. Everything he says is a deprecation of others' intelligence. Ask him what time it is and he says: "You mean *now?*"

He makes a disaster of his children. As for his wife, God help her if he decides to stay home some day. He'll tell her how to reorganize the kitchen and how to dump the garbage. He'll show her how she can say the same thing but spend half a minute less time on the phone. He discounts people, discounts their ideas and their thoughts. It's inherent in him; he can't help himself. The high-drive, high-IQ dreamer belongs in a key staff position, but keep him away from people. The sonofabitch will kill you.

Do not make the mistake of discounting the incredible value of these men, however. They are born intellectual rats with tremendous drive. They can take a failing company that sells suspenders to firemen and turn it into a multimillion-dollar concern producing catapults for aircraft carriers. They can start out selling nail polish in the New York ghettos and become, in a few years, the largest manufacturer of cosmetics in the world. We need them in business, but not around the house.

The low-drive dreamer usually is a good company line officer. You have to be a little lazy to be a good line man. He likes to play tennis or golf with the big customers. He takes them fishing on the company yacht, or moose hunting at the company's camp north of Chibougamau. He's also good at making love, and is smart enough to be discreet about it. But he lets somebody else do the real work and worrying. Do not underestimate him, either, however. He is clever enough so it's hard—if not impossible—to take advantage of him.

What about the schemer-reamer? The schemer part of this executive is the nitpicker. He's always looking for something bad you didn't do, so he can pin it on you and put you at a disadvantage. He's forever trying to corner people. "I gotcha," he says. "You had four days of taxicab fares on your expense account during the time you were sailing to Europe on our container ship."

The reamer part of Mr. Schemer-Reamer tries to squeeze the last ounce of productivity out of everyone around him. And he will not hesitate to use his nit-picking intelligence as blackmail to get it. "You've got to do a little bit more," he insists, "and we'll overlook your past mistakes if you produce. We have a chance to make the best product in the world, but we all have got to pull together."

He, too, discounts people, but in his own special way. We have a client who's a good example of the schemer-reamer. He stands at the window in his posh office overlooking his factory and points to a man walking across the compound. "See that one?" he says. "That's a $40,000 kid jerk. See the one he's talking to now? An $80,000 schmoe." He never calls his people by name. They are the number of dollars per year that he pays them. And he sometimes overpays them in order to squeeze the most possible work out of them.

As for the healer, he's the diplomat. When you've fallen on your face in a simple merger deal, he's apt to salve your damaged pride with something like: "Don't let it get you down. Those lawyers were a slippery bunch. You can do better than that, and I'm sure you will the next time around."

When the executive vice-president has described you to your best customer as a stupid nincompoop, the healer will tell you, "Oh, you know how Walter is. He didn't mean you."

How these fellows can work in concert is exemplified by a pair of brokers I knew—one a schemer-reamer, the other a healer. One of their executives had been royally chewed out by the schemer-reamer for a fairly disastrous mistake. As he came out of the office, beaten down and depressed, the healer type went over to him and said: "Don't let it throw you, Phil. You know how Joe gets when he's tense. Put it this way: life is a bank account. By your mistake, you made a withdrawal. However, you still have a substantial balance and you can keep making deposits. So let's keep it that way."

The schemer-reamer, overhearing the conversation, yelled from his office: "However, don't you make too many withdrawals or we'll damn well lose interest!"

Top leaders in every field will almost certainly reflect at least one of the characteristics described. Franklin D. Roosevelt and Winston Churchill were top-drawer dreamers. They mobilized the resources of their people. At the height of adversity they rose to the challenge.

"We have nothing to fear but fear itself!" Roosevelt assured his people.

"This will be our finest hour!" Sir Winston shouted over the roar of Luftwaffe planes and bombs.

They were great for their countries in crisis. They got things done, were impatient with people and often irritated by them. Once a dreamer comes up with a new world-beater campaign, get out of his way. When he sets his mind on something new, he's impatient. If he can't implement the job himself, he will find the man to do it for him. The chances are the implementer will be a schemer-reamer. They are the people who know how to do it.

Kennedy was unable by himself to get any legislation through Congress. Then along came a schemer-reamer from the hill country of Texas. He could get anything done. He knew the Congress and how to deal with it. When he needed votes he knew how to get them. During his drive for the civil rights amendment he had the gall to call Senator Everett Dirksen of Illinois and tell him, "Ev, I want your vote on civil rights."

As might be expected, Dirksen replied, "That's fine, Mr. President, but you ain't goin' to git it."

Then Johnson pulled the stops. "Listen, Ev," he said. "I just happened to find a copy of a speech you made in 1935, in which you referred to blacks by a very derogatory name. Now if that should get resurrected before election time, Ev, you'd lose Chicago."

Dirksen gasped. "Mr. President, that's blackmail."

Lyndon smiled. "Ev," he said coolly, "let's you and me sit down and reason together." He got Dirksen's vote.

During Johnson's tenure as President, there apparently was considerable opposition to J. Edgar Hoover. Nobody could understand why Johnson—who admittedly recognized him as a potential political hazard—refused to remove him. When confronted with the question of why he wouldn't dump Hoover, he quickly replied: "If you've got an enemy where do you want him—inside the tent pissing out, or outside the tent pissing in?"

We've had healers in the White House, too. Gen. Dwight Eisenhower was one. He kept inflation at 4 percent. The country moved ahead with no major confrontations. He warned us to beware of the military-industrial complex. Everyone said he was a schmoe, but never has this country had a better eight years, according to history. He was a healer—and a mature leader.

The fact is that every company needs these fellows—and has them. In a study of 2,000 executives, we found that more than half were clear-cut corporate bigamists and of these, most could be classified as dreamers, schemer-reamers, or healers, as we have described them here. All had IQs above 120. They were compulsive, with a penchant for numbers. They were suspicious people—watchers with a sense of perspective that kept them from going berserk under pressure. Most had a sense of humor, liked people and parties. Virtually all were workaholics.

The foibles of these people should not be viewed as negative by any means. They are the movers and doers of industry; they are the experts. And what is an expert? According to my favorite definition, he is the fellow who knows just how much dynamite to stuff in the rear end of a bull to blow off its horns without giving it bloodshot eyes.

These are leaders—the captains that people can believe in and depend on and know that with them at the helm "We'll somehow make it." The good chief executive has to be like the captain of the Titanic—able to convince his passengers that he just stopped to pick up a little ice.

4

Executive Sins and Alibis

🖙 A year or so ago my wife and I wrote a book on leave-taking and its impact on the domestic scene in this country. At the time it became apparent that the phenomenon of corporate bigamy often involves *partial* leave-taking—one of the most insidious kinds of parting. In such cases, husband and wife have said good-bye in all essential respects, but still remain lashed together in visible, surface associations.

Recently, a national magazine featured a survey by Barthold's and Company, executive recruiters, of "108 top New England corporations." The article was headlined to emphasize what the editors considered a startling fact—that 93 percent of the chief executives of those companies were still married to their first wives! The implication, of course, was that marriage to a top corporate executive was not, "as commonly believed," a rough and rocky road. Though the magazine article did not report on those 108 relationships in detail, it assumed (naively or otherwise) that they were happy and successful all the way.

The actual findings published were, however, hardly surprising. Most chief executives of the major, old-line corporations listed in those top 108 corporations, still hew to the image of "the stolid family man" as a reflection of responsible stability in the business world. They comprise a staunchly conservative group and will do everything in their power to avoid any public hint of a domestic background that is anything but tranquil and under control. The magazine's findings were, actually, based on the false assumption of *post hoc ergo propter hoc* (after this therefore because of this). Similarly, the old advertisement reads, "Families that pray together stay together." Actually, families that do go to church together may be more conservative and thus avoid divorce even though they may be unhappy in marriage.

Surveys of corporate wives that we have conducted also indicate a high percentage of intact first marriages. But, according to the corporate wives we surveyed, their marriages are—in the majority—a far cry from "happy" or "successful" by any definition. The quality of most such partnerships, in fact, would suggest that they exist only on certificates in the files of the city's marriage bureau.

A typical reaction of one wife who wrote to me about her corporate chief husband:

"He hates birthday parties, Christmas morning, rituals, and sex (which, I suspect, he feels is for primates and the underprivileged). . . . He believes that a woman should be kept 'barefoot and pregnant,' and he hates phonies (a 'phony' is a person who speaks in a sophisticated manner and has inherited wealth). He leaves for work at seven and returns at six. Things must be peaceful and quiet; the children and I must never be at odds, dinner should be ready—and the paper and TV set accessible (absence of the paper has been known to cause full-blown fits). He dislikes drinking, divorce, and men who are not 'good family men.' "

Said another: "My husband's marriage to his company is proceeding as happily as ever. I wish I could say the same for mine."

For many men, as previously indicated, the work scene has been a sanctuary and hunting preserve. At work, the corporate executive or busy professional man can get away from the nagging cares of home responsibilities, form socially acceptable bonds with other men, and work out his aggressive instincts.

To be fair it should be pointed out that the phenomenon is not purely an escape mechanism for competitive business leaders. Business in our society today calls for the engagement of the "whole man." Nobody rises to the top without a total personal commitment—more graphically known as "fire in the belly"—unless his father happens to be chairman and founder of a privately owned corporation, and even that convenient circumstance is no *guarantee* of success nowadays.

The corporate bigamist, however, uses this state of affairs to accommodate his burning inner needs. He gets his kicks, as we've noted, from accomplishment. Sometimes the kicks are quasi-sexual. Dr. Benjamin B. Wolman, a New York psychoanalyst whose practice consists heavily of executives—and sometimes their wives—comments on the typical driven corporate achiever as a man whose penis grows, figuratively, every time he closes a deal. The trouble is, he points out, that the reverse effect is seen when the business coup doesn't come off. Such a man will not be much interested in sex with his wife, or in any other kind of home-oriented activity for that matter, after such quasi-sexual failure. The result, unhappily, is a withdrawal from domestic interaction—a definite psychological if not physical leave-taking from the family scene.

Many other features of the contemporary business community contribute to this sort of partial leave-taking. One hard-driving data-processing executive, seeking a vice-presidency, moved to stepping-stone positions in three competitive companies within a two-year period. Each move meant relocating his family. "This nearly killed my wife and kids," he said, "not to mention my seventy-two-year-old mother. A few months ago, when I had to pull my son out of high school, tears were shed as his friends waved good-bye at the airport. My family really suffered, and I almost changed my mind. But I didn't. The opportunity was too great."

The president of a large materials company in the Southeast maintains membership in a posh golf and country club. When his wife complains about their not spending more time together he has a ready reply: "My dear, I can have a very successful business and make lots of money, or we can do the social whirl. We can't have both, and I don't have the time to sit around and gossip with your friends. Maybe next year, after the merger, but not now."

"That was four years ago," says his wife, "and he hasn't taken me to the club yet. I go alone."

The president of a New York service organization travels almost constantly. On the two weekends a month when he is home, he relaxes by playing golf. His Saturday schedule: up early, out on the course by eight, finish eighteen holes around noon, to the bar for some drinks and small talk; lunch, shower, steam bath, massage, home about four o'clock, nap, up in time for dinner and an evening of entertainment, at which he often falls asleep. Same routine on Sunday. This man rarely sees his wife and children. His wife is beginning to drink. Unaware of any problem until his oldest boy tried to commit suicide after becoming a dope addict, the executive is now seeking marriage counseling. But he has not really varied his routine.

These are examples of "leave-taking interruptus." The parting has taken place in all of the respects which would bring satisfaction to the parties involved in the family association. The formal ties remain in force. They may remain for many years, as the situation festers.

In many cases the corporate bigamist doesn't even realize anything is amiss. One chief executive, when accused of being the worst kind of corporate bigamist with regard to his family, was deeply hurt. "That's ridiculous," he protested. "My family and I are *very* close." Asked when he had last seen them, he thought for a minute and said, "Well, I've been pretty busy lately—it's our busy season. I guess I haven't seen them for any prolonged time since Christmas." It was then March.

The corporate bigamist always has a bagful of excuses or, more properly, "rationalizations." Let's take a look at some of the most common alibis.

Number one: "I'm really doing it for you and the kids."

Nonsense. He wouldn't have any other life. He thrives on long hours and hard work. He picked this kind of life to satisfy an inner need, and he would be doing the same thing even if he had never met his wife.

Alibi number two: "You have everything you want—money, a nice home, every advantage for the kids. What more do you want?"

Who drew up the list of priorities? He did. When a corporate bigamist gives material possessions to a neglected wife, he does it largely for personal reasons: to satisfy his ego and to ease his conscience. If he were ever to ask his wife what *she* wants out of life, he might find that she would trade her mink and her 450 SL sport coupe for a week with him. True, when they were younger, the bigamist's wife thought that these material things were important. But his attitude now imposes on her needs that she has outgrown.

Alibi number three: "You aren't interested in my career."

This excuse is a great favorite. It attempts to shift blame to her, and stir her guilt. But how can his wife be interested in something she knows nothing about? He seldom, if ever, discusses his work with her, never includes her in his important business decisions, and never shares his hopes and fears with her. In fact, she is never drawn into his business circle except as a hostess or a decoration. The wife's perception of her husband's corporate career is that of an adversary which constantly fights her, sucking her husband away. She hears about what he does at work only when he grumbles.

Alibi number four: "When I'm home, you try to turn me into a day laborer, handyman, or garbageman."

On the face of it there's an element of validity in this one. When their weary mates come home after a tough day, many wives are at them instantly: "Fix that leaky faucet; the door is falling off its hinges; the grass needs cutting, check my car, it won't start . . ."

The derogation in reducing a corporate chieftain to plumber or grease monkey is, of course, emasculatory in the extreme. Over the years I have pointed out to a number of corporate wives how this device can backfire, to their great disadvantage. Recently I heard from one of those ladies whose husband chairs a major corporation.

"I think you ought to know," she wrote, "that I think about you every Friday. That is trash day here. Years ago I heard you say that corporate wives shouldn't make their important husbands garbage men . . . I can't help remembering that one of the dumbest regular arguments I had with my husband concerned the weekly trash. It was ludicrous! Fridays have been peaceful for years now—thanks. My new rule is that if something bothers me more than it bothers him, it makes sense for me to take care of the problem (by hiring help) rather than bug him about it. Ah, sweet reasonableness!"

Why *does* a wife resort to emasculatory devices like that? She's not trying to turn him into a garbageman, naturally. She's trying to get him actively involved in his home and family. She has no titles to confer, no corporate bonbons. So she tries to bring her husband closer in the only way she can—counterproductive as this may be. That kind of nagging often is a symptom of deep frustration. Chances are she would prefer a lover to a handyman, but she does not feel she can ask for that directly, and she's not ready to seek it on her own—yet.

Alibi number five: "I'm a very busy man. The company demands every waking moment I can spare, you know that. I just can't give you and the children the time you insist that I should spend—much as I'd like to."

That last is a lie, of course. He wouldn't "like to" at all. A man who loves his family can always find time for them. To build a lasting relationship—or to repair a deteriorating one—time must be found. It is there for the finding. The corporate bigamist can always stretch his day to see an important customer or handle a major deal. We make time for the things we enjoy. The problem here is not lack of time, but lack of motivation to get involved in the affairs of the home.

Alibi number six: "I can't reason with you anymore. Every time I try to talk to you about my work, you turn the discussion into a terrible argument."

This is another common table-turner tactic. The breadwinner may have some legitimacy to his grievance, but there are other aspects. He brings up his work when *he* feels like it. He talks *to* his wife, not *with* her. He does not want a real discussion. When work comes up as a topic, neither party really listens. The introduction of the subject simply acts as a trigger, setting off hostile reactions that have been rehearsed so frequently that nothing new is added. The trouble is that by this time corporate bigamy is so powerfully entrenched that a little conversation about the job accomplishes nothing positive.

The partners to a corporate bigamy situation are frozen in the attitude of leave-taking, like the figures on Keats's Grecian urn. They are not together. They don't talk with each other or understand each other. They see each other occasionally; that is all. And the situation can continue for years, destroying those who are trapped in it.

We live in an era when divorce is no longer frowned on in most businesses, and is much easier, quicker, and more direct than all the "psychological" experimentation and self-examination that might be required to rebuild a crumbling family. "Quick and direct," remember, is the way these fellows like to tackle problems.

There's no reason, of course, why unmarried people can't be top executives—swingers, or whatever. New York's Mayor Koch has done pretty well as a bachelor; in another era so did Mayor Jimmy Walker. And it's true that some families might be better off unafflicted by an autocratic corporate bigamist at the helm. But psychologists know, from study after study, that single people tend to be lonely, dissatisfied, unfulfilled and—often—irascible. And the least "happy" or well-adjusted people in our culture are those who are divorced or separated.

After more than half a career-lifetime in this business, I am thoroughly convinced that the family unit must be preserved at all costs if mankind is to prosper as a species. At stake is our mental health, nationally and individually, as well as the future security of our offspring—bold, brave avant-gardes notwithstanding. Decline of the family unit and rise of cults like the People's Temple and other groups that capture immature, disenchanted, or confused minds may not be merely coincidental.

Jim Hayes, President of the American Management Association, pointed out in a *Wall Street Journal* editorial that Karl Marx, arch-enemy of capitalism, predicted the demise of the competitive entrepreneurial system, but may have failed to predict correctly where the fatal cracks will appear. Marx wrote, said Hayes, of workers revolting, little realizing that the real danger to free enterprise might come from attitudes of the sons and daughters of our corporate executives. It's a fascinating point, and I underscore it unequivocally.

It is interesting that shortly after he took office, President Carter sent the following memo to the White House staff:

"I am concerned about the family life of all of you. I want you to spend an adequate amount of time with your husbands, wives, and children, and involve them as much as possible in our White House life. We are going to be here for a long time, and all of you will be more valuable to me and the country with rest and a stable family life. In emergencies we'll all work full time. Let me have your comments."

Never mind that the "emergencies" soon took over, so that few White House staffers could carry out the President's wishes—or that he himself has become as much of a workaholic, if not a corporate bigamist, as any other President. At least his insights were intact, and his heart was in the right place.

We are living in a time of dichotomies. But this is not a unique condition, viewed against the tapestry of history. In the first paragraph of *A Tale of Two Cities,* Charles Dickens wrote: "It was the best of times, it was the worst of times . . . it was the season of Light, it was the season of Darkness, it was the spring of hope, it was the winter of despair. We were all going straight to Heaven. We were all going straight the other way."

By facing the real problems of marriage and corporate pressures, we can at least point ourselves—humbly but hopefully—in the direction of a culture that, God willing, may produce the best of times rather than the worst of times. And we start by parsing the core of the problem—the corporate bigamist.

5

Corporate Bigamists "Monster" Style

☛ Over the years I have found that all kinds of corporate bigamists, whether administrators, doctors, lawyers, generals, admirals, artists, authors, entertainers, sports stars, musicians—name it—fall into one of four major classifications.

We have already discussed the dreamers, schemer-reamers, and healers among them, but these general labels can apply singly or in combination to any of the four major types we are about to discuss. Bear in mind that the categories described represent the extreme characteristics of the type in each case. Few human beings are pure types of any kind. If you think of the people you know who seem to fit a type, you'll find yourself thinking ". . . but George also has a little of the so-and-so in him." In short, there's usually some overlap. A friend once referred to my categorized entrepreneurs as "Feinberg's Chamber of Horrors." So be it. Let's explore the Feinberg Wax Museum together while I point out the exhibits and explain them. The specimens we examine will include the following:

The "monster" type. He is a monk of industry; a father to

everyone except his own family. He embodies the distinctive characteristics of the eagle—a fiercely handsome bird uniquely adapted to soaring high in the skies, but one that makes a rotten household pet.

The "Janus" type. Like the Roman god of portals for whom he's named, he is a creature with two faces looking, somewhat deceitfully, in opposite directions. He considers himself a great executive and entrepreneur, as well as a great father, husband, and lover. The Janus type is basically a monster who thinks he's a good enough salesman to convince his family that his job deserves his full commitment.

The "need-achiever" type. This fellow is almost what the Janus thinks he is—a balanced executive, based on the excellent model developed by Dr. David C. McClelland, the famed Harvard psychologist, who invented the title I have given him. The need-achiever is financially acquisitive, competitive, a male heterosexual. He *wants* to be a good family man, though this achievement may escape his grasp. There is more hope for him, however, than for the others.

The "Abraham" type. He is the male counterpart of the Virgin Mary; the universal father. His business is justified only as it serves his family. In the bygone days of family-owned corporations, he may have been next to God. Today, it's a rare Abraham who can make it in the brutal political milieu of publicly held diversified corporations—or bucking the competition in the professions. I have been criticized by Biblical scholars for calling him an Abraham, since the patriarch would have sacrificed his son. However, the Biblical text explains quite clearly that it was the most painful sacrifice Abraham could have made. His whole commitment in his life was to Isaac and his family. And only God's supreme test of his faith could have induced him to perform such an act.

In any case, let's first examine the monster type, who epitomizes all the extremes in corporate bigamy. He frequently combines the qualities of the dreamer and the schemer-reamer. It should be made clear at the outset that he is not a "monster" in any pejorative or literal sense. He certainly is no Frankenstein creation, nor is he an evil fellow like Conan Doyle's Moriarity. He is, in fact, the very model of a gentleman in most cases. It is simply that, in any context other than work or career, he is monstrously impossible to live with.

The monster symbolizes the Hannibals of the world. He is invariably high-IQ, high-drive, with a genetic orientation to succeed. As a child, he was "never young." The wife of one monster-type corporate bigamist characterizes her spouse as a driven soul who "was born with liver spots on his acne."

He is an empire-builder and king-maker (the king usually being himself). He is the president of his country, a nation's dictator, a corporate prince. He is the creator of conglomerates, the discoverer of a polio vaccine, and the genius who will come up with a cure for cancer and the common cold.

Often, he is the founder and builder of the empire he rules and, typical of the thoroughgoing corporate bigamist, nothing exists for him outside the sphere of his own creation. He is typified by the father who wrote to his son at Harvard and signed the letter, "Your loving Kuhn, Loeb and Company."

Unlike the mobster, who attains wealth and power through brutal strongarm methods and litte else, the corporate monster uses intellectual means to achieve success. He is brilliant and knows it. In some 2,000 tests that we have carried out on top corporate executives—most of them clearly in the monster category —all scored in the top 10 percent (on IQ) of the general population, and many were in the upper 5 percent. But their intelligence always is sharply focused and honed. And it is applied pragmatically rather than theoretically as would be the case with scholars or academic types. They are more interested, for instance, in *how* to achieve a given result than in bothering to understand *why* it happens to come out this way or that. In short, they want to know "What's the best, most practical and expedient, cost-effective way to build this thing?" They are not the least interested in probing the stress components. They are seldom distracted by theory.

While most monster types would like to be considered as having a "common touch," and frequently give this impression, don't make the mistake of thinking you've been invited to a warm, enduring friendship.

Movie magnate Sam Goldwyn, a man for whom career achievement and the material evidence of it were at least as important as life itself, was famous on the Hollywood scene for wooing prospective talent with all sorts of inducements. Then, when disenchanted, he would lop people off like cordwood.

In her revealing biography, *The Search for Sam Goldwyn*, Carol Easton reports an account provided by an anonymous informant who had been enticed by Goldwyn to move to Hollywood from New York. Early on, he ran into political jealousy problems with studio department heads, and went to see Goldwyn, intending to resign. The producer would have none of it. "You can't leave," he said. "You're too valuable." Throwing an arm around the fellow's shoulder, and lowering his voice to a confidential tone, he suggested that *their* relationship was "different" from all the others, and that the chap should think of him as an uncle. "Call me Uncle Sam," he suggested.

Later, when the newly created "nephew"—who had been diverted from purely administrative duties to direct some pictures —tried to see "Uncle Sam" about some ideas he had, Tycoon Goldwyn wasn't available. Memos and letters surreptitiously directed to "Uncle Sam" and signed, "Your Nephew" went unanswered. One night at a Goldwyn dinner, Anonymous lightheartedly brought up the matter. Goldwyn wasn't amused. "I've been meaning to tell you . . . You are making a terrible mistake with your life," Mr. Nephew was told. There wasn't enough money in directing, according to Sam who, his protege reported, "measured the quality of a person in terms of how much money you had." And, when Goldwyn realized that his advice wasn't about to be taken, it was "the beginning of the end" of their relationship.

Once, when he was heading for Hawaii on a holiday trip, Goldwyn called his staff of long-time loyal slaves together, gave them a pep talk, and then "gravely he walked around," reported Sam Marx, who was present, "and shook our hands, each one of us, and said, 'Bon voyage!' When Goldwyn said things like that you didn't realize it was funny until afterward. When we got outside, somebody said, 'Why did *he* say bon voyage?' A few weeks later, we decided he knew what he was doing—because we were, almost all of us, leaving."

Sam Goldwyn was an outstanding example of the corporate bigamist, monster style. The fierce, burning "need to win" affected everything he did.

Phil Berg, one of Hollywood's top agents during the heyday of motion pictures, tells about a bridge group that included himself, George Kaufman, Chico Marx, Irving Thalberg, Goldwyn, and several other Hollywood lights. Stakes often ran to $2 a point. Goldwyn, he reveals, was a terrible bridge player. If he was losing he refused to let anyone leave the game until he'd recouped his losses. When this happened, the game seldom broke up before two in the morning. According to Berg, it wasn't the money. "It was the game. He just didn't want anyone to have the advantage."

One night, however, when Goldwyn got all the cards and won everyone's money, quite early, he promptly got a headache and went to bed!

Early in the careers of both Goldwyn and the *New Yorker*, the magazine ran a profile of Sam written, according to Carol Easton, by his press agent who described the movie king's philosophy as "outstripping the other fellow by any means possible that doesn't land one in jail.

"Almost everybody in the picture business," the article went on, "has at one time worked for him. He has never been known to praise a man who has slaved for him except for purposes of publicity. There is nothing he likes better than to be photographed holding on to the arm of a celebrity. Nevertheless, Sam Goldwyn is a great man. His insensitivity to the feelings of others is a trait often found in genius."

Despite efforts and lip service designed to make them appear to be "one of the boys," these fellows always insist upon being perceived as "different" from you and me—because they have worked harder, are smarter, or simply because they are firmly convinced that the finger of God is on their shoulder, and that they are uniquely endowed. I heard one captain of industry introduce a speaker at a banquet as follows: "My name is _____ _____, and I am a self-made millionaire. And I didn't get where I am by listening to the schmoes around me, so pay attention to the speaker."

The need to be "different" is sometimes carried to extremes, and may be expressed in eccentricities that often are deliberately acquired to set these men apart. Such idiosyncrasies are like a trademark and become part of their identity.

One corporate chief I know has thrived on the image perpetuated by a story that, when he was younger, someone asked him why he didn't remove a wall in his plant that annoyed him. When he complained about it a second time and someone asked the same question, so the tale goes, he got a sledge hammer and beat the long masonry wall to the ground. On one occasion, I asked him, "Did you really do that?" He smiled inscrutably and said, "Maybe. I like to keep the old myth going. And by the way," he added, "if I did it, I did not clean up the mess."

The founder and president of a large mail order house had a habit of making the rounds of all the offices in the morning, wearing some gadget currently being considered for the catalogue. For several months he might stride the corridors wearing a skull cap with a revolving propeller on top of it; another time it would be a big red bow tie with blinking lights at each corner. He thoroughly enjoyed the reputation he acquired among members of his staff for being a "character." It also served as a cover for his relentless drive. Woe to the employee who underestimated it.

Some quirks may be born of neurotic anxieties or a need for protection. The owner and publisher of a large national magazine and publishing house became known in most of the major cities of the Western world for buying two of everything—two diamond bracelets for his wife, two Lincoln Continentals, and so on. In the case of the cars, he had two of his salesmen drive them—one to a company garage in Chicago; the other to a winter home in Palm Beach. A year later, he complained to one of his executives that his wife's Chrysler and his own Cadillac were both in for repairs, his Lincoln was in Florida, and he had no wheels. The executive asked why he didn't use his second Lincoln. It developed that he'd forgotten he had bought it; the car had been sitting in the garage unused for a year.

True to his dreamer and schemer-reamer characteristics, the monster is truly awful in his relationships with people—particularly those close to him. Charles Revson would call a meeting for all of his top brass for eight P.M. on July 3, and the only item on the agenda would be: "Why do we have so much trouble holding on to key executives?"

Family members are frequent targets of the monster's barbs.

I was at dinner one evening with the top officer of a major corporation and his wife. When we got to our table I asked the lady if I could check her fur coat.

"No *thank* you," she replied with emphasis. "When my husband decides to leave, we *leave*. Right then! I've had to leave a lot of coats behind."

"Yes," her spouse agreed, nodding at her. "And if you don't leave fast enough, I'll leave *you* behind."

Another interesting monster characteristic, relating to interaction with people, is an unerring instinct for the jugular. He knows instantly where a person's deficiencies are. Out of 100 sterling characteristics in a wife, child, acquaintance, or business associate, he will pounce on a single flaw with eerie precision, and punish with it.

Some years ago, after I'd finished a talk before the staff of a huge sportswear manufacturer, the only comment from the company's president was: "You quoted twelve people in one hour." In those days, I was young, insecure, and anxious to make sure my ideas had the proper bibliography and footnotes. I'd gotten a standing ovation, and thought, "Why, that SOB." Later, I realized he was absolutely right. I had, indeed, used authority figures to buttress my insecurities. It hurt me, of course, and that's what he'd intended.

But these fellows always see such things. It's the hunter in them. They know what to watch for and will focus on the single microscopic flaw in a vast surface of perfection. The tactic serves several purposes. Besides being a put-down of the victim, it shifts him to a defensive position, elevates the monster's self-image, and, in a more practical sense, can serve as a mechanism for self-protection. The "chief's" subconscious may, in effect, be saying to him: "We are supposed to climb that mountain together, but I notice that this fellow has a tendency to turn in at the ankle when the right foot is on a skimpy toehold. I'd better watch that, because if that foot slips when we're there on a vertical face, he could bring us all down on the rope."

To focus on someone's strengths would lean too heavily on the monster's optimism—an area largely underdeveloped in him, though he may constantly give lip service to it, pointing to his forward-looking philosophy. It's true that like Sisyphus—condemned to roll the rock up the mountain forever—he never looks back. Not because he's an optimist, but because he is psychologically ill-equipped to stand surprises. Nor is he concerned, as in the case of Satchel Paige, "that something might be gaining" on him. He won't look back on success, either. One key executive gives all his lieutenants a coin imprinted with the slogan: "Always look forward; never look back." His attitude is that if you dwell on previous successes you may get optimistic and drop your guard. Then someone *will* gain on you. Monsters always recognize the fact that someone "out there" *can* get you. And this is where the paranoia mentioned earlier comes into play.

When a top officer of an international shipping combine was sent to head up the company's European headquarters a few years ago, his first move was to replace the entire executive staff of some twenty men with a team of his own. Three of the top officers, whom he particularly suspected would be obstructionists, he had thrown in jail on charges of misuse of company funds. Nothing personal, just good business. Another corporate executive of a major US chemical company, sent to West Virginia as chief of a manufacturing division, cleaned out about fifty members of the former team and replaced them with people of his own from New York.

These men have a great capacity for the compulsive component—not the obsessive (which is the self-doubt). Adlai Stevenson was a brilliant man, but he was totally swamped by Eisenhower in the 1952 and 1956 elections. Stevenson had the obsessive component. When President Truman thrust the nomination on him, Stevenson said, "Let this cup pass from me."

In contrast, Eisenhower put an arm around Richard Nixon and said: "We're going to run a great crusade to rid this country of communism and corruption." And they went on to win a great victory. Stevenson continued with his doubting, obsessive neurosis, and lost twice.

By itself, the compulsive factor drives its subject. "We've got to get the job done!" is the battle cry. The obsessive provides a constant preoccupation with "what I haven't done" or "didn't do." Monster types have no time for such self-deprecatory preoccupations.

While these men are not about to fail in anything they do, they sometimes fan their self-image with displays of great compassion for peer associates or acquaintances who do fail. This may be prompted in part by their tendency to paternalism in business. More probably it leans toward a heroic self-ideal that the strong must carry the weak. This, of course, provides another manifestation of their superiority, but it also reflects the theme in the Boys' Town advertisement of a youngster carrying another kid on his shoulders, and saying, "He's not heavy. He's my brother."

Richard J. Whalen in his book *The Founding Father* tells how when Joseph P. Kennedy, founding father of the political clan, was busy acquiring the first corner on a billion-dollar empire in the years before World War I and worked with a partner named Harry O'Meara. It was a seat-of-the-pants Boston real estate venture known as Old Colony Realty Associates, Inc. Joe and Harry comprised the staff and operating officers, buying, refurbishing, and selling houses. By dint of shrewd bargaining, working seven days a week, and fast turn-around, they managed to put together a substantial business. One day, a friend dropped by, soliciting pledges to help a young Irish buddy in serious trouble. The friend's sick child had died the previous day; he'd lost his job; he and his wife were about to be thrown out of their dingy apartment for nonpayment of rent. The child's body was wrapped in a sheet in the bedroom for want of funds to bury it. O'Meara was writing a check for $50 when Kennedy walked in, heard the story, and told his partner to tear up the check. "What good will $50 do a guy with all that trouble," he asked. "Either do it right or not at all." He told his friend to bring the man in. When he arrived unkempt and ragged the partners recognized him as a neighborhood acquantaince when they were all altar boys together in a local parish church.

Kennedy wrote him a check for $150 and sent him out to buy a suit, shirt, tie, haircut, and shave. Then he arranged a decent burial for the child, straightened out the back rent with the landlord, and, when the man returned, offered him a job with Old Colony. During his tenure with the company, the man attended night law school and later became a successful attorney.

Unfortunately, this positive compassionate characteristic seldom extends to the monster's business subordinates. Nor does it often apply to members of his family except in rare circumstances.

When it comes to the family, these fellows have what I like to think of as a one-way mirror in the head. Such glass transmits the scenery through itself from one side, but if you try to see through it from the other side, you're confronted by an opaque wall.

With monster types, the business influences sometimes get through to affect the family situation, but family influences never get through to affect the business regimen in any way. The separate lives are lived in different compartments. Remember that tunnel vision!

I know the president of a college who, not long ago, was carrying the burden of three major family crises simultaneously. His son had been in an automobile crash and was in the hospital with both legs paralyzed. His wife was suing him for divorce. He had just been offered another presidency and had it under serious consideration. In spite of all these stress-building preoccupations, he seemed totally absorbed by the small matters of business I had for him.

I was amazed, and asked him how he did it. "I live in airtight compartments," he told me. "Those other pressures don't leak in on me here."

The average man, when his wife is seriously ill, or when a son or daughter is having problems in school, sits worried and preoccupied at his desk. He can't work effectively at his job until the problem is solved.

Not so with the monster type. That imaginary one-way window in his head closes it off and it doesn't get through. But he'll go home depressed about something that happened in the office, and be a complete boor all through dinner. If he ever comes home to dinner, that is.

The monster usually has little time for his family, except under special circumstances. In an emergency, for instance, when he can bring his power and influence to bear, he's in there like gangbusters. If a daughter is held by the police for a traffic violation, or a son is arrested for possession of marijuana, he will mobilize all the forces necessary to resolve the problem immediately. He's on the phone instantly to get his lawyer busy; he'll call the judges he knows, and mobilize all the city officials including the mayor to intervene.

One of my clients had a daughter who, traveling in Morocco, collapsed from a too-heavy drug indulgence and went into severe mental depression, creating a serious problem. Local officials put her in a government hospital. removed her passport, and refused to allow her to leave the country.

For four weekends in a row, this top corporate executive flew to Morocco every Thursday night, and was back at his desk, refreshed, on Monday morning. He never let anyone know where he was; his close associates thought he was just taking long weekends to relax a little.

In those four weekends, he studied the Arabic dialect from tapes on the plane, learning enough so that he could talk to the doctors about how to obtain the girl's release. During three of those visits the doctors swamped him with bureaucratic gobbledygook, insisted that the girl required intensive care under their expertise.

"On the last trip I finally found the words to get her out," he told me.

"Marvelous," I said. "What were they?" I thought he'd come up with a new psychiatric diagnosis.

"Very simple. I merely told the head doctor, in Arabic, 'This will be my last trip. I have just run out of money to pay her bills.' They released her immediately."

The incident reflects the shrewdness and compulsive dedication of the monster for any challenging job he undertakes. It also shows that he *can* become concerned with family. Unhappily, it is usually on a temporary basis, reserved for emergencies which he takes care of by the numbers via the shortest, most expeditious route. That's where his training is finely honed. But to respond to family needs on a daily basis is out of the question for this fellow.

At a recent meeting of top executives of a large food store chain, we distributed a confidential questionnaire to the wives who were present, asking them to "characterize" their husbands as one of the four categories of corporate bigamist. About 20 percent considered their husbands "monster type," and the descriptions they gave, in most cases, bore them out. One typical response:

"He *always* puts the company first, above wife and children. He expects the same feedback from his family that he gets from his managers. I was in the hospital for surgery and he would not leave the job long enough to be there. When I came back to my room, I needed him then more than at any other time in my life. We have discussed this and he doesn't understand my attitude."

Being married to a monster type is a terminal illness. For him to be a good husband and father is a non sequitur. As Sam Goldwyn exemplified, he has to win *all* the time. He seldom has the good grace to get sick. His need for perfection in everything makes him a menace even in a well-ordered and -run household. He'll go into the pantry, look at the canned goods, and chew out his wife because all the labels aren't facing forward.

A good marriage is based on tolerance of mutual deficiencies, and these people can't admit to *any* deficiencies, much less have any tolerance for deficiencies in others. Further, they are incapable of emotional involvement with anything—issues, ideologies, women, children—anything. For them, a family is a handicap. It not only consumes valuable time but, more important, reduces any hope of flexibility or a capacity for the detached calculations required to take maximum advantage of continually changing circumstances. The widow of a fighter pilot killed in Vietnam wrote me some time ago to this effect: "He was a fighter pilot first, a husband second, and a father third. We loved each other dearly but I knew he never really was mine. He belonged to the sky, and the sky has now claimed him." This woman found, as many have, that if you are married to such a man you just fan him and feed him between rounds.

The monster's domestic relationship is characterized by what I call "the three I's"—Irrational, Impulsive, and Inconsistent. When I questioned one corporate giant about the pressures of his job, he looked at me, puzzled, and said: "I have no pressures on my job. I take no calls from home." Another magnaté client sees himself, in dreams, being carried around by family members and associates on a palanquin. How would you like to have *that* gem around the house?

The late Mamie Eisenhower, wife of the man who liberated us from the Nazi horde and then became President of the United

States, recalled that during the first two weeks of their fifty-three-year marriage, Ike drew her aside and said, "Mamie, I have to tell you something. My country comes first and you come second."

"As a bride I couldn't understand this," Mrs. Eisenhower recalled. "But that is the way we fundamentally lived our lives." It's the way most wives of such men must live their lives. The wife of Connecticut's Republican Senator Lowell Weicker, Marie Louise, who elected to end their twenty-three-year marriage, said recently: "Whether I'm there or not does not seem to make much difference."

The problem is not just limited to Republicans, in case you wondered. When a reporter interviewing Mrs. Lyndon Baines Johnson asked her to define "a politician," Lady Bird replied: "A politician is someone who ought to be born a foundling and remain a bachelor." She should know.

Monster types, ironically, are usually aware of their effect on the family. As one executive expressed it to me: "My family suffers most. I suffer from fatigue, but they suffer from loneliness." The problem lies in the fact that, outside the confines of their finely honed business talents, they are fish out of water. These men march to a different drummer.

Psychologist Benjamin B. Wolman says in his book *Victims of Success: Emotional Problems of Executives* that his business-success patients all have trouble relating to other people, relaxing, and doing anything except their work. He tells about one businessman with a special talent for complex financial deals. In the office he was "cheerful and full of energy." When his wife dragged him on a vacation to the Caribbean, however, he was miserable. "His only pastime was playing with the pocket calculator to determine the possible income of the hotel owners, or the number of meals served in a week's time, or the number of spoons and forks used at dinner by all the guests together. Once in a while he occupied his mind figuring out the percentage of guests who used the swimming pool and the total sum of the tips given to the beach boys."

The drive of these people is not just for money, nor even for power, but just to be on top, to compete, compulsively, until all acknowledge they are number one. This drive is so all-consuming that nothing else matters. And, as indicated earlier, it permeates all fields of endeavor.

Professor Ann Roe, a famous psychologist, wrote a book attempting to analyze the motivations of eminent scientists and found that the large majority of these people loved their work above all else. In fact, her study revealed that outstanding scientists frequently could not differentiate work from leisure; their work was their life. They preferred it to golf, tennis, or any other recreational activity enjoyed by the average person.

Even in more esoteric fields, like philosophy, the monster types run true to form. Bertrand Russell admittedly wanted a wife who would serve his needs without asking much in return. He was always disappointed. His women were always flawed; none provided him with that perfect blend of intelligence, selflessness, and sensuality he doggedly sought. The fault, as he pointed out to his fourth wife when reviewing the murky history of his unsatisfactory relationships, was basically theirs. Russell's failure to establish genuine contact with other human beings had a devastating effect on his children. Adoring them in his own way, he could never conceal from them, as his daughter Katharine Tait writes in her memoir of her father, that "we were not loved for ourselves, but as bridges out of loneliness. We were part of a charade of togetherness, acted by a fundamentally solitary person. He played at being a father . . . but his heart was elsewhere, and this combination of inner detachment and outer affection caused me much muddled suffering."

The bald fact is that monsters should not marry. Many of them are married only because they originally reasoned that a wife would be a useful adjunct to their drive for success. Perhaps, in a better-ordered future society, the monsters of this world will be identified early on and placed in an elite corps, like the Janissaries who once served as Turkish shock troops. Janissaries were totally dedicated to their trade of warfare. They never married. The ranks were replenished through selection of strong, promising youths.

So much for our portrait of the monster type of corporate bigamists. They are tough customers, but don't sell them short. They are marvelous people to be friends with if you can get that close, but not to be married to. Everything comes before the family. As a friend observed about one of them we both knew, "As an executive you couldn't put a hand on him. As a human being, you wouldn't want to."

For the dedicated, dyed-in-the-wool monster type, there is little that can be done to make a human being of him unless he admits his unbalance and wants to change his ways. It's a little like joining AA. But for most other types of corporate bigamists, there is hope other than all-out leave-taking.

6

Of Januses, Need-Achievers, and Abrahams

☛ When *Playboy* magazine interviewed rock singer John Denver some time ago, the insightful interviewer, who'd been plying him with questions about his domestic affairs, finally nailed him down.

"What about you? It seems to us you're pulled between the family and the world outside the family."

Denver replied: "You've hit the nail on the head. The constant joy to me of seeing Annie with our children—her womanliness, her being a mother—God! But I am a complex person. Annie doesn't fill every space for me, nor I for her. Many people don't face up to that and can't live with it, so it ruins their lives. I'm not willing to let that happen, so I'll be straightforward about it. And Annie knows about my drive to sing. I cannot give that up. I cannot. I would cheat myself, my family, everybody I love. I would take something away from all of them. Annie doesn't like much of the life I lead. That's one of the differences in us. And yet there are aspects of my life that she really enjoys and wants to take advantage of. If I go somewhere she would like to go or where we have mutual friends and she and I have a chance for some time together, she might come along. And certainly she can bring the kids, or not, as she wants. But, as I told you, I was home last year for a total of four weeks."

And there you have an example of a Janus type. This professional corporate bigamist has many of the attributes of the single-minded monster; but he has two faces, front and back. He looks both ways. He is brilliant; he knows it; and he feels he can bridge the gulf between family and job, while giving the job highest priority.

Many a Janus suspects he probably should not have married, and that having children probably was not a good idea in retrospect. One Janus-type chief executive told me that he had decided to marry a committed Catholic girl because she'd *have* to stay married to him. Unlike the monster, however, the Janus does give thought to his family. He thinks he can make the situation work. The job comes before the family, of course but he is confident he can cope with both.

The difference between these types of corporate bigamists is readily discernible in their attitude about the role of the family in their lives. Recently, Joanna Bendheim, profiling six top New York executives for *Westchester Magazine,* characterized Edwin ("Jack") Whitehead, cofounder and Chairman of Technicon Corporation, as follows: "Whitehead doesn't buy the theory of the happy corporate executive. He . . . has been married three times, has terrible relationships with his children, is arrogant, a free thinker, and a nonconformist." Whitehead readily admitted to all of this and described himself as "insecure as they come . . . an unhappy kid. I was fat and had acne and was very unsociable."

On the other hand, William Ellinghaus, vice-chairman of AT & T, who fathered a family of eight children, assured his interviewer that he was happily married, and spent a lot of time with his children, though "more with the first four than I did with the last four. I had more time years ago, every weekend and longer vacations. The whole family must learn to adapt when daddy moves up the ladder and a well-adjusted family learns to cope with that.

"Having a big family," he added significantly, "has been a great thing for my wife."

The trouble with the Janus's optimism is that his coping mechanisms, powerful on the work scene, usually are inadequate to the challenge of family life. His wife tells him their son is on drugs. "No problem," he responds, "I'll handle it in three weeks, when my schedule is a little lighter." He is always in the process of devoting a proportion of his time and energy to making the marriage work. This gives the family hope; but not a great deal of real hope, because the schedule never does get "a little lighter," and everyone—including him—knows it won't.

The Janus, as previously indicated, really believes he can sell his wife and his children anything. Like the monster, he has an instinct for the jugular that may serve him well in business, but can be self-destructive in the family situation.

On his anniversary, when his wife says something like: "Today, dear, I am going to do anything you want me to do," he's apt to ask her to fix him two eggs for breakfast—one boiled and one fried. Then, when the eggs are presented to him, he'll look at them and snarl: "You boiled the wrong egg."

The wife of a Janus type I know asked him one evening, "Do you love me, Joe?"

"Of course," he said.

Then she said, "Do you love me very much?"

He said, "Of course."

"Do you love me very, very, very much?"

"Hell, no!" he said. "Two verys are enough for anyone."

These men are ambivalently torn. They would like to do everything. And wherever you have ambivalence, you also have guilt. The Janus has a lot of guilt and it shows up at odd times.

Not long ago, a client of mine who heads a giant conglomerate was busy with a new merger. He invited my wife and me to dinner, and brought along his own wife and son. The boy was auditing several courses at Baruch College where I teach, so I knew him. The client and I had just finished discussing the president who would come with the company being merged, when my client's wife observed, "Well, he seemed like an *honest* man."

Her husband instantly snapped at her: "Since when did you join the company?"

Within five minutes there was an equally sharp put-down of the son by his father, who asked him, "How do I know you're learning anything in those audited courses if you don't have to take exams?"

"Guess you'll just have to trust me," the lad answered.

"That," said his father, "is a difficult thing to do!"

Then, as we were getting up from the table, the father made a great point of helping the boy on with his topcoat, adjusting the collar and dusting the shoulders with the palm of his hand.

There is little doubt that the Janus, in many cases, would *like* to do better by his family. And I think we can help him.

The next specimen in Feinberg's Wax Museum is the need-achiever type of corporate bigamist. He is far more balanced in his interests than the monster or the Janus. He acknowledges his responsibilities on the domestic front, and does not feel that his marriage is a mistake. He sets goals for himself at home as well as on the job, and he is willing to invest effort to achieve those goals. He does not invariably put success ahead of family.

The multimillionaire president of a national brand apparel company that has used our services, exemplifies for me many of the basic characteristics of the need-achiever. This man has two daughters and a charming wife. He considers most corporate leaders immature, insensitive, and unbalanced in their avoidance of family concerns.

"Life is like a wheel," he says. "If it's out of alignment you go swerving and wandering and bumping along. So I like to align my life.

"To be too involved and absorbed by business is unbalanced," he says. "The options in such total commitment are less desirable —running around all the time with other women, the endless search for the big turn-on, and so forth. For me it's not worth the effort."

For years this man has bridged the gap by taking the summer off with his family at their country home in Connecticut. It is his season for family togetherness, if you will. It doesn't mean that the business is neglected by any means. He is on the phone to his office every morning, but the afternoons and evenings have always been devoted to his daughters, his wife, and their social life.

When his daughters came of college age, he encouraged his wife to pursue a career of her own. She now heads up public relations for a large organization. When she became embroiled in a political power struggle in the outfit, he called in a consultant to advise her. He used to help his youngest daughter with her homework when she was stumped. His eldest daughter is the editor of a national publication. When he reads something he thinks may interest her, he clips it and sends it to her. He often takes her to lunch with interesting people who may have something to add to her knowledge and outlook.

Like all corporate bigamists, however, the need-achiever is a driven overachiever and his relentless drive often extends to his dealings with the family. The wife of one need-achiever told me, "We're like a football team. I hold the ball, he kicks it, and the kids cheer us on."

Unlike the monster, who can compartmentalize his separate lives so that the traumas of one don't impinge on the crises of another, the need-achiever frequently can become a serious victim of stress from the conflicts he experiences in trying to hold both his lives together.

One such young executive I know inherited a place in the family business. He's a third-generation Yankee blueblood, brilliant, with a Harvard education. He has two children, and has deliberately held in check his ambitions and intents in the company because he believes it "may have a negative effect on the kids."

He has avoided contact with and exposure to the chief corporate officer, and has deliberately missed meetings that would make it appear that he was looking for more responsibility and control in the business.

He has been warned that he may miss his opportunity to take his place in the organization. I sent him that wonderfully pertinent quote from Eccles. 3:2–9:

A time to be born and a time to die.

A time to plant, and a time to pluck up that which is planted.

A time to kill, and a time to heal. A time to destroy, and a time to build.

A time to weep, and a time to laugh.

A time to mourn, and a time to dance.

A time to scatter stones, and a time to gather.

A time to embrace, and a time to be far from embraces.

A time to get, and a time to lose.

A time to keep, and a time to cast away.

A time to rend, and a time to sew.

A time to keep silence, and a time to speak.

A time of love, and a time of hatred.

A time of war, and a time of peace.

What hath man more of his labour?

For our need-achiever he "hath," perhaps, to make sure he picks the right time. The problem is that his opportunity in business may not always be available at the time *he* chooses. The need-achiever usually climbs to the top only under special circumstances: if he inherits a business, or if he is a genius. Many of them do and are.

The definition of a genius that I like best is: "a person who has the infinite capacity to shape commonly shared information in a unique fashion." Many need-achievers have this capacity, and most of them need it to succeed in a material sense.

In spite of his family orientation, the need-achiever often becomes trapped in the corporate-bigamy mire. Like most executives with one eye on the glittering goblet of success, he can become overabsorbed with the requirements of the job, and neglect his home life. This state does not, however, grow primarily out of his personality, as it does with the others. It is, rather, a response to contingencies of the moment.

These are the reasons why I believe that there is more hope for the need-achiever. He may be heavily preoccupied with the demands on his career, but he doesn't have to stay that way. Often his realization of the fact that his course may lead toward a dramatic parting with family interests—hurting those he loves—will motivate him to make adjustments. But the insights that can bring this about may have to be provided by his wife. He may not see things clearly on his own, blinded as he is by the drive for success in his business career.

The last exhibit in my museum displays the Abraham type—the self-sacrificer. His is a father/husband above all. Even this benevolent fellow suffers a home-job conflict, but it takes a different form. The stronger pull is toward home. If it's a choice between getting into the accounting books or leaving work early to make paper airplanes for his son who has a cold, he will leave early.

The Abraham type is never going to view the world from the peak of Everest, IBM, a Nobel podium, or any other work pinnacle. Early in the game he may think it will happen. Usually he has come from a sophisticated background and been inculcated with the ideal of material success. He bought the proposition that he carried a marshal's baton in his knapsack, but somewhere along the way the knapsack was lost and a "Tevya" of the world —like the famous fiddler in *Fiddler on the Roof*—emerged.

What was the great appeal of the fiddler? Perhaps it was the homey, if sentimental, portrayal of a father who said, "My family is more important than anything else." He was worried constantly about his daughters and how they would marry. He was trying to balance their pressures against change. He was a man caught in a world of change. Remember the way he described it? He said, "On the one hand she loves the butcher; on the other hand she should do what I tell her to do. She should marry the man picked out by the matchmaker; on the other hand there is love in her eyes." Everything in the fiddler's life revolved around his children.

My own father was similar in his dedication to his family. He cared little about what the world thought. He cared only about what his family thought. While we never wanted for any necessity, my father never made a mark for himself in the world. His entire life was devoted to us. My brother is a physican and I am a professor and this was the realization of his great dream.

For the Abraham type, if he refuses to part with that dream—and most do—destiny demands that he go down as a dutiful and—on the whole—good family man. But not necessarily a happy or fulfilled one.

These, then, are the types of corporate bigamist: the monster, for whom material success comes first, last, and always; the Janus, who says, "Let's do both; let's tango. I can carry both of these responsibilities on my broad, athletic shoulders"; the need-achiever, who will defer success "because my family is more important right now, but I'll achieve material success later to fulfill myself"; and the Abraham, who says, "My family is all that counts in this greedy world."

For extreme types of corporate bigamists, there is little that can be done to make more than a convenient formality of those marriages that may already have become nothing more than a tenuous facade. The dedicated monster is incurable. Abrahams, of course, do not need counsel. But something can be done to help the Janus and the need-achiever, who are less fully committed bigamists. The resolution may be a reconstruction of the marriage in which both partners must play a sincere and dedicated part. It is vital that workable strategies be chosen, thought through, and executed adroitly. Wounds often go deep. We are not dealing with scratches to be covered by Band-Aids and then forgotten.

There's no great mystery about what tears marriages apart. Several years ago J. Krupinski, E. Marshall, and V. Uhl published in the *Journal of Marriage and the Family* an analysis of the breakup of 641 executive marriages. The problems presented by both spouses, in terms of when they felt things were starting to become unglued, were pretty prosaic. The order of destructive events went approximately like this:

- Interpersonal hostility shown in frequent violent arguments, aggravated by practical problems, management of money, childbearing, and a lack of emotional control. The wife in the early stages is the partner most likely to bring the complaints.
- Mutual alienation, manifesting itself in a lack of communication, a difference of aims and interests. "You don't understand me anymore. I don't understand you." There is intolerant behavior on both parts. The wife, sensing her husband's hostility, may suggest a walk in the moonlight "like we used to, so that we can talk a little without the kids

around." This will meet with a blunt rebuff, such as, "Did it ever occur to you that I am tired and have a tough day tomorrow?"

Stung, the wife retaliates. "You weren't too tired to watch the whole ball game on TV . . ." and they're off and running.

• Indifference, reflected by one or the other partner in scathing put-downs. "Do you think the romance has gone out of our lives completely?" the wife asks, in the middle of a sentimental TV show. "Check me during the commercials," her mate replies.

• The wife's loneliness is aggravated by her husband's now-excessive drinking. Coldness creeps into the relationship. The wife becomes indifferent to and totally unable to cope with all the domestic problems. Each accuses the other of being cold sexually. Both may become emotionally ill.

• A new version of power struggles appears. Here the wife is described as aggressive, domineering, nagging, distrustful, embroiled in her own little world.

• The husband avoids his home. Apathy develops. There is no intimacy. It is characterized on a marital-judgment scale as the "intimacy avoidance period."

• The husband (usually) finally throws in the sponge. He says there is nothing he can do and, in traditional situations, he seeks the divorce. The wife is not terribly unhappy about his seeking it.

Putting the pieces of such a mess back together before it reaches the final stages takes hard work. First, the important principle is what you can do together. I don't care whether it's drinking a martini, having lunch together occasionally, making a date to visit a museum, or spending a weekend with nearby parents. What makes it work is doing it *together*, as a working team, to restore a zest for living. Marriages survive when they have built emotional capital that they can draw against in time of crisis.

It is not enough to suggest that the man should talk about his work at home. This is difficult. He wants an island of calm; his own Bali Hai. She wants a peninsula to connect his life with hers. Continued isolation—even when modified by a little sporadic conversation—will erode the relationship. What is needed is the application of some management.

Most of us who do jobs of any importance apply certain management skills to our work. Successful family life needs managing too. Oddly enough, individuals who are highly gifted on the job seem to forget all of their experience when they step over the threshold at the door of their house. The corporate bigamist compartmentalizes his life so completely that he leaves his brain in the desk drawer. In responding—or, more accurately, in not responding—to the needs of his family, he becomes a management imbecile.

This is understandable. We can't keep on operating at full throttle all the waking hours of the day. We need some "down time." However, the corporate bigamist—who is good at work because he goes to extremes in effort and dedication—retreats to the opposite extreme when the faintest trace of a family question impinges on his consciousness.

One day the president of a market research organization was sitting in my office when the phone rang; it was his wife. It had begun to snow. Couldn't he possibly get an early start to avoid the traffic jams? He said, "My dear, I am neither a clock-watcher nor a snow-watcher!" Then he slammed down the phone. The actual subject of his wife's call may have seemed trivial. But the motivation for it was not trivial. His wife was trying to make some kind of a human connection with him.

The corporate bigamist tends to classify every approach from his wife or children as an interruption—of his work or of his leisure. He does not want to be interrupted during the working day; he does not want to be interrupted in the evening or on weekends. One wife told me: "The kids and I are not really like a family. We are more like the retinue of a championship fighter. Everything is geared to getting daddy ready to go back to the wars on Monday morning. He must not be disturbed; he needs his rest; there should be no noise. Our function is to get him into shape for fights that we never see. Apart from this, we don't exist."

Let's take this particular point about interruptions and comment briefly on what we mean by the application of a little management skill. The individual who does not want to be interrupted at inconvenient times learns in business to interrupt *himself* at inconvenient times to do certain things in order to accommodate priorities. In that way he controls his day. The person dedicated to his job can certainly find a few minutes to make phone calls home. Frequent contacts of short duration, rather than rare and protracted grudging contacts, spell "thoughtfulness," and say that home and loved ones are on your mind. It is not the same thing as being there in person, but it may be the best available substitute and can work wonders.

In business, as in family life, we are constantly making trade-offs. The initiation of contacts of adequate frequency—even when nothing too meaningful is discussed—has real as well as symbolic or emotional value. For an anxious wife, there is real benefit in knowing that she does not have to sweat out an opportunity to talk with her husband—about something important, or just to get a few things off her chest. If the working executive would equate contacting his home with the manner in which he maintains the good will of an important client, he could do much to forestall a domestic catastrophe. Of course this is predicated on the assumption that he is interested in maintaining the family connection to at least something approaching the degree to which he wants to maintain his important business contacts.

I have known any number of corporative executives who felt that "checking in" with a spouse occasionally was pretty simplistic. While it certainly is no panacea—nor is it the only suggestion that we will cover in these pages—its importance cannot be overestimated.

Not long ago I was asked to address a group of corporate presidents and their wives. A secretary to one of them chatted with me before the talk and observed that it would be interesting to know how many of the wives present would rather have twice as much husband if it meant half as much money as their high-priced partners brought home. So, when I finished my speech I told them this, and said I would like to poll the wives present. All but a handful leaped at the opportunity to express their feelings in the matter, and all of the women polled—some fifty ladies—turned in slips of paper with anonymous comments in full or partial agreement with the premise. Typical of their observations:

"Yes! I would not only get more husband, but the children would get more father."

"Sure, I would like twice as much husband, but only if he were in one place long enough for someone to introduce him to me . . . I think he's that tall fellow over there."

"Oh, maybe not half as much money, but I would rather have more of him than *more* money."

"I'll trade another promotion for just one night a week that he doesn't bring work home."

And there you have it.

7

The Making of a Corporate Bigamist

Do you know that your soul is of my soul such a part
That you seem to be fiber and core of my heart?
No other can pain me as you, son, can do;
None other can please me or praise me as you.
Remember the world will be quick with its blame
If shadow or shame ever darken your name.
Like mother, like son, is saying so true
The world will judge largely of mother by you.
Be this then your task, if task it shall be,
To force this proud world to do homage to me.
Be sure it will say when its verdict you've won
She reaps as she sowed: "This man is her son!" *

☛ Those lines were written in 1900 by Mary Hardy Mac-
Arthur, mother of General Douglas MacArthur, when her son
was a cadet at the Academy at West Point. He was about to appear
as a witness in a special Presidential court of inquiry into the
matter of hazing. Young MacArthur knew he would be asked to
reveal the names of upper classmen who had run him through a
physical drubbing until he'd lost all muscular control of his limbs.
But his parents had instilled in him two immutable principles—
never lie; never "tattle." He also knew that if he disobeyed the
order of his superiors, it could mean his dismissal from the Academy and the end of his military career before it had fairly begun.
Mrs. MacArthur, who knew the torment tearing at her boy's soul,
sent the rhymed message from her room in the old West Point
Thayer Hotel, where she lived most of the time when he was attending the Academy—"just to be with him."

* *Reminiscences,* by General of the Army Douglas MacArthur, McGraw-Hill
Book Co., © 1964 by Time, Inc. All rights reserved.

In his 1964 book *Reminiscences*, MacArthur confessed that his mother's poem put an end to his indecision. "I knew then what I would do," he said. "Come what may, I would be no tattletale." He *was* asked the question. He skirted it, ducked and dodged it, and, when finally pinned down, refused to reveal the names. He then fell on the mercy of the military court, pleading for any punishment rather than be stripped of his uniform. He was remanded to quarters, court was recessed, and presiding officers got the names elsewhere.

MacArthur went on to become US Army Chief of Staff from 1930 to 1935, Commanding General of US Far Eastern forces in World War II, commander of occupation forces in Japan, and supreme commander of the UN forces in Korea until "relieved" by President Harry Truman. His "sin": outspokenly advocating measures to halt the aggressive support of North Korea by Communist China, in conflict with administration policy. For MacArthur, twice married, country and service to it came first. Politics was far down on his list of priorities. He emphatically turned down a Presidential nomination bid.

As Chief of Staff, MacArthur had locked horns bitterly with Franklin D. Roosevelt when, prior to World War II, the President slashed a military budget that the General considered far below minimal basic defense requirements. MacArthur indicated pointedly that his chief was putting politics ahead of his country. He threatened to resign and take his fight to the public. Roosevelt was livid with rage and obdurate. Then, MacArthur spat out his famous, unprecedented parting shot: "Mr. President, when there's a boy dying on a foreign battlefield with an enemy bayonet in his belly and an enemy boot in his head, I want the last curse on his lips to be for the name of Franklin Delano Roosevelt!" With that he saluted, turned on his heel, strode from the White House, and threw up on the lawn.

A moment later a Presidential assistant appeared and told him that Roosevelt had ordered him back. On the General's return, Roosevelt had quieted down. "Douglas," he said, "You can't say that to me. Why did you?" MacArthur replied: "I could not let my mother down." The President suggested that he "grow up" and get on with his work.

Roosevelt, however, told his people to drop the fight for some of the military cuts he had originally proposed—though he never referred to that bitter encounter.

The roots of MacArthur's driving force were clear. In one of his last public appearances, he referred to Mary Hardy MacArthur as "my sainted mother." Besides having lived practically on campus while her son attended West Point (where he achieved the highest grades ever recorded up until that time, which since then have only been equaled once), Mary MacArthur followed him to various posts overseas until her death in Hawaii in 1935. She was a woman of great character and strength, and the weight of her influence on Douglas's life was considerable. His father, Arthur MacArthur, had achieved the rank of lieutenant general and was also a strong personality. But career requirements kept him preoccupied and the influence on his son's life was more passive and less pronounced than the mother's.

The point in reviewing these phases of General Douglas MacArthur's life is that they provide us with interesting psychological insights regarding the factors that help to mold the unique characteristics of the overachiever, or corporate bigamist.

In endless surveys, almost all dedicated top executives have described their mothers as the guiding force in their early lives. It is usually the mother who was the aggressive, competitive factor in their development. Fathers of such men usually are described by them as having been strong and intelligent, but a relatively passive influence.

If you check the biographies of United States Presidents, you'll find that mother played the major role in most of these childhood scenarios. Harry Truman constantly referred to his mother as the parent who gave him his love of history and pointed him toward politics instead of the haberdashery. Former President Nixon in his farewell address to the nation referred to his mother as the most powerful force in his life. Eisenhower has described a powerful mother. Franklin Roosevelt's mother—a real tiger of a woman—was far-famed for injecting herself into his affairs—all the way to the White House. As every visitor to Hyde Park has discovered to his awe, surprise, or horror, for years before he became President of the United States Franklin occupied the master bedroom in the southwest corner of the building, Sarah Delano Roosevelt occupied the one in the southeast corner, and Eleanor chose to sleep on a narrow cot in the dressing room between the two. Roosevelt's father, a wealthy landowner, was Vice-President of the Delaware and Hudson Railroad and also held diplomatic posts in the Cleveland administration. He was obviously no slouch, but no match for his aggressive wife where their child was concerned.

What we've seen in the mother of such men is a burning desire for the power and success of their offspring. It does not appear to be a compensatory mechanism, but a really calculated drive.

I once interviewed the mother of an entrepreneurial international conglomerate empire-builder. She told me that she had always had ambitions for her son; was always pushing him, always doing something to further his career even as a child. His father, a brilliant mathematician, was passively interested in the boy but had no sense of the practical. Mother was the pragmatist who imbued him with the competitive drive and motivation for material success.

In probing the backgrounds of top executive clients, we often get comments such as: "My mother taught me how to handle money, and the technique of making lists. She always encouraged me to believe that whatever job had to be done, I could do it." When they came home from school and said, "I got 90 in math," is was usually the mother who asked, "Who got the other 10 points?"

Harvard's Dr. David McClelland, whose studies in the field of motivation are now famous, found that first-born (or only) children usually are more likely to be destined for high achievement. Our experience indicates that certainly one of the reasons for this might have to do with the uninterrupted and "new-experience" mother-attention that a first child receives. An aggressive, competitive mother might easily instill those achievement-oriented qualities in a bright first child by her example and suggestions. But as others come along, she gets too busy to provide quite the same attention. Dr. Sigmund Freud believed himself to be his mother's favorite, which, he said, gave him confidence in later life.

When you look at the childhood of these men, you find them highly competitive very early. As one of them said to me, "The lead dog is the only one that gets a change of scenery. I decided this when I was about ten."

A budding corporate bigamist will be the kid on the block who sets up a stand to sell lemonade, or the vegetables he grew in his mother's garden. He's the one with the paper route, who soon splits his profit to hire others to run it so he can pick up an available adjacent route and expand. He's the Tom Sawyer, who gets the contract for a job and then inspires others to do the work.

Some of these boys, by the time they're ten or twelve years old, seem to have an uncanny ability to determine what another youngster can do, and how far he can be pushed. You'll see them watching the hands and the eyes to corroborate their own hunches. How much of this is in the genes or is triggered by parental training and discipline is debatable. But there is no question that the potential corporate bigamist is, as that young wife said about her monster-type husband, "never young." From childhood they will show decisiveness, a willingness to take risks, and—through training, environment, family life-style, or other factors—they have learned to separate themselves from the family.

The founder of a great conglomerate who is now a Hollywood tycoon was only fourteen years old when his mother, cleaning out the pockets of his dirty jeans, discovered papers indicating that he had just bought two moving picture theaters, using collateral from his uncle for bank loans.

Billie Sol Estes, whose questionable financial dealings built a $150 million empire that earned him one stretch in jail and a clutter of new indictments, nevertheless is a striking example of how these driven men get their start. Estes's business career began at thirteen, when his Texas farming parents gave him a five-dollar ewe lamb for Christmas. Billie Sol bought a ram for another borrowed five dollars and, two years later, was the owner of a flock of 100 sheep. The wool and the livestock grossed him $3,000, with which he bought 400 sows and feeder pigs—and so forth. At eighteen, Estes was worth $38,000. He was a millionaire before thirty.

Another fifteen-year-old entrepreneur who later became the international conglomerate head mentioned earlier proved his mettle when he and his mother and younger siblings were stranded in a Paris hotel at the outset of World War II. The father, making a business swing through Europe, had left them with enough money for a week or so, and plans were for them all to meet elsewhere. Meantime, war broke out, reservations were canceled, visas expired. Mother and children were unable to get transportation for several weeks and ran out of money. The young achiever, making friends with hotel personnel, got help in getting the visas extended. He borrowed money from the desk clerks and hall porters, promising interest and using his mother's jewelry as collateral. He then bought tickets, mobilized the family, and got them out of the country.

The achiever's exhibition of early independence was brought home to us in a study our organization conducted involving 5,000 newsboys. These youngsters, ranging in age from about twelve to fifteen, delivered newspapers in rural areas of the country. We were retained to find out the factors that differentiated the boys with flourishing routes from the others. We discovered that the successful ones used the money they earned as they themselves saw fit. Often it was in ways aimed at enlarging their business. The less successful were those who had to have parental approval on how they spent their own money.

The characteristics that seem to predispose such kids to leadership include intelligence, decisiveness, ability to function in total concentration excluding all extraneous problems, a need to avoid repetitive work, high ego bordering on grandiosity, and an abundant competitive drive to win. People who were neighbors and playmates of Franklin Roosevelt in Hyde Park, when he was seven or eight years old, tell us that in simple games like hide and seek, nature projects, boating on the river, he had to be the leader and top winner or he would stalk off for home in a violent fury.

For most achievers, the background is one that has both roots and wings. These are youngsters sufficiently secure so that they can leave the family situation without qualm or guilt, and without looking back. In their famous experiments with baby monkeys given chicken wire or padded cloth "mothers," Drs. Harry Harlow and R. Zimmerman found that those with the wire mothers didn't want to leave them. They had to be taken from them, flailing and screaming. Among those raised by softly padded cloth mothers, a high percentage left the bosom more easily to explore the environment for goodies on their own.

Contrary to some popular concepts, it seems far more probable to us, based on many surveys and extensive questioning of top executives, that many young people leave home *not* because they had bad relationships with their mothers or fathers, but because they had such good relationships that they don't have to look back for approval.

And, as indicated, the formula appears more often than not to involve in the balance a dominant mother with a relatively accepting and nonpunitive father. Apparently it is important that he be nonpunitive. Dr. McClelland, in his Harvard studies, has found that in a significant number of cases where there is a driving mother and a punitive father, there can be all kinds of trouble with male offspring, including homosexuality, drug abuse, and the kind of nonconformity that goes with such problems.

Our own studies would indicate that the real driving force behind the highly successful corporate bigamist seldom if ever is his wife, despite what you may have heard to the contrary. There is not the slightest doubt that a castrating or "bad" wife can stand in the way of a high achiever, drain him, and deprive him of opportunities in the pursuit of his career, or for peaceful interaction in his home life. But a good wife, while she may be cooperative and decidedly *helpful* in making the way easier for an ambitious mate, will not do him as much real good as a bad wife can do him harm.

A fascinating sidelight on maternal influence in the making of an overachiever is the possibility that, if a strong mother's aggressiveness and drive can rub off on a favored son, perhaps some of her maternalism rubs off, too.

This curious idea was pursued not long ago by Dr. Gene Gordon, MD, of Children's Hospital in Washington, DC, in a paper entitled *Maternal Identification in the Male,* delivered at a symposium sponsored by the American Association for the Advancement of Science.

The idea was triggered when, scanning a new Bible he'd been given, Gordon was struck by Moses's appeal to God when his people grumbled about the monotony of a manna diet. "Am I their mother? . . . am I called upon to carry them in my bosom, like a nurse with her babies?" The quote got Dr. Gordon wondering how much mothering there might be in leadership.

"Mothers nurse, love, and protect their children," he observed. "Do leaders and executives care about their followers, employees, 'people'?"

To get some input on the question Gordon rounded up eight top executives—four in government, four in the business world. The interviews, he emphasizes, were neither "subtle nor scientific," but were aimed at finding out if these top leaders had ever been "forced to become involved with associates or subordinates in dealing with their personal problems in a maternal way."

Actually, he used the word "paternal" because he knew that "maternal" would scare them off. The word "fatherly" didn't work. It provoked anxiety. Even "parental" was too much. It made them "uneasy."

"The tendency to equate leadership and manliness," Gordon reports, "is evident today as it was 2,000 years ago" (in Moses's time). An executive he calls "Andrews" (he did not use real names) at first denied that he ever got personally involved with employees. Another, "Baker," thought the premise logical and interesting because he'd noticed it "in others" but it didn't apply to him. A third, "Campbell," denied that personal relationships existed "at the level I operated at. . . . Don't think we were babying our employees."

Later, Andrews recalled a hard-working, loyal, middle-aged employee whose retirement replacement trainee the older man had always praised until retirement drew near. Then the imminent retiree criticized the younger man's competence relentlessly, suggesting that his own expertise was irreplaceable. The problem was a subject at board meetings, and Andrews admitted he devoted half a day every other week for a couple of years to "work this out to the satisfaction of both men."

"What would you do?" Gordon asked.

"Sit and talk. More than anything else—there was no substitute for that . . . or have him come over to my home. . . . Just sit and let our hair down and talk . . . I tried to stress three things: There has to be a shifting of responsibility . . . better we make [it] orderly than under crisis conditions. You have been well rewarded and are financially secure. Are we going to welch on our commitment to this [younger] guy? Is it fair?"

Upshot: the older man retired on schedule.

Baker at first related another executive's experience with a workaholic employee on the edge of a breakdown. The troubled man was given a lot of attention by several executives including Baker. Baker then remembered a young woman on his own staff who came to him with husband problems and confessed she was in love with someone else. "I concluded it was me she was in love with. But . . . it turned out to be someone else," he revealed.

"What did you do?" Gordon asked him.

"I took it upon myself to try [to help] in spite of the fact that she would be in love with someone other than myself [laughter]. I told her she shouldn't feel so guilty . . . I said, 'It's . . . important to recognize what your husband's reaction would be, and the chance you'll destroy your marriage.' . . . I treated her as if she were more or less normal."

It turned out Baker also had shown great concern for a young woman employee who came to him for advice about taking hormones for sterility. He said he had handled that in a "normal common sense way." He advised her to find out how much was known about the treatment, the doctors involved, and the risk she might take. Apparently she did the recommended research, took the treatments, and produced several children.

Campbell, too, it developed, had played Good Samaritan to a loyal employee who'd been advanced beyond his capabilities, and had taken to the bottle and absenteeism. As he put it: "We had to . . . demote him; but do it in a way where he wouldn't lose any self-respect. We moved another officer from a different department, put him over Harry, but Harry kept his title. That was a year ago, and it's worked out very well. We went to considerable pains to make this thing work . . . I called his wife, too, at one point and talked to her."

And so it went. All the interviews were much the same. These examples were cited as vivid illustrations of the "concern, sensitivity, involvement, and, yes, tenderness" of these executives in dealing with the lives of employees.

David Ogilvy, founder of the advertising agency bearing his

name, observed in his book *Confessions of an Advertising Man* that "The executive is inevitably a father figure. To be a good father, whether it is to his children or his associates, requires that he be understanding, that he be considerate, and that he be human enough to be *affectionate*."

But far and away most explicitly revealing on this subject is Mr. Saizo Idemitsu, founder of Idemitsu Kosan Co. in Japan. In an article in MIT's *Technology Review*, author Mitz Noda, senior staff engineer at Hughes Aircraft Co., quotes the Nipponese tycoon as follows: ". . . Years ago mothers came to my company with their sons fresh from primary school. At their request for me to take care of their children, I made up my mind to bring them up in place of their mothers. Ever since, I have translated maternal love into action on every occasion and in every appropriate form to my employees. This is what now is called paternalism. When my employees or their children get married I give them housing and family allowances. *I profess myself to be their mother* (authors' italics) and take a parental attitude toward their joys and sorrows. In short, affection and loving kindness produce respectable people. My company has many employees who carry on my parental love, guaranteeing the perpetuation of my ideas."

Lending further psychological weight to Dr. Gordon's tentative thesis is Freud's observation that pure masculinity or femininity is not to be found in human beings either biologically or psychologically. In addition, he points out, psychiatrists today have pretty well determined that significant identification with one parent or another begins "probably as early as the first few months of postnatal life, and the parent who gets identified with in those early years is the 'mother.' This 'mother,'" Gordon proposes, "is the power in the child's life . . . the first leader, organizer, and executive; and 'her' domain is the child's universe which 'she' runs with omnipotence and omniscience. That is why the child identifies with 'her.'"

Which parent "she" happens to be can make a whale of a difference for the son or daughter (we'll get to her later).

Dr. Gordon concluded by suggesting that "in addition to the usual manly qualities of courage and charisma which are the standard attributes of leadership in our patriarchal, chauvinistic society, executives and leaders may also manifest qualities of tenderness and nurturance which facilitate the executive function." These qualities, he believes, "are maternal and feminine descriptively and metaphorically, but . . . may also derive from early identifications with the mother. . . . In short," he quips, "there may be as much deep psychological truth as there is obscenity in the often-heard complaint that the boss is a 'mother.' "

As far as our corporate bigamists are concerned, it is difficult to identify such maternal qualities of "tenderness and nurturance" in those chummy, conniving monsters and Januses, although the blessings they can bestow on the office family, when they feel like it, could well reflect some such maternal shepherding instinct. In any case, the concept is an interesting one that bears consideration since we are examining the many complex factors that go into the making of these people.

Certainly the same sort of instincts and feelings that went into the creation of Mary Hardy MacArthur's poem, quoted at the start of this chapter, are reflected in the prayer written by the General himself many years later to his own son during the early days of World War II in the Philippines:

> Build me a son, O Lord, who will be strong enough to know when he is weak, and brave enough to face himself when he is afraid; one who will be proud and unbending in honest defeat, and humble and gentle in victory. Build me a son whose wishes will not take the place of deeds; a son who will know Thee—and that to know himself is the foundation stone of knowledge.
> Lead him, I pray, not in the path of ease and comfort, but under the stress and spur of difficulties and challenge. Here let him learn to stand up in the storm; here let him learn compassion for those who fail.
> Build me a son whose heart will be clear, whose goal will be high, a son who will master himself before he seeks to master other men, one who will reach into the future, yet never forget the past.*

* *MacArthur: His Rendezvous with History* by Maj. Gen. Courtney Whitney. Alfred A. Knopf, © 1955 by Time, Inc. All rights reserved.

And after all these things are his, add, I pray, enough of a sense of humor, so that he may always be serious, yet never take himself too seriously. Give him humility, so that he may always remember the simplicity of true greatness, the open mind of true wisdom, and the meekness of true strength.

Then I, his father, will dare to whisper, "I have not lived in vain."

Last year, as a point of interest, we asked a number of top executives among our client corporations to send us recollections of any childhood incidents or circumstances that they felt might have influenced their present material success in the business world. Most answered—some briefly, others in detail. In every case, a heavy maternal influence was emphasized or clearly implied. Here are a few typical responses:

Thomas Turner, a former corporate vice-president of Fairchild Industries, now with Falcon Jet Corporation, wrote: "The only childhood experiences I can recall that affected my business life [were] a hard-working father who instilled in me the work ethic without my knowing it; a realistic mother who advised me to be an engineer, not a starving artist. A close family, lots of love and children."

Wrote Michael Kievman, Vice-President of Cox Broadcasting: "Both parents worked full time . . . to provide for four children. My mother was always able to keep a clean house and fed us well, despite the fact that she had to work sixteen to eighteen hours a day. My earliest memories are of being taken to the shop . . . and having a hot meal prepared by my mother in the back room . . . I had to help in the shop and had little time for extracurricular activities . . . all four kids had to do the same. My oldest brother is one of the world's great violinists. My sister was a harpist and went to Juilliard."

The Chairman and Chief Executive of Beatrice Foods, Wallace Rasmussen, taped a 4,000-word manuscript for us, detailing a childhood of hard physical work and raw courage on the family farm. "When I was about four," he reports, "I remember a winter so cold that my mother made us sit on chairs. We could not play on the floor because our hands and feet would freeze."

His mother, he revealed, "got up early in the morning and worked until late at night . . . she kept our clothes and the house very clean. At the age of five I started working in the fields with my father. I tilled corn, walking behind the harrow with a team of sometimes six horses. . . . Also [that year] I started school. I liked the problems and I liked to learn to read . . . it always seemed easy for me to read. [Early] in the third grade the teacher asked if my mother would permit me to go to fourth grade, and skip third. I convinced my mother that I could do the work, and she agreed.

My father was a gentle person. He worked hard and when an animal would get sick, he could not bear to put it out of its misery. My mother would tell me, 'Go get the shotgun and put that horse (or cow) out of its misery.' I was in my early teens at the time."

And so it went—mother, mother, mother.

Mother, needless to say, is not the end of it by any means. But she appears to be a powerful beginning. The successful high achiever, which includes the corporate bigamist, usually spends his twenties acquiring know-how and judgment in his field, along with his workaholic tendencies. Those were the years when Howard Johnson, for instance, was putting a restaurant chain together. "We were open from seven or eight in the morning to twelve o'clock at night," he told a reporter from *Nation's Business* some years ago. "I could always find something to do. I was always checking.

"From a distance I would sit in my car and watch the operation and then go over and watch it again a little bit. I think it certainly wasn't because I was a genius. I was a hard worker and I happened to have a good idea . . . I had no other interest but building that business. I think that was my only form of recreation."

By the time these people are forty, their career is established (MacArthur was already a general at forty—youngest brigadier in the regular army), and interests outside their immediate position often are developing.

One other characteristic of the up-and-coming corporate bigamist is that his ethics usually are above reproach. Even the most unconventional of them insist on this. Technicon's Chairman,

Jack Whitehead, put it bluntly to *Westchester Magazine*'s reporter: "I don't think that bastards win. Guys with no ethics and morals usually don't make it to the top. People who sacrifice their principles and compromise never do."

Berry Gordo, the astute black Chairman and President of Motown Industries, recently observed: "Many people, in their rise to success, are so busy running to the top, stepping on their competitors, stepping on their enemies, and, saddest of all, stepping on their friends and loved ones in the process, that when they get to the top they look around and discover that they are extremely lonely and unhappy. They'll ask me, 'Where did I go wrong?' My answer has always been 'Probably at the beginning.' "

The upshot of all this is to establish the fact that we need our corporate bigamists desperately. Harvard's David McClelland has demonstrated that the rise and fall of civilizations is dependent on the number of people that are achievement-oriented in a society. He did this by analyzing children's fables and hero stories. Throughout history, when a country's hero books and tales dropped their achievement orientation, he found a collapse in the culture. In short, the phasing out of Horatio Alger often spells the doom of a culture.

And, as far as those driving, guiding mothers are concerned, the thought has occurred to me that, as the Catholic Church removes the best from its genetic bank by making them priests, our new society may lose its competitive mothers. They will be going out to fulfill themselves directly, rather than through their sons. If that happens, we may lose the wellspring of our male executive entrepreneurs.

8

The Perks of Power

☛ An up-and-coming advertising salesman for a national magazine (he later became a top executive in publishing) was recognized by his publisher boss—who told us the story—as a remarkable producer. But his expense account tariff came high. The regular run included items such as hundred-dollar luncheons for himself and clients behind the velvet rope at New York's "21," rented chauffeured limousines, prime seats for top Broadway shows and big-league baseball, country club, yacht club, and luncheon club dues, chartered yachts for deep-sea fishing, and first-class air fares or chartered flights everywhere.

Finally, word got to the top brass via nickel-and-dime-watching accounting department clerks, and the magazine's publisher was told to do something about it. So the boss wrote a scorching memo to his star performer, chewing him out for the record, and threatening to put him on a rigidly limited expense allowance if his profligacy with company funds was not curtailed noticeably, and immediately.

A day or so later, the memo was returned to the publisher,

with a note from the salesman scrawled across the top in red marker pen. It said: "Harry—look what some sonofabitch sent me and signed your name to it!"

Management reacted with laughter and relief. If the salesman had come back with apologies, excuses, or an angry defense of his spending, he would have lost completely the respect of his superiors.

Among the motivations fueling that fire in the belly, which burns to drive the overachiever ever upward, not the least important are the perquisites of power and position that set him aside in the pecking order. Most top corporate executives know this. IBM's founder, Thomas Watson, used to buy promising young executives $500 suits, because "it makes them want it!"

For a junior executive or creative entrepreneurial type recognized upstairs as a "comer," indulgences at company expense usually are tolerated or overlooked. A well-known *Life* magazine photographer, after a three-month assignment overseas some years ago, turned in a huge expense account that included nearly $1,500 in taxi fares. An eager accountant checked out the assignment and sent the expense claim upstairs, recommending the man be fired or forced to repay the company. The late Henry Luce, then the magazine's chairman and founder, called in the photographer and chastised him verbally—but not for the $1,500 claim. The upraiding was for his poor judgment in listing the item as "taxicab fares" when the assignment involved covering naval maneuvers aboard an aircraft carrier in the Mediterranean! It was gently suggested as well that the amount might be considered a little excessive by some people, and there the matter was dropped.

To a corporate chief, the size of that kind of caper doesn't amount to a pocketful of produce from President Jimmy Carter's truck patch in Plains, Georgia. "Perks," as they're called, have been offered for years to top company executives to motivate and reward them for services rendered. You begin to get some idea why such perks that go with leadership are a major factor in the making of a corporate bigamist when you know what really *is* involved—over and above huge salaries, bonuses, and stock options. Recent investigations by the Securities and Exchange Commission, and a survey of 400 top US corporations by Hay Associates, a management consulting firm, turned up details of company jets for personal use, interest-free or low-interest loans for home financing, free life insurance, complete medical, financial, and legal services for top executives and their families, company-provided servants, lodges, beach mansions, and mountain hide-aways, twin-diesel yachts provided for personal commuting to and from homes on the shore. One oil company executive who makes nearly half a million dollars a year in salary and bonuses is provided a free apartment near the company headquarters in Los Angeles, plus a company plane to run him back and forth from his home in New Mexico.

Another president of a giant manufacturing company was loaned $1,800,000 at 6 percent interest (when the prime rate was 8 percent) to buy 60,000 shares of the company's stock. The directors told him he would not have to repay the principal if he achieved certain business goals of the company.

Such goodies—most perfectly legal (even top-echelon civil service and military jobs carry many of them)—have little to do with the money or the material value they represent. After people move up into higher six-figure income brackets, the money becomes relatively academic. As one of them put it, "Hell, you can only drive one Rolls Royce at a time." The perks—like the big, decorator-furnished corner office and private elevator—are the symbols of their power for all to see. It marks them as a breed apart, and some of them use their perquisites to maintain their distance from the "herd."

These are the things the company can and will provide that they can never hope to get at home. It is why they are conscious of being "big shots" in the office. It's what brings the bow from the head waiter who ushers their party to a ringside table and calls them, respectfully, by name. It is the essence of "being some-body," and it is one of the gut reasons they "marry" the company.

Furthermore, the perks stand as symbols of the corporate biga-mist's importance that he can bring to bear on the home front. When his wife would like him to take the garbage out, there's the limousine and chauffeur out front waiting for him, to make her think twice. And who else has a helicopter land on the back lawn to pick him up? Not that damned tennis pro you can be sure. (In many novels corporate wives, when they do throw in the sponge, run off with the tennis pro at the health club, or with their hairdresser.)

The perks don't just make these people more comfortable. They fill their need to demonstrate their competitive superiority. They will always be first on line. It's part of the game for them.

Certainly, most of the corporate bigamists we know love the trappings of power, especially those perks that reinforce their sense of omnipotence; that demonstrate to the chief himself and the world that he is the boss. Recently I had the privilege of riding a private jet with the president of the company that owned it. We had almost reached our destination and had begun the letdown when the pilot's voice came over the PA system advising us politely to fasten our seat belts.

The chief was not about to fasten his belt. He wasn't taking orders from any chauffeur up on the flight deck. Instead, he turned to his secretary and said, gruffly, "Go get me some hot coffee."

The poor woman went forward and came back with the cup of steaming liquid, staggering, and juggling the cup on its saucer as the plane lurched through gusty ground currents seconds before touchdown. I was sure the coffee would spill all over me as well as her boss, and that she'd lose her footing, fall, and hurt herself. By a miracle, it didn't and she didn't. The president took the coffee as though nothing unusual had happened at all.

There are some chief executives, of course, who consider a company jet ostentatious. I flew to the Midwest recently with the president of a large meat-packing concern. We went tourist because that's the way he likes it. I asked him why he kept a company plane. "Well," he said, "I can prove that it's cost effective." Other officers of the company use it, but not the president. He prefers flying tourist because he considers it more democratic, and he is one of those men mentioned earlier who likes to give the impression of having a common touch.

Occasionally junior executives on the way up will deplore extravagant company expenditures for big perks like jets. But when they get to the top spot themselves, most undergo a dramatic change of perspective. A president of an international consulting company used to criticize his predecessor for extravagances with company money. "Damnit," he once said to me, "Joe even has to have his own private plane and pilot. I think that's terrible."

Then, when Joe retired and Jim took over, I accompanied him on a business trip. We went in the private plane. I reminded him of what he'd said and he replied: "Well, I need it because I have to travel around so much making speeches." I nodded. "So did Joe, didn't he?" Silence.

Sometimes there is a slight conflict about it. One young president said to me, "This Mercedes is really great—it's got all this room back here. And you know, it's a little hard on me because of what I used to say on the way up."

However, most of them love the perks and have to have them. When they don't there's usually an ulterior motive. Amadeo Giannini, late chairman and founder of the Bank of America and Transamerica Corporation, refused to move into a fancy office that had been built and furnished for him on the top floor of his then brand-new building in San Francisco. He called it "a bird cage" and turned it over to his executive vice-president. He had a desk set up for himself in the vast, unpartitioned top-floor sanctum with some two dozen vice-presidents. It was right there in the middle of them where he could see and hear everything that went on—and where they'd see him. He told us, "I never lock my desk. Anyone can see anything I've got there anytime." Later, one of his VP's, when that phrase was quoted to him said, "That's right. No need for him to lock it. There's nothing in it."

Actually, Giannini was anything but an ostentatious man. He lived throughout his life in the same modest San Mateo middle-class neighborhood house he bought when his bank was making small business loans to help rebuild San Francisco after the great earthquake. But his apparent modesty in the new bank building was purposefully planned. He had the smartest banking talent that money could buy working for him, and he was shrewd enough to know that he had better keep his eye on it.

Recent attempts to diminish executive perks, starting with President Carter's attack on the "$50 martini lunch" and the US Treasury Department's eyeing of some of the abuses which certainly exist, have not made much headway. Nor are they apt to except in short-term efforts, and intensified crackdowns on flagrant abuses and violations of existing regulations. Mr. Carter hasn't yet given up Air Force One, or Camp David, nor does he exactly work out of an energy-efficient log cabin. The imperial dictum about official limousines had virtually no effect. They're busier than ever. For most high achievers, if the rewards are trimmed, so is incentive.

And in some cases, perks are far more than just goodies for the top dogs. The expense-account lunch, for example, while it may be something of a status symbol in part, also is a long-accepted way of doing business that serves some psychological functions as well. Lionel Tiger, Rutgers University's outspoken Professor of Anthropology, told *The New York Times* in an interview that the business lunch "makes officials into persons, which is difficult to do in a tolerable way within the office."

While there are stories of top executives paying upward of $1,500 for ten-course dinners for six, including $250 wines, truffles, and smoked salmon stuffed with Beluga caviar, most expense-account meals at good, but not ultraposh, metropolitan restaurants will run from $25 to $50 for two. Affluent companies will usually tolerate expenses of up to $12,000 per year for their top-echelon executives, below president and chairman for whom there is seldom a limit. Middle-level managers will run about half that in a major corporation.

Last year, however, Treasury officials estimated that by clamping down on the "travel and entertainment" category of business deductions they could achieve a "significant gain" in tax revenues. They estimated "losses" due to the allowable procedure for handling air travel, hotel costs, nightclub and theater entertainment of clients, along with business luncheons and dinners, somewhere between $500 million and a billion dollars a year.

At the President's mere suggestion of disallowing the personal half of such expense, the National Restaurant Association, representing some 125,000 establishments, promptly demonstrated that any such plan would not only put an end to most business lunches entirely but would deal the entire industry a devastating blow, ma'or victims being small independent neighborhood restaurants employing tens of thousands of unskilled people such as dishwashers, busboys, and waiters-in-training. They threatened to organize a march on Washington in protest.

In short, the perks of power are not simply goodies for the

privileged few; they constitute a big business affecting large sections of the economy.

The hard fact remains, however, that without perquisites business in general would be hard pressed to find enough leaders to go around. Most of these men consider their perks nothing less than their just due. And one of the hardest things for them to face is the fact that some day they will have to give them up. It's a prime reason why the corporate bigamist hates to retire and will do everything in his power to avoid it. Without his corporate army to direct, and his cornucopia of privilege, he is virtually emasculated. He no longer commands a company plane. Gone is the exclusive use of the chauffeured company limousine. He now has to pay the groundkeeper to keep the garden pruned on his exurban estate—which used to be done by the company in return for occasional business lawn parties. You can hear these fellows crying and gnashing their teeth about it in any of the "golden ghettos" like Miami or Palm Springs. They've got $3 million and they groan pitifully about digging into capital to pay their own way. But there's no question about it; it's hard to have to travel commercial when you've been flown around in your own private version of Air Force One for a decade or two. And for the chief corporate executive these things are very important because— above all—they tell *him* that *he* is the boss.

9

The Fragile Structure of Executive Marriage

Charles Luce, Chairman of the Board and chief executive officer of New York's giant utility Consolidated Edison, once told an interviewer, "If you're head of a large corporation you have little time for family activities. . . . Families have to adapt as a man climbs up the ladder and wives have to find a life of their own."

The well-known chief executive officer of a national corporation, a classic corporate bigamist, prides himself on the fact that he puts in seventy hours a week in his office. He admits to bringing home about two more hours of work on most evenings when he gets there, spends at least the better part of one day every weekend on business-related matters, and is out of town on business some five to seven nights per month, on average. When asked how his prolonged absences from them affected his wife and children, he shrugged and replied, "I suppose it's a little hard on them, especially on my wife. But they understand that it's the name of the game, and my wife is a great little manager."

These career-bigamous executives, all "married" to their jobs, reveal by their attitudes a distinct preference for the business "spouse." And yet somehow their more conventional marriage to a living, breathing human wife seems to last. Top-echelon executives and professionals have the lowest divorce rate of any group in the country, according to every survey conducted on the matter.

Given the strains and pressures, the time devoted to nonfamily activities, the conflicting loyalties, and in many instances the constant uprooting of children as the home base shifts to accommodate corporate "progress," how do these men and women achieve such a record of marital longevity and implied—if not actual—happiness? To gain some insights into the mechanics of the phenomenon, we prepared a questionnaire, with the assistance of Dr. Walter Reideman, and administered it at meetings of the Young Presidents Organization, the American Management Association, and other executive meetings throughout the central states. Three hundred executives and two hundred of their wives responded to it.

A quick first look at their responses appeared to verify the idyllic state of things indicated in the rosy reports published by popular women's magazines. For example, 94 percent of the executives and their wives proclaimed their marriages to be "good in every way." Further, 91 percent of the executives said that marriage had changed their lives for the better. Sixty-four percent said that if they had not married they would have found it harder to achieve business success. The picture presented was one of a successful and job-satisfied man returning home to his loving wife and adoring children on their exurban estate for an evening of family togetherness. In sum, it reflected joyous achievement of the American dream.

However, a closer look at the responses showed some startling contradictions that alerted us to the probability that all was not as serene as it had first appeared. Hidden behind the simple tally of "yes" and "no" answers were curious comparisons where husbands contradicted wives on the same question and vice versa, and where write-in comments clued us in to behind-the-scenes factors that seriously qualified many of the pat answers. Maintenance of anything approaching a really successful executive marriage, it became clear as results were studied, leans heavily on a very delicate mechanism requiring constant adjustment by both partners. Like every delicate mechanism, if the adjustment is not exactly perfect, it will cease to work. The process by which the executive and his wife adjust their marriage to the powerful demands made on them by the corporation is fascinating and instructive. It also takes its toll in the form of guilt, anxiety, and suppression of feelings.

The major adjustment made by the executive's wife is a denial of the anger she feels for her husband and the demands he makes on her and their marriage. She, in effect, turns off these feelings and substitutes the belief that her husband is fulfilling all her needs and desires; therefore, the marriage is a good one.

One typical set of answers came from the wife of a corporate president—thirty-nine years old, married eighteen years: "My marriage is good in every way." Then, in another place: "My marriage relationship is good, but I'm personally unhappy." Why is she unhappy? Did she blame her husband? No. He was described as "intelligent, loving, generous, understanding, loyal, dependable, ambitious, hard-working, and has a sense of humor." But the wife was doing it all. She raised the kids, managed the house, hosted her husband's business dinners and parties, stroked and fanned him when he came home whipped, and suppressed all of her own needs to attend to his.

If there is a genuine mutual respect, such accommodation will work. But it takes a remarkably well-adjusted wife to handle it. Lady Clementine Spencer-Churchill, wife of Sir Winston, carried it off with astonishing success. An insightful review of her life in *The New York Times*, when she died, pointed out that she was a truly exceptional person, yet it took all of her intellectual brilliance and strength of character to deal with Churchill's angry resentment of criticism, his tempestuous outbursts, and black fits of despair that he referred to as "the black dog." Her stalwart common sense bolstered his sagging spirits when he was a political outcast between the great wars, and anchored his soaring imagination to earthbound realities during his years as Britain's Prime Minister in World War II. Throughout his roller-coaster political life, in addition to managing a household, she was continually at his side, helping, encouraging, and critiquing his public appearances.

She was no mouse, however, and was observed on more than one occasion surreptitiously rapping his knuckles with a fork when he sulked or got obstreperous at the dinner table. Despite the reaction she knew she could expect, she did not hesitate to criticize or rebuke him for boorish behavior in front of friends. At a dinner one evening he was discussing a volume of his memoirs and called on her for confirmation of a comment he'd made about the book. She calmly observed that the volume was "too full of minutes and memos, and is all rather dull."

Winston flushed lobster red and roared an insult aimed at her judgment in the matter, while guests examined their plates in embarrassed silence.

Clementine rose to the occasion. "Now, Winston," she said, "you really can't talk to me like that you know." And, in a farcical simulation of anger, threw her napkin across the table at him. Everyone howled with laughter, including Sir Winston.

She once told Churchill's doctor, Lord Moran, "I don't argue with Winston because he so often shouts me down. If I have anything important to say, I write a note to him."

The Clementine-Winston relationship was far from a one-way street, however. His respect for his wife was enormous. In a public tribute to her, Churchill once wrote: "My marriage was much the most fortunate and joyous event which happened to me in the whole of my life, for what can be more glorious than to be united in one's walk through life with a being incapable of an ignoble thought."

And in a toast to her, he said: "I could never have succeeded without her."

Clementine's technique in marriage involved no secret, devious manipulation or subtleties. Her methods were forthright and willingly shared. In a talk on men and marriage to a graduating class of her school, she told the young ladies:

"If you find yourself in competition with men, never become aggressive in your rivalry. She who forces her point of view may well lose her advantage. You can gain far more by quietly holding to your convictions but even this must be done with art and, above all, with humor."

Problems for the executive husband in a marriage relationship, our survey showed, are seldom less trying than for his wife. He adjusts by trying to separate his two major roles in life—executive and husband. As an executive, he directs people and organizations under considerable pressure. To do this, he finds he must shut out his feelings about home. Any intrusion by his wife or family often becomes more than he can cope with. If he is a Janus or need-achiever, when he stops work he believes he can effectively shut out his business responsibility and become a devoted husband and father.

But he cannot do this, no matter how hard he tries. As he ascends the corporate ladder he finds more and more of his time and attention devoted to work-related activities just to stay abreast. This arouses guilt: he is "not a good husband." He tries in various ways to compensate. "I'll make it up to them," which he rarely does. "I'm doing it for their sake," which he knows is untrue. A third rationale is to mentally make his wife a part of his success: "I couldn't do it without her," although he never tells her what he is doing. In short, his adjustment technique is to convince himself that his wife is an important part of his life. He usually succeeds, since she seldom complains and tends to idealize their relationship. One manager's comment: "My wife has been a mother and father to the children. It's been very hard on her but she's done a terrific job with them."

That the executive works long hours already has been pointed out. Of those in our study 87 percent reported that they worked all day, evenings and weekends. So it is obvious that the major portion of most executives' time and energy—corporate bigamists or not—is dedicated to work. They know it, and not all are necessarily pleased about it. A typical response: "If there was one aspect of my job I would change it would be not having to put in so many hours." But, of course, he has his reasons for doing it: "I raised my family to expect a certain economic level. I feel the pressure of maintaining that level even if I must neglect them."

Actually, his wife is seldom involved in her husband's work or instrumental in his success. Only two of the wives surveyed said they were helpful in their husband's career. Most of the others saw their primary contribution as being "an understanding wife and making a comfortable home for him." At best, her involvement is limited to being a sounding board, with no actual help for his problems expected or given. The wife of a civil engineer, owner of a construction company, said: "I want him to tell me what is troubling him. . . . When he does something that particularly annoys me, I try to understand his action from his point of view and act accordingly."

Yet the wife does not feel that her husband's job interferes with their marriage. In response to direct questions, only a handful said their husband's job interfered with their home lives. Most said they never feel neglected, and half of them said their children never feel neglected. Although these wives reported that their husbands were away on an average of seven days a month nearly half said they have learned to adjust to it. About 20 of our 200 ladies said they always mind it and always will complain about it. One wife put it this way: "If your husband is working toward a goal for his wife and family, the word 'sacrifice' is a very poor choice. Let's say it's a mutual sacrifice of time with one another over the years."

The study results indicated that executive wives, though alone a great deal, do not feel neglected. One might expect a wife to feel angry at her husband and resentful of his occupation because it keeps them apart so much of the time. Apparently the psychological mechanism at work here is that she suppresses her anger, becomes oblivious to her frustrations, and adapts to the situation with a sigh of resignation. Said one: "What good will being angry do? If I get upset, he'll get upset and then what do I do?"

Curiously, when the wives were asked directly about feeling neglected, or being upset, they denied such feelings. When the questions were *indirect* ("Did you or your husband ever work out a specific compromise because of the demands of his work?") approximately a third of them admitted being alone too often, described a lack of communication with their husbands, or complained that their husbands worked too many hours. A typical response: "I have many small children and no help and my husband is gone most of the time. . . . I would like him to do more things around the house. We have moved many times and there are periods when my husband is gone a great deal." Even in these responses, they rarely attributed negative feelings to themselves. They worried that their husband's health would suffer from the long hours of work, or they wished their husbands had more time for the children. One wife puts it this way: "He really works hard and I worry for his health. . . . He eats and drinks so fast."

Behind these concerns lurked the wife's own wishes, desires, frustrations, and anger, rarely given expression, but which leaked out in unsuspected places. Apparently to justify their desires, it was necessary for the wives to idealize their husbands' commitment to the family. This was reflected in the overrating of the husbands' involvement in raising the children. The wives said that their husbands were involved to a greater extent than the men said they were. For example, a majority of the executives said they were not much involved in any aspect of rearing their children. But an identical percentage of the wives of these same executives maintained they *were* involved in *some* aspects of child-rearing, and many of them said their husbands were involved in *all* aspects of child-rearing.

This idealization was further revealed in contradictory responses to questions about neglect. In every instance, the husband believed he neglected his wife to a greater extent than she said he did. Said one typical husband: "The most important personal sacrifices my wife made was having to raise the children without me, due to my traveling." According to his wife, "He was very sweet with the children and a big help in their development."

Given the hours of work and the commitment to his job, it is likely that this executive evaluated the situation realistically, while his wife distorted and suppressed her feelings to satisfy her intense need to believe she had an ideal marriage—in which the husband is a kind of superman, hard-working, successful, attentive, and involved with the children.

There are two reasons for this particular adjustment. First, the wife believes her husband does not think he is neglecting her. Second, she wants to believe that she is the glue holding the marriage together. "It was the third time we moved in four years," one of them wrote. "The children were miserable. If I showed my unhappiness, everyone and everything would have fallen apart. I had to make sure he was not disturbed by all this."

When the wives were asked, "What do you believe is the *major* contributing factor to extramarital relationships?" nearly half responded, "Lack of understanding, love, and affection of the wife." Few attributed the major cause to the husband. The husbands tend to agree on this, thus supporting the wife's belief that she is responsible for the marriage and indirectly reinforcing her suppression of negative feelings about his career involvement and her idealization of their relationship.

The executive's use of the compartmentalization technique to solve the dichotomies of his life often has a serious effect on a number of critical areas. Most of the men said that they never noted a relationship between events at their office and enjoyment of sex, and only a dozen or so said that they always see such a relationship. This is highly unlikely, since sexual enjoyment is dependent on mood, which is related to other activities. For executives, work is the major activity. So it isn't surprising that more than half of the wives said they sometimes see a relationship between business events and their husband's enjoyment of sex. About twenty of them said they always see such a relationship. It appears, then, that wives are more perceptive of the relationship between business and family life in this regard than are the men.

There is no question that executive husbands make a serious effort to separate their business and domestic lives. Their ability to bring it off is highly doubtful. Most men were convinced that they were able to suppress office problems at home. Questions on the subject brought responses like: "Her biggest complaint is that I don't share my problems with her. I just don't care to rehash them after I get home."

The wives, however, did not buy this. Most said that they knew their mates were trying to suppress office problems. Only a few said they were unaware that their husbands have business problems. Thus, the husbands try; but most do not completely succeed.

The study makes it clear, too, that domestic problems do interfere with the husband's routine. This is especially true of younger men in the early years of marriage, when the children are young. The executives themselves admitted that wives interfere by calling the office for help in solving home problems. A good number of the husbands were resentful of these interferences. A typical response: "I wish she would take more responsibility for the children and learn to stand on her own. She comes to me with every little problem."

What does it all add up to? In a vast majority of cases, the executive's wife, sensitive to her husband's needs, assumed almost total responsibility as caretaker of the home and children. Relieved of this burden, most husbands devoted themselves to the consolidation of their business power base—at the cost of the close family orbit, and a penalty in guilt. Said one: "My wife dropped her career as a talented artist when she married me. She felt there was insufficient time for art and family."

In most cases the conflict between home life and work life was rationalized with observations such as, "It isn't the quantity of time spent with the family, but the quality that counts." Not a few of the executives claimed to be an example to the children of the rewards of hard work and achievement, extolling the virtues of being a good provider of necessities and luxuries.

Most of the executives appeared, in their responses, to remain in a state of some conflict—though not to any harmful degree, since the wives did not complain. The men adjusted, rationalized where necessary, and operated as "paper" husbands and successful executives.

The dynamics of this adjustment appeared to lead, in most cases, to a rather touchy balance in the husband-wife relationships, interpreted as "good" marriages by the participants. The homeostatic condition almost has to be, however, a precarious one for most such partners. Its maintenance depends on the suppression of feelings by the wife, her continued idealization of her husband and their relationship, the continued ability of the husband to compartmentalize his roles to a reasonable degree, and his ability to control feelings of guilt. If any of these elements change, the marriage is in trouble.

The study also revealed that all of these adjustments to the demands of the corporation deprive the couple of many pleasures that marriage can provide. Both husbands and wives reported that communication is a problem. This is not hard to understand. Communication must be kept to a minimum to prevent suppressed conflicts from coming into the open and threatening the delicate balance that the marriage has achieved.

An interesting consequence of the communication deficiency uncovered in the study was that husbands and wives often were unaware how their mates felt on important issues affecting their lives together. Wives rated their sex lives much better than their husbands thought they would rate them. Among the men who said that their sex life was unsatisfactory, three-quarters of their wives thought they had found it "adequate or better."

Other curious differences turned up. In cases where the husbands said they "shouted" when annoyed at their wives, many of those wives called the shouting "a discussion." When husbands said they "sulked," a substantial number of their wives saw this as "discussion." Of the husbands who said they had worked out compromises to solve domestic problems, most of their wives reported "no compromise."

It became evident that the sex life of the executive and his mate is less than optimal—certainly less than one would expect in a marriage described (as most were) "good in every way." Only 39 percent of the husbands described the quality of their sex life as "good in every way." Given the stigma that our contemporary culture attaches to inadequate sex, the figure probably is inflated.

We know there was a minor amount of amusing collusion on some of these answers. Not long after one meeting, a company president called me and said, "You'll get a kick out of this. As you had instructed us, my wife and I filled out the questionnaire separately. But we compared our answers when we finished. I had checked our sex life as 'not satisfactory.' She had checked it 'good in every way.' She asked me if she should change her answer, so I said, 'Of course,' and damned if she didn't hunt up an eraser and change it."

Our study reflected the unique fulfillment that executives derive from their careers, as opposed to their lesser satisfaction from sex-related activities. Sex is not as important as what happens in the office. This is part of the price an executive pays for dividing himself between his marriage and his corporation. He must lose something somewhere; and he appears to lose it at home. More than a third admitted to sexual fulfillment "less often than frequently." More of them felt that their wives were unsatisfied but said that if they had more time and could relax, sex might be more enjoyable.

All told, the executive's marriage is best described as a utilitarian device in which the relationship is largely dependent upon business success, and at a heavy cost in excitement, passion, and spontaneity. What passes for a partnership "good in every way" often is a bland, nonexciting, adjusted marriage of convenience for both—an existence in which the husband and wife cope with the demands made upon them by the corporation.

Wives who were able to adjust by "making a good home," submerging negative feelings, and serving as a sounding board apparently were able to classify themselves as "happy" or "contented." For others, however, this type of adjustment was insufficient. They classified themselves as "incomplete and unfulfilled." In most cases, these wives were not using their intelligence, education, and ability to their satisfaction, and were not content to live in the reflected glory of the husband's success and children's accomplishments. Most of them endeavored to fulfill themselves outside the household, and still make adjustments to the needs of the husband and the corporation. The most common activity was community work, and the majority of them admitted that they did it for self-serving reasons. Less than half indicated that they did it as a service to the community.

So, it becomes clear that the outwardly serene marriage of the top corporate executive is built upon an extremely fragile foundation, in a delicate balance that can easily be disrupted. The single group of people in America that comes closest to fulfilling the American dream of wealth and happiness has achieved not the ideal happiness of the dream, but a will-o'-the-wisp that exists in their heads and may evaporate in a careless instant.

One caveat may be in order regarding our study. It was based largely on the traditional single-breadwinner family in the mid-1970s. What changes lie ahead for the already-fragile structure of the American family group is anyone's guess.

10

Prescription for a Better Domestic Bottom Line

☛ If you trim all the hogwash from the problem of the corporate bigamist and his home life (or lack of it), I suspect that "twice as much spouse and half as much money" lies at the core of what we are dealing with—if not literally, certainly in the broad concept. As the lady said, "maybe not *half* as much money, but rather more of him than *more* money."

Unfortunately, for the entrapped corporate bigamist present income is never the golden pot at the end of the rainbow. If next year's business and next year's income do not exceed the figures for this year, "progress" has come to a standstill; he has *failed!*

A few years ago, the American Telephone and Telegraph Company completed a massive study, conducted over a period of eight years by Drs. Douglas Bray, Richard Campbell, and Donald Grant of the company's Human Resources Division. The purpose of the study was to determine the personality and environment factors that led to, or hindered, advancement of its

110

college-graduate trainees through the company's management levels.

The researchers interviewed subjects annually, probing nine specific "life themes" for each person; observing how emphasis on one or another theme changed as the subject climbed the corporate ladder. They also audited changes in emphasis among those who succeeded, versus the relatively unsuccessful trainees.

Each of the life themes chosen was an indicator of things such as orientation, drive, and purpose in the subject. They included the subject's attitude toward his job content, supervisors, promotion, and the company in general; his educational pursuits, and exercise to maintain or improve physical condition; attitudes toward accumulation of wealth—real estate, securities, etc.; reactions to the kind of neighborhood lived in, and housing desired; activities and concern for spouse, in-laws, and children as well as premarital relationships, such as dating, engagements, and life-style; attitude toward parents, siblings, and relatives; leisure-time pursuits; ethical, philosophical, or religious involvements; community activities such as Chamber of Commerce, Boy Scouts, voluntary civic and charitable efforts, and political activity.

By analyzing changing attitudes toward these life themes by the "successful" versus the "unsuccessful" management trainees, the authors of the study discovered that the subjects fell into two distinct, contrasting types, which they labeled the "enlarger" and the "enfolder." The enlargers were those who were most successful; the enfolders the least successful.

The results are similar to those that we have observed in our consulting work with many organizations. I do not believe that they apply just to mammoth, multinational organizations such as AT & T.

The enlarger's life is oriented toward goals of innovation, change, and growth. The enlarger moves away from tradition and places his emphasis on self-development, and extending his influence outward into his work and community activity. He looks for more responsibility on the job and, as a result, is likely to achieve a position of more influence in organizations. His self-development and career development are in the areas he stresses. Earlier ties to parents and formal religious practices weaken as he grows outward.

The enfolder's life is oriented toward goals of tradition and stability. Rather than project himself outward, he seeks to cultivate and solidify those things with which he feels most comfortable in his own familiar sphere. He forms close attachments to a small circle of friends and most of his socializing is done with relatives. Status considerations sometimes embarrass him. He values informality, sincerity, and genuineness in his human affairs.

What it all adds up to is not so surprising: the more successful men become more committed to their work, more outward-oriented, away from the family.

Less successful men become more involved in their families, in their religious, recreational, and social activities. The enlargers are the Januses and the need-achievement people of the world. The enfolders are more like the Abrahams of the world.

Is it possible, then, for the enlargers who do move up in corporations to develop some kind of genuine family relationship? I am reminded of F. Scott Fitzgerald who said that one characteristic of a first-rate intellect is its ability to entertain two contradictory ideas in the mind simultaneously. In this context, and stealing a thought from that first-rate mind, we can consider the prospects hopeless but, at the same time, determine to make them otherwise.

With this established, we can presume to make some recommendations for the successful corporate executives who recognize a deficiency in their domestic relations and would honestly like to do something about it.

First, we need a picture of the person we are talking about. Let's say he is an enlarger. He's forty-three years old and married. He is aggressive, ambitious, and loves his work. He spends ten or eleven hours each day in his office, and comes home dead tired. But after dinner he will shuffle papers from his briefcase until past midnight. In short, he is a "typical" executive family man; a need-achiever on the way up. The only fly in his ointment is his wife. Or, if our subject is a career woman, the "fly" would be the husband.

Eleanor Hicks, a beautiful thirty-two-year-old woman who heads the United States Consulate in Nice, France, makes it clear that, with her foreign-service ambitions, any potential husband will have to accommodate his career to hers. The spouse of such a career-oriented woman would have to be someone who isn't geared to one place; someone like an artist or writer who can move around and enjoy it. The government now tries to make it easier for married women to have careers in the foreign service. Today, things are changing for both the career woman and the man.

In more traditional times, Eleanor Roosevelt wrote to a friend in the armed services, advising him as follows: "There is one thing I have always wanted to say to you. When you go home and get engrossed in work, see that you stop long enough now and then—even when she is working with you—to make her feel she is first in your life, even more important than saving the world. Every woman wants to be first to someone sometime in her life."

So, to our recommendations. They are observations which I think can be helpful toward achieving marriage harmony for the busy executive. Put them where you will stumble over them frequently, and use them as references.

Stop hiding behind alibis. Eliminate the standard excuses we've already discussed, plus those you've invented. Your wife is intelligent (or you wouldn't have married her) and she won't buy them. Sit down with her and convince her that you are ready to face the responsibility of helping to find solutions to the problems you both face. Then make a sincere effort to *do* it.

Schedule time exclusively for your family. This should not be regarded, grudgingly, as a favor you are doing for your wife and kids, or as precious moments wrenched from productive working time. Even if it is, don't ever let it show. Think of it as a business proposition. You are a problem-solving, result-achieving machine, which is why you got where you are in business. But machines need care. You need the break. Furthermore, by taking such breaks, you are improving a situation that may harm your capacity to do your best job. Serious emotional problems besetting your wife and/or children will suck away far more of your creative ability than the modest investment of a little time in family living.

If you can't spend evenings and weekends at home, plan your

schedule so that you can take a few days off every couple of months to be with your family. I know a General Electric executive who takes off to a private island every three months for a few days with his family, though he rarely sees them in between these times. Another takes his wife to a cabin he owns on a lake for a quiet day or two of sailing, reading, and planning.

An otherwise neglected wife will look forward with anticipation to such periods together, and *thank* you for making them possible.

So, decide for yourself if the maintenance of a healthy family life is important to you. If it is, then self-respect should impel you to take the steps necessary to achieve success at home as well as in the office.

Not every corporate bigamist *does* consider the family relationship important to him, of course. When Hubert Humphrey's illness forced him to retire from the Senate to spend his remaining life back home in Minnesota, a number of his colleagues were seriously concerned that he would be climbing the walls in short order. Scotty Reston told them to relax. "Hubert can go home to Muriel because his home holds no terrors for him," he said. Most of the others couldn't understand what he was talking about.

Capitalize on the small things in life. Emotional capital is easily piled up by celebrating minor anniversaries. It doesn't have to be a big event; a luncheon or dinner out on Valentine's Day can be a great surprise. It even can be just a thoughtful thing like bringing home flowers (the kind she likes best) or just getting up early in the morning to see a sunrise, enjoying a sunset, or suggesting a ten-minute walk under the stars. The fact that you thought of it means more than what you do about it.

A number of busy executives I know arrange to have lunch downtown or—if it isn't too far away—at home with their wives one or more times a month, to help bridge the gap between business and family affairs.

When I suggest this to men who haven't tried it, I frequently get the icy stare. I know what they're thinking. After a decade or more of marriage, lunch with a wife has all the appeal of an unexpected call from the IRS, or a flat tire on the way to a board meeting. "What the hell," they are wondering, "do you talk about at lunch with a wife of a dozen years?" According to men who follow the practice, there's plenty to talk about, and they thoroughly enjoy it. Recently, *The New York Times* interviewed half a dozen top executives who habitually lunch with their wives when they can, and here's what they said:

Such mid-week noontime meetings with his wife, says William Fine, a former Hearst executive now associated with the Frances Denney cosmetic firm, gets more accomplished than talking at home; and afterward there's a tingle of romance. His wife, Susan, who is creative director for the same firm, agrees. "It's . . . a nice quiet way to catch up and get everything out of our hair. . . . It's completely relaxing, and Bill's very interesting to talk to because he has so many projects."

Thomas Amory, president of a New York executive recruitment firm, lunches with his wife of ten years whenever he has no business appointments. "I'd rather lunch with my wife than with anyone," he says. "We enjoy each other's company and are as interested in each other now as we were when we got married." Mrs. Amory notes that their evenings usually involve business functions and·dinners, "so there's no lack of conversation at lunch. . . . We talk about business, children, social life, frivolous things, and we flirt."

Walter Hoving, chairman of Tiffany, walks a good half mile home to his East Fifty-second Street apartment nearly every day to lunch with his wife, Jane. When the *Times* reporter asked Mrs. Hoving if there was ever a problem with conversation, she promptly replied: "With *Walter?*"

The head of New York's Citizens Committee, new Dean of the Columbia University School of Journalism, and former Editor-in-Chief of *Newsweek* magazine, Osborn ("Oz") Elliott, calls lunch with his wife "a happy event. . . . We never seem to have the problem of nothing to say." His wife, Inger, who is President of China Seas, says the luncheons with Oz give her "a delicious feeling." Food isn't the object, she says. "I like being with him, and I like being with him in the middle of the day."

An important thing to remember if you decide to take your wife to lunch or dinner: don't skimp. These should be special occasions, so try to make them just that. And whatever you do, spend your own money—not the company's or the tax collector's. Several corporate bigamists we know have learned the hard way that bad situations are made worse, not better, when rare moments of recreation with their wives are obviously on the expense account.

Be open-minded to criticism and tolerant of it. One has to be able to evaluate a mate negatively and take criticism in good grace. My wife is one of my best critics. I came back from a seminar conducted by the late Senator Hubert Humphrey and former Secretary of Agriculture Ralph Hodgson, and I said to her: "I listened to those fellows and I tell you I am as bright as they are." And she said, "That's the trouble with the United States." She needs the freedom to tell me off. And I don't mind (most of the time). In this case I was up against leaders on whom the fate of the country depends. Her dig wasn't in a class with the wisecrack of the wife who, when her husband said after a speech, "I brought down the house!" replied sourly: "So do termites."

The best words to describe this kind of essential accommodation are flexibility, empathy, and motivation. As one great statesman, Carlos Romulo, once put it, "The taller the bamboo, the lower it can bend." Empathy is knowing what hurts the other person. "If you love me, you know what hurts me." Finally, motivation is the inner fire that drives you to maintain the family and the marriage as extremely important factors in life's journey.

If you travel a great deal, call home frequently. As indicated earlier, brief but frequent contacts that show concern are better than rare, grumpy visits that grate. Don't wait for a reason to call. Check in with your wife the first thing in the morning. Ask her how she slept. Any home repair problems? Talk briefly with each child individually before they leave for school, and don't talk in generalities. "Did you put up those shelves for mother?" "What dress are you wearing to school today?" Call again in the evening around bedtime. Ask your wife about the PTA meeting; your boy about the ball game. Such calls will demonstrate to your family that you can still be close to them when you are far away. They also enable your wife to get things off her chest; to lean on you for advice and opinion if the furnace isn't heating the house properly, your daughter is flunking math, the boy dented the car fender. You may not be able to do much but sympathize at the time, but she will have communicated her anxiety and found some release in sharing it. Furthermore, she won't save up all the bad news and let you have it in a chilling broadside when you return home exhausted from the trip. Don't be disappointed if you picked the wrong time to call and your wife is not in the mood to chat. Maybe she is in the midst of reprimanding your son, or stopping the roast from burning. As the wife of a sugar company executive put it: "Why can't he give me the same courtesy he would a customer, and call back?"

Work for the company part of the time and for the family part of the time. Two young executives I know have made compacts with their wives. One goes to work early, stays late at the office, and frequently brings work home at night. Until recently theirs was an unhappy marriage. Lately he has been giving all his in-town, meeting-free weekends entirely to his family. Starting Staurday morning, he doesn't conduct any business for forty-eight hours. He even gave up weekend golf to be with his family. He does whatever the young children want to do; boating, walking, movies, bowling. Saturday and Sunday nights he socializes with his wife and friends, or he and his wife take in a concert, opera, play, or a movie together. The other fellow devotes every available free moment to his family now, while the children are growing up. But he has agreed with his wife that once the youngsters finish high school—about five years hence—he will spend more and more time advancing his career. Then she will see him less and less, except when they steal away together. His wife has accepted the idea, knowing that, though he loves his work, he is sacrificing advancement now for the sake of the kids.

Don't be a perpetual Santa Claus to the children. Grand-parents usually lavish gifts on the children so there is rarely a need for father to do the same. Too many gifts often are regarded by bright youngsters as an attempt to buy their affection. An occa-sional gift, justified by an achievement or event, is fine. Make sure it is something the child wants. A doll unique to a foreign country you've visited—for a young daughter's collection—will bring smiles and appreciation. If the boy is a student of history, bring him an appropriate book on the Civil War rather than a fancy bike. Try to bring thoughtful gifts for each one, including your wife. On a trip, pick something characteristic of the area in which you find yourself; modest but attractive handmade silver jewelry from Mexico, orchid pins from Caracas, local crafts items from various states. Once in a while, of course, it's good to be splashy with something extravagant for your wife—a "thank you" for her hard work.

Share business successes and failures as they occur. The idea that wives don't understand business, find it dull, or aren't interested, is a common fiction often employed by the corporate bigamist to excuse himself from any obligation to communicate. Don't delude yourself on this subject. Most wives of executive husbands *are* interested and have the education to comprehend fully the implications—if not the technicalities—of business transactions if they are graphically presented. She'll be interested to know that "Old Jackson" approved that marketing program you've been working on nights. Or that he arbitrarily kicked out your proposal on employment policies.

No wife can be enthusiastic about her husband's career if he never bothers to tell her about his experiences. Wives of our clients often lament to us: "He never talks to me."

One president of a university said to me, "I can't give a performance all day then come back home and give one at night. I don't want to recount all the traumas of the day over my dinner. I want an island of calm and quiet." Well, unfortunately he (and you), are going to have to develop a peninsula instead of an island, because she wants to be involved.

Use your influence, position, and business skills to help your family. If you own the company or run it, and your son needs copies of a map for geography class, have your secretary make copies (ask her to do it when she's not busy, or she'll hate you). If your wife is writing a report for the PTA, have someone in your office type it up in spare time and make copies for distribution. If your daughter needs to interview someone for a school project, introduce her to an appropriate business associate. Take members of your family to lunch with interesting people you know, when business permits. Years ago, one of my sons was interested in biology. At that time, a client of mine had acquired a chemical company. Scientists at the company helped to set up an insecticide experiment for my son and provided insects for him to study. I carried his observations and questions to the scientists for answers. I might add that my son is now resident physician in neurology in a leading university hospital.

Another client of mine used his business acumen to help his son out of a jam. The boy was waging an apparently unsuccessful campaign for an elected office in his high school. Taking time out from a busy schedule, the executive helped the boy to organize and plot an effective political strategy, taking pains to instruct him on the reasons for each step of the campaign. The boy took advantage of his father's savvy and won the election. That boy is now a Congressman from the State of Massachusetts.

Things that may seem unimportant to you can be really big stuff to a youngster. An insurance company vice-president I know had a promotional association with a famous football hero, and obtained an autographed picture of the man. His young son took it to school and was a proud six year old in "Show and Tell." Obviously father grew taller in the son's eyes as a result of the experience.

Begin by making small compromises. Some minor changes in your working habits will be necessary in order to warm up a cooling domestic front. You don't have to give up all business trips, or evening work. But perhaps you can cut down on the number of trips you take. Surely *some* of those trips can be delegated to an assistant who may welcome the opportunity to pinch-hit for you. Try making it home for dinner at least two or three times a week. Avoid bringing home extra work unless your wife is going out. If you need extra time in the office, try going to work earlier in the morning. Few families object to this. Small compromises are always possible, and are critical if you are to make a success of your marriage.

Make really significant use of your family time. If you are really good at your work, then you are good planner. Organize time with your family the way you would business time, and make it meaningful. Set yourself as the chairman of the entertainment committee.

Most important, *be involved.* If you take your wife out to dinner or the theater, don't go to sleep (many men do!). If you were with a client, you'd damned well stay awake. Make an effort to show your family that you have a strong emotional involvement in your home. Later, you will discover that these small efforts have accumulated to build substantial emotional capital and helped to maintain a surprisingly good relationship with your family.

When his son was elected to the Presidency, the late Joseph P. Kennedy said, "There is no other success for a father than to have made some contribution to the development of his children." The elder Kennedy was frequently away from home for long periods, and it was his wife who provided him with lists of questions to ask the children when he did get home. But the crux of the matter is that he made it a point to ask those questions. Your wife is the key to your relationship with your children. She is the gatekeeper. One sociologist did a study in which he found out that a woman can be a great mother and a terrible wife, but that a man cannot be a great father and a terrible husband.

Dissolve role-playing injurious to family relationships. Too much "macho" can destroy a marriage. Old saws, such as "That's not a man's work," for instance, will quickly raise hackles in this time of new life-styles. I notice that my son, for example, prepares meals now for himself and our friend-in-law, with whom he shares his life. I would never do that. My mother always taught me not to be caught carrying a shopping bag. I have spent forty years trying to overcome that hang-up to help my wife do some of the shopping occasionally. I still have trouble. Recently I had to rush to a client and asked my secretary-assistant, Elsie Quinn, to put some necessary books in a shopping bag for me. (They wouldn't fit in the stuffed attaché case.) She did, and I went off without them—shades of Freud.

It is important that people of opposite sex are willing, at times, to take on so-called feminine or so-called masculine roles. A tiny thirty-one-year-old blonde I know drove a tractor during spring planting a few years ago, for the first time since her marriage to a successful farmer husband. Her three sons are now all in school. Her husband lets her use a $12,000 air-conditioned crawler with a glass-enclosed cab that protects her from rain, wind, sunburn. Here is what the wife said about their relationship after a season of tractor-driving. "We get along better since I started working with him in the fields. Now I realize why he works so late. I hate to quit, too, when it is still light and there are a few more rows to finish."

There are always "still a few more rows to finish" and if you can finish them together, you will build the emotional capital we've already mentioned that I firmly believe is a clinical component of a successful marriage.

Maintain a mature attitude about sex. Marriages do not break up because of sex alone. Sex is a sensitive barometer of problems in other areas. People in a marriage relationship should react whimsically to sex—like two puppy dogs playing in the grass. People should realize that the major sexual organ of the female is the cerebral cortex. It is how she sees a given situation. When a man comes home at night, unfortunately, he wants that Bali Hai—isolated from the pressures of the world. The woman craves adult communication. She would like to discuss what he's done during the day, to be connected to the main part of his life, to bridge the gap. Having understood that, they both can interface with each other so that sex becomes a normal, flowing consequence of their emotional commitment to each other. Sex should never be just sex.

Masters and Johnson in a brilliant article warned against bringing the work ethic into bed. (The wife of one executive we know complains bitterly that he has "finally" begun bringing his briefcase into the bedroom and works in bed.) The work ethic is goal-oriented while the sexual experience should be process-oriented. They pointed out that impotency among top executives is on the rise. Men committed to fulfilling obligations under pressure of time tend to want the sex over and done with—like any other "chore"—so they can get on to other goals. "Grab 'em and stab 'em." "Bim-bam, thank you ma'am" is too often the attitude of the dedicated corporate bigamist. This time-pressured attitude blocks the full enjoyment of the sensual aspects of the experience. Masters and Johnson point out the need to be "sensate" rather than goal-focused. Kissing, holding, talking together lovingly should be as pleasurable as the consummate act.

Communicate! Any corporate executive or career professional person knows that the life blood of his business is communication. Family relations are no different. Communication is a two-way street. Problems are solved mutually, not by one-way pontifications. When family problems arise they can be worked out only by husband and wife talking them over, planning together, working on them together. They work it out.

In a going business concern, you evaluate the operation on a regular basis with the whole top staff present. There is nothing so different about a family organization. Marriages can just as readily be based on a mutual renewal of contracts. Husbands and wives *must* take time out to discuss how well or badly the domestic business is going, if it is to survive. Where can it be improved? Where have they disappointed each other? What steps can be taken to achieve a smoother-flowing, well-oiled operation? Marriage lends itself uniquely to practical analysis and pragmatic solutions—a near-perfect arena for the trained analytical approach of the top corporate executive working in concert with a mate who is trained and experienced in the operation of a usually understaffed domestic plant.

All kinds of marital problems can be solved mutually by talking over the pros and cons calmly and rationally: Should mom go back to work if the kids are grown and off to school? Should dad accept a new job offer on the West Coast that promises more money and career advancement, if it will disrupt the children's schooling, tear them from associations just established. More lives than dad's will be affected, and more voices than his should be heard before a decision is made.

These are the sort of crises that will tear marriages apart when a corporate bigamist insists that his trip up the ladder is all that counts. Where intelligent people are concerned—and most of the people we're talking about *are* intelligent—compromises can be reached and successful conclusions achieved.

While husband and wife do these things together, they are building that emotional capital, a lack of which can unglue the best of unions. Emotional capital, my father used to say, "is the blanket that hangs over the bed that gives you the most warmth." It's what you draw on when a child is sick; when your son is caught in the school john smoking pot; when neighbors gossip maliciously to destroy your image.

"The kid got killed in an automobile accident and that is what wrecked their marriage."

Baloney! The marriage was destroyed because there was no emotional capital from which to draw. There was no doing-it-together. There was no mutual problem-solving approach. There was limited—if any—empathy. You have got to have cash flow for emergencies and for most of us the capital for it is built on a daily basis.

If you think all this is impossible to achieve for a man with heavy career responsibilites, it won't hurt you to take a look at the man presently holding down (whether you like the way he's doing it or not and regardless of your politics) the job reputed to be the toughest in the country. President Jimmy Carter was described by Saul Pett in a highly insightful Associated Press profile as follows:

"A man who can keep twenty-five complicated projects in his head without stumbling over a detail, a man with a Bible on his desk and a finely honed schedule that includes: '12:15, Lunch, Oval Office, Rosalynn Carter.'

"A man of diverse parts which ordinarily don't connect in most human beings, a man who likes poetry and music and uses words like 'maximize' and 'support capability' and wrestles with his daughter on the floor after dinner.

"Or spends hours helping her build a lean-to at Camp David. Or holds her on his lap on Air Force One and, when she asks, 'Where does the moon come from?' gives her a patient, detailed lecture on the solar system.

"Or takes her to a movie when momma is out of town.

"An urbane man who told *Playboy* what he did, and with Amy watches his wife disappear in the sky on the way to South America, watches until the last moment and turns and says, 'I miss her already.' And no one who heard him doubted him.

"A Baptist who advises sinning aides to marry the girl, a family man who invites an assistant with marital troubles to come to the White House with his wife and kids and see how the Carters get along. A father who could not prevent some marital trouble in his own son.

"A complex man, a private man, who holds more news conferences than anybody before him, ducks fewer questions, and remains in command the way Jack Kennedy and Franklin Roosevelt did, without the wit of the one or the guile of the other.

"Back in the Oval Office, the President said he enjoys the job and indicated he plunges with relish into 'the complexities [which] are almost incomprehensible'—nuclear proliferation, nuclear disarmament, the Mideast, southern Africa."

11

The Troubled American Family

A year or so ago the parents of a twenty-four-year-old Colorado youth were treated to what must have been a high-voltage shock by a letter from an attorney announcing that their son was suing them for $350,000. They were charged, they found, with neglecting his requirements for clothes, nourishment, shelter, and "psychological support" at certain specific times in his life when he felt he was entitled to them. The lad's lawyer explained: "Basically what we are doing is bringing suit for malpractice of parenting."

According to a contemporary dictionary, "malpractice" is defined as the "failure of a professional person to render proper services through reprehensible ignorance or negligence."

Russell Baker, who discussed the case in his *New York Times* column, pointed out in pained protest that parenthood for most of us is strictly an amateur operation at best—especially in the beginning—and it seldom achieves anything approaching professionalism until after three or four kids and a decade or more of field experience. Even when reasonably competent parents remarry after forty and produce new offspring, on purpose or otherwise, they may find to their bewilderment that their hard-won knowledge is completely out of date; that they are still amateurs. Even specialists in child raising like Dr. Benjamin Spock, Baker noted, are unclear about what constitutes malpractice, as evidenced by Spiro Agnew's attack charging Spock himself with malpractice on the grounds that his theories begat the evils of permissiveness.

Mr. Baker, in his own amusingly delightful fashion, wrapped up the item with the observation that he'd be hard pressed to raise $350,000 for a suing son, but might be able to pay off parking tickets or raise hell for the kid if he got in trouble. Now, though, he'd hesitate to do that, he said, and leave himself open to a charge of malpractice of parenting by the Spiro Agnew school.

Unhappily, there is nothing really amusing about the implications that Russell Baker made abundantly clear in his column. Can you imagine what an upper-middle-class father would have done to a son who tried to sue him on such grounds at the turn of the century, or even in the late 1940s? The young man would have been disowned and no self-respecting lawyer would have touched the case.

In approaching the whole area of contemporary family life, and factors such as the social and corporate pressures that impinge on it today, it is essential for all of us to understand that the future is not what it used to be, and neither is the present for that matter.

Young marrieds today have a whole new approach. Once taboo subjects such as the possibility of divorce and its implications are apt to be discussed with the same candid objectivity as projecting possible plans for a trip abroad. When my son's wife asked him what would happen to his stock holdings if they should divorce, he casually informed her, "In that case they're mine. I bought them in my name." Though she apparently had not liked the response, she'd had no inhibitions about asking the question, nor had he about answering it.

Another interesting sidelight on contemporary couples is that none of them will admit that they have a problem. It's not fashionable. For instance, there is no longer any social approbation for a wife who complains that her husband is a corporate slave who almost never comes home. Years ago, such a wife might take pride in her "big businessman" mate and bask in his glory, even though she complained bitterly about her problems. Friends and neighbors could be counted on to recognize that the complaints really were a form of bragging about her sacrifices and envious social position, and she could get social approbation from them: "We ought to give her a little sympathy. She has been long-suffering with that rich old goat." It's like the old story about the Klopman diamond, which supposedly carried a deadly curse. When asked what the curse was, Mrs. Klopman responded, "Mr. Klopman."

Nowadays this approach doesn't work at all. The present generation of young marrieds will deny that a problem exists. Now the cry is: "You must be some kind of nut to stay married to such an ape." The modern wife cannot complain. "If you're unhappy, get out!" she is advised by her buddies. Yesterday's housewife didn't think she had that option. She was in the same cultural bind as wives in Islamic countries: her husband could divorce her, but she could never initiate such an action.

Many more changes are in the offing, you can be sure. The children who are the product of these contemporary young adults will impose their idiosyncrasies on the culture, and some of them may be even more individualistic than anything we have yet seen.

Nearly 20 percent of today's children are being reared in one-parent families. In most cases that parent is a working woman. In more than half of the dual families, both mother and father work, so there's nobody home to take care of the children. Those that can afford it hire children-sitters, or taxi the kids back and forth to a day-care center if they can find a reputable one. Presently there are far too few to cope with the demand.

All of this has been pointed out with flourishes by Professor Urie Bronfenbrenner of Cornell University, bolstered by many studies he has conducted on the subject. In terms of child-rearing, he points out that the old American concept of the clustered family haven, ruled over by mom while pop brought home the bacon for a passel of duty-devoted, home-loving youngsters, exists in fewer and fewer American communities. Most European and Asian cultures still are structured around what social scientists call the "nuclear family." In this country, however, the family has ceased to provide a real nucleus for a neatly structured culture. Life-style is influenced by a kaleidoscopic montage of economic and business world demands on the old homestead, and by problems that arise when both parents work—a burgeoning phenomenon we'll explore. In addition to the problems already mentioned there are all the domestic chores, the transporting of a commuting husband to the railroad, of children to school, the dentist, ballet lessons, scout meetings, band practice. Then come the social and civic activities in the evenings.

The proper development of a day-care child "physically, mentally, socially, and morally," says Dr. Bronfenbrenner, leans on one vital requirement: namely the "irrational involvement" of one or more people in the activities of that child. "Somebody's got to be in love with that child—love it more than other children."

It's hard to find that in a day-care center. When he visited Russia, Dr. Bronfenbrenner asked a Soviet colleague why the Soviets played down the day-care system they had developed to such a high degree. The Russian psychologist's reply: "You can't pay someone to do what a mother does free." In short, adds Bronfenbrenner, "You can't buy an irrational commitment. But a child needs that interactional involvement; it needs people crazy about it as well as people *not* crazy about it."

Whether or not a child gets this in the American social milieu today depends on the kind of family environment to which he or she is subjected in formative years. Which years those are depends on who's talking. Dr. Spock, agreeing with Dr. Sigmund Freud, tagged the first six years as the most critical in the development of human potential. At a recent symposium, when Senator Robert Taft asked Dr. Bronfenbrenner what he thought, Bronfenbrenner surprised him by pinpointing junior high school. Those years, he said, are "most critical in what happens destructively—when they should be the most constructive." The junior high scene, he pointed out, is a "disorganizing, alienating, segregating world, a system in abcission, cutting off from everything and everybody, a system where warm, able, compassionate kids become like kids in *Lord of the Flies*. They're cut off from family, from their next step—the world of work—from their neighborhood.

They need a passport to go to the bathroom. There's no challenge; no responsibility." Nicholas Hobb, former president of the American Psychological Association, says that what's distinctive about American society today is its nonutility of childhood. "We don't let kids do anything important. They have no functional role, no experience in being responsible for other human beings."

It should be emphasized that this was not always the case. Up until about thirty years ago in rural America, nearly every youngster had specific chores. Before breakfast there were cow stalls to be cleaned, wood or cork floors in barn and pig house to be hosed and scrubbed, the day's stove wood to be split for mom. After school, it was get the cattle in, help with milking, collect and candle the eggs, weed the kitchen garden, clean and fill the oil lamps and trim the wicks, feed the livestock. Farm kids were very much a part of all that.

Children raised in well-ordered American city families usually had jobs assigned, too. Somebody was designated to get dad's daily paper and tobacco, bring in and sort the mail, make the beds. Certain housekeeping chores often were assigned and, in large families, swapped around. This often was true in families with servants. Offspring of the less affluent had tougher jobs. I can remember as a youngster being told it was my responsibility to work at the fruit and vegetable stand of an uncle who'd been wiped out in the 1929 crash. And I can remember, during summer vacations, the pungent aroma of my sweaty father as I worked with him delivering packages to his customers.

American children certainly *did* have a role and a sense of responsibility. It was the rule for most well-bred American children up until thirty or forty years ago; today it is the exception.

As for the family environment, it is first necessary to know what you're talking about when you say "family" nowadays. In contemporary America the word is bandied about to describe all kinds of people clusters: mafia, Charles Manson family, communal families, the family of man, and so on. You frequently hear people say things like, "George is really close; he's family."

Already, some bureaucrats are champing at the bit to redefine the word, with input from what one of them—Mr. David Snyder, Planning Officer for the Internal Revenue Service—has called "alternative primary group forms," such as "intentional communities, worker co-ops, self-help organizations, group and con-tract marriages, etc." Mr. Snyder would also like to see his newly defined "families" incorporated—for tax purposes, of course. That's what planners are for, I guess.

According to Noah Webster, however, a "family" is "the body of persons who live in one house, and under one head; a house-hold . . . a group comprising immediate kindred; especially, the group formed by parents and children." And *that* is the only family with which we are really concerned here. It is the nuclear family upon which cultures, rather than chaos, have always been built and probably always will be, regardless of federal labels or even the very real influence of dramatic social changes boiling up around us in a generation of young people with a whole different set of values.

Let's look at a few more of the changes besetting today's young people now moving into familial partnerships. The youth prob-lem today has to be understood in terms of the historical perspec-tive of what happened in the 1960s. Significant changes occurred in that decade which carried a tremendous impact on school-age children. First, there was an educational explosion. A quote from a primer for behavior of kindergarten and first-grade children—six year olds—provides a striking example of what we're talking about:

"This morning Peggy felt as grouchy as she could be. One shoe was hiding under the bed. She reached for it and combed her hair. She had no breakfast. She was late. The school bus wouldn't wait. At school she had a fight with Rose. She punched Miranda in the nose. What do you think is the trouble with Peggy today? Why do you think she feels this way?"

This is sensitivity training at the six-year-old level! That's a little early to get involved in sensitivity training before one under-stands motivation. It reminds me of a friend who went to one of those group sensitivity sessions. They told him to undress and wander around in the nude—which he did. One of his peers in the group asked him, "What's your motivation?" He replied: "When-ever anyone asks me about motivation I lose my sensitivity!"

But to return to the six year olds, in order to give their sensi-tivity training some perspective, we have to ask what the same type of little girl as Peggy worried about sixty or seventy years ago. One such young lady wrote to the *New York Sun* and asked the editor if there was really a Santa Claus. He replied that "Yes, Virginia, there is a Santa Claus." He went on to point out that Santa was love and generosity and devotion and gives to our lives beauty and joy, and how dreary the world would be if there were no Santa Claus—as dreary as if there were no Virginias; that there would be no childlike faith to illuminate our existence.

The core of that concept should be obvious because the Bible told us thousands of years ago that when you increase the educational level and fail to couple it with faith, the result is bitterness and futility. When W. C. Fields was in his middle sixties and dying, somebody said to him, "Why are you reading the Bible? You never did that in the fertile, productive years of your life." Fields replied, "I'm looking for loopholes."

That generation of the sixties has been one of unfulfilled expectations, due in large part to the explosion of those new concepts in education. When you grow up, the new little girl was told, you can wear makeup. But when she got there nobody was wearing makeup. When you grow up, they promised, you can dance. But when she got there, nobody was wasting time dancing.

Besides the new nature of education add the fact that our most sacred institutions are being challenged. Even the Catholic Church is in ferment. Today, almost the only people who *want* to get married are priests. Few others—even among Catholics—think it's such a hot idea. Liaisons by the numbers and production of multiple families without benefit of formal marriage have become the order of the day among more progressive free thinkers. This process is one I like to call "sequential monogamy."

The pill has had tremendous impact. Almost no college girl can go to the infirmary for cough medicine without the school physician asking her if she wants the pill. It is the first time in the history of mankind we've been able to guarantee the prevention of pregnancy in animals, which is what many seventeen year olds are. At that age, they're burning with sexual desire. *Anything* will turn them on—a stocking, a shoe—even a door knob! Perhaps the difference is partly biological. Today's young women menstruate six months earlier than did their mothers; a year and a half earlier than did their grandmothers. Everything they eat turns to hair. Come down to Baruch College and see them—in their blue jeans, and their soft shirts, and smoking their marijuana cigarettes. They look like Napoleon's army in retreat from Russia, or the remnants of an explosion in a Salvation Army warehouse. And they are standing the world on its ear. But not by insidious design. There is a sad naiveté about it. However, I must say it's getting a little better—their appearance is improving.

My wife has an M.A. in psychology and is an expert on the Rorschach test, and we have noticed an interesting response in the young people using our services for vocational guidance. A common interpretation of the ink blot cards has been that they see young children running around in a circle—like we used to do as kids, during recess, until we got dizzy and had to lie down. This can be interpreted psychoanalytically as an attempt to control one's environment: "Look, I can make the world turn around." Such a fantasy is childish, but it accurately reflects the need today's young folk have to somehow order their chaotic lives. They feel so incompetent and fearful of a world changing too fast for them that the only way they can deal with it is to make the world dizzier.

The search for identity in cults and communes and the proliferation of a drug culture is hardly surprising in the face of all this. And on top of it comes an intensified drive for sexual equality; mothers and fathers each fulfilling themselves through separate careers, bringing down on the already-rugged obstacle course of traditional marriage a whole new and unprecedented set of hazards. Not the least of these are reflected in a deluge of new theories about sexual gratification and its place in the new lifestyle, as promulgated by a growing number of analysts.

"Marriage can be happier with sexual freedom," claims a California State University sociologist, Lewis Yablonsky, citing a typical study involving some 800 married men averaging thirty-six years of age.

Professor Yablonsky told a reporter from the *Los Angeles Times-Examiner* that he had concluded, after his interviews, that "life would be far more pleasant" if married men would "follow their natural inclinations to have a wide range of affairs with women."

Yablonsky reported that adultery, practiced by 50 percent of his interviewees took the "boredom" out of their domestic sex, and "reinvigorated" their performance with their own wives. Those who were becoming impotent, he said, "rediscovered their potency with another woman," came home "recharged," and loved their wives all the more for it.

As for the 800 wives involved, the professor claimed that psychodrama sessions he held for them indicated that when they realized that they had the love and respect of their husbands, they no longer felt rejected and that any jealousy they might have felt "may diminish." In his study, he said, he found that the galavanting husbands did not approve of sexual promiscuity in their wives, however, because it might "damage their role as mothers and nurturers."

It should be interesting to see how these 400 freewheeling marriages have fared after, say, a decade of one-sided chauvinism. There's nothing much new about such "chasing" behavior. Kinsey's figure in 1948 for promiscuity in married males was the same 50 percent found by Yablonsky. What *is* new is the crass, ubiquitous way it is carried on nowadays. A generation ago, it was limited to an affair or two, indulged in with great discretion, mostly by those affluent executives and professional men who could afford it. The rest sneaked what they could away from home, or shared with President Carter "lust in their heart." It reminds me of the gossipy woman in County Cork, needling her neighbor. "They be tellin' me your hoosband is after chasin' women," said she. "It is not to wurra," her intended victim retorted. "Dogs chase motorcars but they'll not drive!"

While all these macrochanges are developing, microchanges also are bringing pressures that badger and trouble the modern American family. Every familial partnership goes through specific stages—some eight of them, all told.

In our modern family group, we start with the beginning partnership which goes through several substages that have been beautifully analyzed by two scholars named Rawlins and Feldman.

In brief, the couple is married (or otherwise joined). From zero to five years there are no children. It is an easy time—the honeymoon stage. Marriage, you may have observed, is the only meal where the dessert comes first. Some people find that this is the best stage of togetherness.

Stage two is the child-bearing stage when the oldest child is anywhere from one day to a year and eleven months old.

In stage three the family has preschool children. The oldest child is somewhere between three and five years old.

Stage four finds the family with school-age children. The oldest child is six to twelve years and eleven months.

At stage five the family is involved with teenagers; the oldest child is thirteen to twenty years old.

Stage six sees the family as a launching pad. Just as an arrow leaves the bow, the child leaves the home. As someone aptly put it, the best part of Christmas for the folks is seeing the tail lights on the departing cars of their young college students.

Stage seven is the family in the middle years—the empty nest and the home stretch to retirement.

Stage eight is the aging family—from retirement to the death of the first partner. All of this, of course, presumes that there is no breakup.

The most difficult stage for the traditional marriage comes between stages two and five. The double whammy is that it is just as tough for the man as for the woman. Mother is locked in; the kids are hovering around her. She wants to watch nonsense television programs; the outside world is saying to her via all the media: "Have fun. Have instant gratification. You're aswim in a sea of erotic possibilities. You've come a long way, baby." But she is locked in with the children and with the pressures of housekeeping. And now she is told she can be doing *much* more than just having fun. The magazine articles say, "Make a career for yourself." Sure. And cook three meals a day and clean the house but look beautiful when your husband comes through the door.

At the same time, the husband is locked into his career, doing his thing which he must do to put bread on the table. If he is a reasonably concerned and responsible family man, he is positioning himself so that, hopefully, one day he will be able to enjoy the empty-nest period with his wife.

Hence, the marriage is most vulnerable from that second stage through the fifth. To indicate why, it is only necessary to listen to the hopes and dreams of contemporary young people about to embark on a mist-shrouded future. What does an educated woman, ready to become a mother, think about her own tomorrow? She graduated, say, in the seventies and hoped to have children early. What is she like? What dominates her thinking? A commencement prayer delivered by a young lady on graduating from college provides some insights:

> We pray that you will hear us as we think about our graduation, even though we have trouble using the traditional language in talking to you. And though many of us no longer feel a part of a religious community, graduation brings together the past and the future in our minds, so that we think with mixed feelings and we do not know what to affirm. It is especially hard for us because the events of this year have forced us to have a personal reaction to public events. We do not feel that we are a cool, swinging generation. Somehow this year, more than others, we have had to draw lines to try to find an absolute right with which we could identify ourselves. There is a strain in all we do; a sense that time is now, added to what we would feel anyway as we graduate. We are grateful for what we have learned in experience here and we are not sure we have done the best we could. We feel we have gained a certain competence, but we realize we have fallen far short of what we can do. We pray that you will help us accept the past, and face the future with courage and dignity. Help us to leave our friends with love that does not depend on geography. Helps us to prepare a kind of renaissance in our public and private lives. Let there be borne in us a new voice that will help us to live and to die if we must to remake the soul of our time.

These words of a young potential mother typifies the thinking of a current generation of parents-to-be. It is a clear clarion call that reflects the dimensions of the problem. As a wife goes through her difficulties, her husband is also on the way up through those trying stages two to five. But he must answer some of the questions that his wife poses for him. And he has to be able to respond to some degree to the kind of defenses we all develop when we are in crisis. His wife is coming up with her ways to defend herself against the challenges of those stages and he is coming up with his ways. Whether or not there can be a meeting of minds depends, of course, on the partnership and how much each partner wants it, and how much each is willing to *give* in order to keep it from foundering.

In his book *A 158 Pound Marriage* John Irving suggests that marriage is a middleweight's attempt to solve a heavyweight problem; a shaky structure for controlling the uncontrollable. Maybe marriage is all that. But survey after survey has shown psychologists that married partners are happier with their lot than singles or members of informal partnerships. So perhaps it's well worth a try to apply the "middleweight" solution to our modern-day cultural shambles. There's little doubt that the most imminent factor threatening traditional family life as we have known it is the growing drive for sexual equality, and the two-career marriage. The array of problems it can impose on a family are impressive, but a substantial number of partners have managed to solve them and make such unions work.

12

Some Family Solutions to Corporate Bigamy Problems

> To keep your marriage brimming,
> With love in the loving cup,
> Whenever you're wrong, admit it,
> Whenever you're right, shut up.*
>
> OGDEN NASH

🖝 Not long ago, the president of a large apparel company complained to me that there was nothing his family could do to turn him on any longer. "I love my wife," he said, "and the kids are good kids. But I go home and nothing happens to me.

"Then I go to Hong Kong to work with a Chinese executive. We decide how many pieces of this or that fabric will be on the backs of 20 or 50 or 100,000 women next season. Designs we create and arrangements we make to convert those dreams to reality bring to life all the strings of my inner self.

"Then I go home to my wife. I have listened to her conversations and seen her in all the stages and situations of our life together, and she is comfortable to be with. But what can she do now to strike music from these strings of mine?"

The message from this lucid gentleman strikes with no little pathos at the core of the corporate-bigamy problem. There is little the family can do about it when only the job situation can satisfy

---

such a monster, with his all-pervading need for power, stimulus, and the pumping of adrenalin. Nothing at home can compensate him for the clout, glory, and excitement he gets from being the big boy on the block that his business universe provides. In that world, there is always another plane to be caught, another speech to be made, another article to be written, another battle to be fought, another foe to be bested. The corporation, which provides the field for games, manipulation, and control, plays on *all* the strings of his personality. At best, the family can only pluck at a few.

Even sex loses much of its magnetic quality on the home front and earlier in a marriage than might be suspected. After the age of about thirty, men's sexual drive calms down. Marital sex continues, of course, and may do so for many decades, but there is no longer the overpowering need. As a means of attracting a rising successful executive to his home and family, it can be largely discounted.

For the executive who can discuss at least some of his business problems with a wife who is interested—a wife who understands what he's talking about—home may hold fewer terrors. But even in such cases, there are sensitive areas and other difficulties in communication that cannot be brushed aside lightly.

"Frequently we dine with business associates who serve on the boards of a variety of other companies in diverse industries," one corporate chairman pointed out to me recently. "If I should discuss a merger problem with my wife and inadvertently neglect to swear her to secrecy, and she should thoughtlessly talk about it in the ladies' room to the wife of a corporate head (whom she would not know as such), a multimillion-dollar enterprise could blow sky high—along with my career in business."

The same gentleman explained why he is reluctant to discuss even less important problems at home: "Let's say I come home tired and she asks what the trouble is, and I tell her, 'Jones screwed up again and we lost a million-dollar account, and I'm going to have to fire him.' That should be that. But suppose next morning I change my mind, for complex business and political reasons, and I go home that evening and my wife says, 'Well, did you fire Jones?' I say 'No.' Naturally, she wants to know why not.

"Then I have to explain myself, get into a lot of background

which perhaps should not be revealed to anyone, and the whole
thing sounds as though I'm trying to defend myself—which I certainly am not. The trouble is that my wife is at ground zero.
Before she can understand the development she must be brought
up to standard—deftly, so as not to reveal anything confidential.
That sort of thing drains anyone."

And that's what they mean about being "drained" at home. For
these men, home is a draining experience and not a fulfilling one.
They do not realize the importance of what the Menninger Clinic's
Dr. Tony Brocher calls "the need to diversify our emotional port-
folios." Businesses are not set up to provide emotional satisfaction.
Families are. What these hard-driving executives don't realize is
that when they retire, they will have no place else to turn.

Recently my wife and I were in Japan on business. One of the
many things that fascinated us was how, in the Japanese culture,
the corporate giants and their lieutenants are cushioned by custom
from the family strains and drains in their lives. After a day of
concentrated work in the office, they do not head for home right
away. First, they go to a geisha house where they are fed and
entertained with light conversation by highly trained and talented
geisha hostesses. In the dignified circles traveled by top corporate
people, these are extremely proper establishments—cultural centers in the highest sense.

The men are relaxed and congenial. They may talk a little
business, but no big deals are consummated at the geisha house.
The chatter may involve things such as the progress of this or that
silk or electronics company, the trends in international currency,
or light banter about sports and cultural events.

By custom, wives and female guests are not welcome at such
gatherings. The geisha houses are strictly men's territory. While
we were in Tokyo, I was invited by the president of a company to
join him for dinner at the house he patronized, and I mentioned
this to my wife. She promptly asked me what I thought she should
wear. She didn't understand that she was not invited. But she was
not about to be put off when I tried to explain. I had to intervene
with the president to make an exception on the basis that my wife
was a professional psychologist and my partner in business—something he and his associates had trouble understanding. But I pre-
vailed, and Gloria was accepted as a dinner guest in the forbidden

environs. Needless to say she was the only woman present. To bring a wife to a geisha house gathering like that is highly inappropriate behavior, and I was being extremely gauche in insisting that she be included. My hosts would never have understood that my motive was self-preservation, nor did I attempt to explain the Western concepts involved in *that* rationale.

In any case, by the time these Japanese gentlemen get home following their social hour at the geisha house each evening their wives have baths ready for them and the tea is steeping. Maybe there is some conjugal intimacy, a good night's sleep, and they go back to work the next morning refreshed and ready to tackle another day in the competitive world of business. Aside from the usual pressures of business and the group functioning it involves, these corporate executives are protected from the morass of family problems by their wives. The author of a recent article on the subject has suggested that the secret of Japanese success relative to this matter is the fact that they are "group-oriented." I can't agree. My own experience indicates that top-level business people of virtually all nationalities *must* be group-oriented in order to achieve growth and power. If the Japanese have a partial formula for the corporate-bigamy problem, I would say that it is the role of the geisha house and the family in the culture. The former provides a relief valve; the latter preserves the energy and the business commitment of the top men. Whether or not it is as great for the wives and families of these top men is doubtful, however.

A recent sociological study of "corporate widows" in Japan indicates that the housewives are no better off than corporation wives anywhere. In many ways they are worse off than their American sisters who, at least, live in spacious suburban homes of their own or in comfortable, convenient urban apartments. In Japan, "families of the organization" live in company- or government-owned concrete housing made up of stark, cubicled units in vast complexes known as *danchi*. Here, isolated from their company-enfolded and often absent husbands, wives—often college graduates—are expected to achieve total personal satisfaction in the "joy" of rearing the children and keeping the home fires burning against the brief and sometimes rare visits of their husbands.

Although the commuting husbands are, indeed, pampered and rewarded by the company they live for as they struggle up through the pecking order, no such company-sponsored morale boosters apply to their cell-bound wives. The result is "an almost-obsessive concern for the future of their children, forcing most to attend heavy schedules of extra classes." This situation has, in fact, bred a nation of mothers (and fathers, too) with a grimly competitive drive for the material success of their offspring, and an almost-total preoccupation with the primary value of their culture—business. The trend is so pervasive that "pushy" women anywhere in Japan today are derisively called "danchi mammas."

Among these women, the survey revealed a significantly increasing incidence of "high-rise neuroses, alienation, loneliness, rising suicide, and mental decay."

Possibly the day will come when American corporations will enfold the entire family; when all employees from top brass to lowliest worker—female as well as male—will bring the kids to the office nursery and where the teenagers will find programs in the company compound to keep them busy after school. That would be the ultimate in "organizational focus" and it could be a reality in the future if present trends continue.

Meantime, most executive families in America will deal with the classic husband-job-spouse love triangle in their own individual ways. A hard look at the common trouble spots, the solutions that some families have applied effectively, and the recommendations of knowledgeable analysts, should help to throw some light on the problem so people can live with it.

No one questions the existence of the often-bitter stresses and strains that are imposed on marriage by top corporate executives. They are there, all right, as we've already observed. But perhaps the most rigorous ordeals are experienced in those marriages where one or the other spouse is a public figure—political, military, show business, etc. Even the George Washington family had corporate-bigamy problems.

In the midst of his military campaigns, harassed by a more numerous and better-trained enemy, the failure of the Continental Congress to provide funds for basic provisions—let alone payroll—and the miserable rations supplied by exploiters, General

Washington unexpectedly received word on the battlefield that Martha was upset and annoyed because he wasn't writing often enough!

During preparations for a Bicentennial display of letters, prints, and documents from the American Revolution, the New York Public Library turned up among its special collections a letter that Washington had taken time out to write in the midst of these conflicts and frustrations. The note scolded Martha gently, and asked whether she *really* thought he was "without excuse" for his lapses in communication.

Like her sisters in other fields, the modern political wife usually is expected to run an efficient domestic establishment (sometimes in two or more homes that she gets to visit but never gets to live in), and raise the children with little or no support from her "leader of men." A politician's wife, says Ellen Proxmire, former wife of the Wisconsin Senator, in her book *One Foot in Washington*, "is first and always a mother, a cook, a chauffeur, a seamstress and homemaker, but she is also an adviser, a social secretary, a campaigner, and even a TV personality."

That's not all. Unlike the wife of an executive in other fields, besides getting out to stump for votes, she must know the policy issues so she can make knowledgeable and sparkling speeches at fund-raising luncheons—at the same time being careful not to outsparkle her spouse. Eleanor McGovern, according to a lengthy feature on political wives in *Time* magazine, ran afoul of her husband's campaign in 1972 when the press notices of her speeches became better than his. She was admonished to "cool it."

An active political wife must arrange and hostess elaborate banquets and cocktail parties and help keep things rolling at campaign headquarters. All this, of course, makes her very much a part of her husband's career—a source of personal satisfaction that few other wives ever achieve. It may be the reason why, in most cases, the political wife wouldn't trade her situation for anything, despite the fact that if and when the battle is won, she may well be brushed aside while the winner is hustled off to his rewards by the party bosses.

On top of all that, the forgotten wife has to put up with her "big man's" usually overbearing personality, an almost essential part of the equipment of every successful politician. An internist

who spent thirty years treating many of the nation's leading politicians and their wives told a *Times* reporter: "Politicians are not
a loveable lot. They are self-serving egomaniacs, and I take my
hat off to their wives. I don't know how the husbands get away
with it. . . . There's a lot of resentment under the surface. The
wives always start out with 'my dear, darling husband' and how
much he's doing for Cayuga County or wherever the hell he comes
from. But if you listen long enough, you find out she doesn't give
a hoot about Cayuga County. If you really establish rapport with
one of these wives, she will come right out and tell you how hor-
rible her life is."

If that is the case, then how does one account for the fact that
a fairly large percentage of the marriages of highly successful
politicians remain intact? Probably for the same reasons that
high-level corporate marriages are "good in every way." In reality
the marriage may be tacky, but success and money are important
factors even when the glory is reflected. It should also be mentioned that a divorce action does not enhance the prestige of a
politician, just as top corporate executive candidates are often
bypassed if their marriages are in trouble.

How these people make adjustments to keep the critical factors
in delicate balance is sometimes subtle, sometimes obvious. There
are no pat formulas, but a lot of ingenuity. Much of it is subconscious, such as the suppression of feelings already discussed.
Other techniques are calculated, deliberate, and highly individual. And usually it is the wife who takes the active role in presenting a domestic scenario of well-being—or otherwise.

A few women are able to fulfill themselves, like Clementine
Spencer-Churchill, with the rearing of children and achievement
of a power-behind-the-scenes role in the lives and careers of their
husbands. Lady Bird Johnson, according to former White House
aide Liz Carpenter, was the "gentle hand" that salved the wounds
Lyndon inflicted (inadvertently and otherwise) on staff members.
She was the arbitrator of in-house spats, quarrels, and joustings
for favor, and a driving force in winning over many of her husband's opponents. She was, revealed Ms. Carpenter, "a WIFE in
capital letters."

Rosalynn Carter, an even more forceful behind-the-scenes
Presidential aide, attends cabinet meetings because "if I didn't

there's no way I could discuss things with Jimmy in an intelligent way." She has lobbied successfully for her husband on federal budgetary measures, represented him on important international matters with foreign ministers and heads of state, served as an influential adviser and sounding board for him and his staff at frequent lunches in the White House.

During Jimmy's campaign, Rosalynn told Abigail McCarthy, exwife of Senator Gene, about an ardent feminist whose point of view was completely beyond her. Said Rosalynn: "She couldn't understand how I could do all this for a man—you know, all this work—and I was not a candidate myself! I'll have my identity if Jimmy is President." And she has—with flourishes. She has been called "the most influential First Lady since Eleanor Roosevelt" and, according to some of the inner circle, even more influential politically. Nor has she sacrificed the Carter domestic front to the Carter political cause. When Jimmy was depressed by defeat in a Georgia election, Abigail McCarthy points out perceptively, "his sister Ruth brought him religious experience, but Rosalynn gave him Amy. Her security lies in the life they have shared. . . . She knows her value like the virtuous woman of the Old Testament who sets her hand to strong things so that her husband can 'sit honorable in the gates . . . the heart of her husband trusted in her.' And that is her power."

A wife like Rosalynn Carter can hardly be considered "submerged" by her husband's career since she finds such fulfillment in it. While that is not a common phenomenon, neither is it rare among wives of public figures who have achieved the zenith. Elsa Einstein's letters reveal that her "lion among thinkers" was a classic male chauvinist whom she tended like a child. It was she who organized and carried out the myriad details involved in meeting his obligations and appearances—and in just surviving. To her now-famous scolding for his arrival at a formal dinner without his socks, he replied, smiling, "What use are socks? They only produce holes." And when the wife of a friend noted that Elsa waited on him hand and foot and asked him what he did in return, he replied, "I give her my understanding."

Einstein himself, in a letter to a friend in 1930, admitted, "I am truly a 'lone traveler' and have never belonged to any country, my home, my friends, or even my immediate family with my whole heart. In the face of all these ties, I have never lost a sense of distance and a need for solitude."

In spite of all this, and even acknowledging her frequent disappointment in his lack of personal warmth and tenderness, Elsa found satisfaction in playing her supportive role to the hilt, permitting the famous professor to devote full time to his work. She wrote to a friend: "God has given him such nobility, and I find him wonderful, although life with him is exhausting." Her only real joy in their personal relationship, she confessed, was in reading about his accomplishments in his press clippings.

For most wives of public figures, the compensations in helping the "big man" to achieve and maintain his fame, are not all that great. Jane Muskie told one interviewer, regarding her husband Ed's Presidential aspirations, "His ego is constantly fed. A little kick in the behind sometimes helps."

A number of wives of famous fellows have taken fairly dramatic action to achieve just that. Among the memorable ones were Eleanor Holm Rose who had the lock changed on the door of her New York City penthouse to keep her famous producer husband Billy Rose out in the cold for a considerable number of days. Angelina Alioto managed a complete disappearance for seventeen days in 1974 to punish her husband Joseph, then Mayor of San Francisco, for failing to introduce her at parties and neglecting to give her credit for her stories and jokes that, she claimed, he plagiarized.

In most families of public figures dramatic adjustments sometimes are made by one or both partners to keep things glued together. Betty Wright, wife of Texas Congressman James Wright, got fed up watching her husband leave the house at 7 A.M. and come back to bed exhausted at midnight, day after day. "We finally made a pact that every third weekend we would spend one day alone with each other," she says. "It's not much. But I knew what I was getting into when I married Jim. It's the price a politician's wife has to pay."

Some political wives with children have struck harder bargains than that. Virginia Congressman M. Caldwell Butler's wife, June, told a reporter: "If my husband doesn't like my image, he can get a new model. If his constituents don't like my image, they can get a new Congressman. I feel my part is to have a solid family."

One of the most common complaints among wives of all corporate bigamists, but especially those in the public area, is their feeling of stress, frustration, boredom, and abandonment. Random interviews by *Time* magazine reporters revealed that many feel wife and family are the last items on the husband's list of priorities. When Abigail McCarthy had serious complications following childbirth and was rushed into emergency for tests and x-rays, her former husband, then a senator from Minnesota, took off to make a roll call on the Hill. Hospital personnel were stunned. Mrs. "Mac" took it as par for the course. The exact percentage of Congressional husbands who have been busy elsewhere when their children were being born has never been tallied. But people who should know indicate that it probably would represent enough votes in any given session of Congress to pass a piece of legislation.

Senator Edward Kennedy's wife Joan recently told a group of Washington women that she had turned to alcohol at one critical point in her married life to cushion the multiple problems entailed in being the spouse of a highly popular, preoccupied husband. When she emphasized that she had had far too little opportunity to be with her charismatic mate, a chorus of "Amens" rose from Congressional wives in the audience.

The complaint that political wives can have no life of their own, however, is labeled a "myth" by Ms. McCarthy, who points out that those who really want one manage to make one for themselves. She herself, a syndicated columnist and writer of consequence, is a shining example. She also points to June Bingham, wife of a New York Congressman, who writes outstanding biographies; to Shirley Bellmon, an Oklahoma Senator's wife, who designs and manufactures uniforms; to Georgia Senator Herman Talmadge's wife Betty, who developed and runs Talmadge Farms, a livestock enterprise with an annual gross of some $4 million; and many others.

Mrs. April Evans, wife of Billy Lee Evans, a first-term Representative from Georgia, typifies a new breed of younger political wife who has no intention of becoming stultified, bored, or beaten into the Washington limbo, despite her husband's dedication to his "other marriage"—the job.

Billy, Mrs. Evans points out, left a highly successful law practice and a two-home setup to become a freshman Congressman with a personal campaign debt of nearly six figures, and a century-old Washington townhouse that they rent for $850 a month. Their new abode has holes in the walls and exposed, leaky plumbing. When Billy takes a shower, says April, "it rains in the foyer." Their Congressman's income of $57,500 barely makes ends meet in Washington and their Georgia weekend retreat "will probably have to go."

April Evans can recite the entire litany of political wife woes. Her husband gets home between ten and midnight most nights, and wakes her to say good-bye at 7 A.M. "He has been gone as much as two weeks without seeing the children," she notes. "You feel sort of left out. You kind of get to feeling like a widow." She chauffeurs their children to public school daily, and drives twenty miles into Virginia to shop for food because it's cheaper there.

While Billy Evans wants his wife "home with the children," she is far from committed to that role indefinitely. She has a degree in political science and a year of law school and intends to continue. "Billy knows I have ambitions," she told *The New York Times* * a year or so ago. "It's easy for a wife to be totally left out." Right now she'll postpone her career for him because he told her before they married that he wanted to be a Congressman. "It's not like I didn't know," she says. "I'm not trying to sound unselfish, but it's more important for him to have this right now. If he's not happy, I can't be happy."

Few people will deny that any husband who's up to his neck in a high-powered career often is hard put to include his wife and family high on the list of daily priorities. When your every act carries with it responsibility to stockholders, bankers, and backers for millions, if not billions of dollars not to mention the livelihood of thousands of employees in a business enterprise, there is an understandable tendency to develop at least a modicum of preoccupation with the problems involved. In fact, if you hope to be top honcho for more than a few days, you'd better.

Nevertheless, any number of top executives and career head-liners somehow have managed to solve the job-family dichotomy with considerable effectiveness. An outstanding example is Jack Nicklaus, a perfectionist among perfectionists who has difficulty finding enough time for the crushing demands of the pro-golf tour circuit. Nicklaus now heads up Golden Bear, Inc., a multi-million-dollar company employing nearly 200 people to handle its sales of golf clubs, bags, balls, and clothing; a golf course de-signing and engineering firm; a travel agency; a car dealership and leasing agency; a radio station; housing developments; cattle ranches; and a utility company.

In spite of the pressures all that entails, his family comes first as far as Jack is concerned. "When I first turned pro," he told sports writer John Dorschner recently in *Family Weekly*, "I made a rule that I wouldn't be away from home more than fourteen days at a time, and I've broken that rule only twice."

"Home" is a comfortable, sprawling "contemporary" in North Palm Beach, Florida, where Jack, his wife Barbara, their daughter and four sons enjoy themselves in low-key family activities, and plan fishing and skiing trips. The Palm Beach social set is politely bypassed. Jack's interest in skiing is relatively new. He took it up because he thought it would be "great for the whole family." When some sponsors worried about him busting an arm or leg and missing a whole golf season, Jack told them: "If I don't go, I'll miss a whole ski season."

On one occasion, a major sponsor organized a tournament and called to tell Nicklaus he was in the top lineup. Jack turned it down. He'd promised his sons he'd take them fishing in Alaska on those dates, and did. He's been known to walk out of business meetings to watch his sons play basketball. "You have to know where to draw the line," he says.

Not all headliner husbands are quite that cavalier about the career "wife," but many of them have set up special ground rules at home to deal the family into their lives.

Alan Alda, star of "M.A.S.H." and a rocketing success as a film and TV writer, actor, and producer, was busy in Hollywood a few years back producing a series involving family togetherness, when he suddenly brought himself up short. His family was in New Jersey. "For weeks at a time," he confessed to West Coast writer Joseph N. Bell, who quoted him in the *Christian Science Monitor*, "the only contact I had with them was by phone. I finally realized how absurd it was to be writing and coproducing a show about family solidarity while I was neglecting my own family."

Nowadays, he informed Bell, he commutes back and forth to New Jersey by plane every weekend during his Hollywood stints. His wife and two of their three daughters fly out to California each summer. The eldest, Eve, works back East.

Even on the Washington scene, some high-powered officials have found it possible to be fathers some of the time. Stuart Eizenstat, President Carter's Assistant for Domestic Affairs, makes "a very conscious effort to preserve some sort of family life." An important part of that effort is to swing by his home every evening in time to see his two youngsters before bedtime and chat with them, even if it's only for ten minutes.

Vice-President Mondale, when he's in Washington, usually manages to get home by six-thirty or seven for dinner. Then, after "family hour" is over, he goes back to work.

Former Energy and CIA Director Secretary James Schlesinger takes time out to play cribbage and backgammon with his eight children in highly competitive contests. "If you can't play games you can't do anything," he says. He makes a point of getting home for dinner and encourages the family to challenge his political and social concepts. He takes his family role seriously! When he was CIA chief, he arrived late in his office one morning with a bandaged hand and explained that he'd had problems with a son, "a good boy, but I had to deck him."

Most executives who make the effort to establish ground rules with their wives work out family time on certain evenings or weekends. But some "contracts" go even further. While his children were young, a marketing vice-president of the Univac Division of Sperry Rand Corporation, told me, "I made a conscious decision to stay out of the New York area in order to avoid the killing pace. I did not compete for positions of great responsibility; I was strictly a family man.

"But now," he said, "my children have grown. I am based in New York, and I spend more and more time at work and less and less time at home. The pace is killing, but I told my wife, 'You had your fun; now I'm having mine.' And although I haven't been home in three days, I guarantee you I'll be greeted with warmth and affection, because we made a deal."

There is increasing evidence that new young executives coming along have a whole new approach to the corporate-bigamy problem. In a recent interview for *Across the Board* magazine, Robert S. Sweeney, Jr., a 1978 Harvard MBA, told business author Judson Gooding that he not only expects business to improve its performance in meeting society's new goals, but also to be less demanding of executives. "Few people are willing to be company slaves now," he said. "My career is not my number-one concern in life. It's important, but what is most important is getting married, and my closeness to my family. . . . I may not end up the richest person, but I will do all right. I've had a close home and family life; my father always took time for us when there was reason to—and there were six children, so there were lots of reasons. I've seen the warmth of this kind of life and what it means. I want that, and I'm not willing to go all day and night for the company. There's just not that much time. Pretty soon it takes over everything.

"You gotta have some time off—take a weekend. I have a theory. I call it my 'big bath' theory. The idea is that you do intensive work; you immerse yourself in it, and then you have time off, rather than nibbling at the work and stretching it out so's you're never clear of it."

While Mr. Sweeney has all the apparent qualifications of a typical need-achiever, a respectable number of today's crop of MBAs and junior executives are voicing similar sentiments. Since these are the people who will be formulating industry's policies in the next few years, there is every chance that many more empire builders will be taking Sweeney's "big bath" in the foreseeable future.

Baths or otherwise, the examples of successful executive marriages we have presented here are intended to illustrate that such unions *can* be more than tenuous paper partnerships that rely on suppression of feelings, careful manipulation, and a need for security and privilege at all costs—*if* a genuine *shared* effort is made by both parties to put them on a solid footing.

There have been any number of treatises spelling out the characteristics of successful marriage. Most are pure pap. However, in his book *The Sexual Wilderness*, Vance Packard listed seven excellent traits that he believes "seem particularly likely to enhance the enjoyment of *any* marriage." He emphasizes that "enjoyment" does not imply "adjustment," but *does* contribute to "an enduring sense of love."

1. A large capacity for affection. Differentiated from love, affection is what cements a marriage in shared experiences year after year. It is revealed in thoughtful acts by both partners and the enjoyment of each other as persons, for reasons other than erotic stimulation. They can and probably will remain best friends throughout their lives.

2. Emotional maturity. This involves lack of selfishness and wishful thinking, a willingness to accept responsibility, innate self-discipline, and ability to control preoccupation with pleasureable stimulation. It is "the best dowry you can bring to a marriage."

3. The capacity to communicate effectively and appealingly each other's thoughts and feelings. The ability of partners to really enjoy talking with each other on a substantial variety of subjects, openly discuss problems that bother them, and to be comfortable being with each other during long periods of silence, is a characteristic vital to a successfully functioning family.

4. A zest for life. This is what makes a marriage enjoyable rather than merely well-adjusted. It involves doing things together—even fixing a screen door—for the pure enjoyment of it, seeking new experiences together "rather than an adulterer's way of seeking new experience as an escape from a partner."

5. The capacity to handle tensions constructively. A marriage where the partners never raise their voices in anger is probably unrealistically based. This trait means keeping the tensions in proportion and at times even enjoying the process of discharging them.

6. A playful approach to sex. Occasional tender romps should be a part of sexual encounters between men and women who have a fine total relationship. They should not just involve the formidable mechanics of the act displayed in current books, the serious business of reproducing the species, or reducing tension.

7. *The capacity to accept fully the other person with full knowledge of his or her shortcomings.* There must always be respect, and even admiration. Only in such an environment can two people dare let down their defenses and truly be themselves, which is a requirement for contentment and for a sense of completeness in marriage.

One more trait that may help to keep romantic love alive in a marriage is "shared vulnerability," or the capacity of the partners to be completely open with each other to ensure mutual self-disclosure. While this would by no means entail revealing company secrets, such dissembling in any area probably is seldom achieved in the rarified atmosphere of the executive world. Certainly both admiration and shared vulnerability are counterindicated for the monster type of corporate bigamist. Most monsters we know have very little admiration for anyone and, secondly, they literally cringe from exposing *any* vulnerabiilty.

In his book, *Fire and Ice,* Andrew Tobias tells how, when Charles Revson bought a spectacular diamond bracelet for his third wife, "Ancky," he showed it first to a lady guest who was with them—instead of presenting it to Ancky directly. "Do you think Ancky will like this?" he asked. Any display of warm emotion to his own wife would have exposed more vulnerability than he dared show.

13

Guidelines for Corporate Bigamists

☛ "When I was in college, I made a list of the physical, mental, behavioral, and family background characteristics that I would demand in any woman I might marry," the president and chairman of an international conglomerate admitted to me candidly. "The woman I did marry had most of these attributes, or I wouldn't have married her. Nor, I am sure, would we still be married today—forty years later. I knew I would need a self-sufficient wife who would enjoy managing a large home and raising a family without interference, and who would be secure and mature enough not to interfere with me. I was determined to make something of myself, and knew, too, that I would have no time for irrelevant domestic details."

The arrogance and lack of any emotional consideration in that format for marital compatibility can, of course, only be found in a real monster type. Not every man—or even every potential corporate bigamist—is coldly objective enough to set out a marriage prospectus the way he might plot a merger acquisition. But that is precisely what this fellow did.

While it certainly does not follow that every prospective executive husband should attempt this cut-and-dried method of acquiring a wife, there is something to be said for the careful choice of a partner beyond just emotional and/or erotic attachments. After all, the gentleman just cited *is* still satisfied with his partnership and, we happen to know, so is his wife, who was nearly as calculating in her choice of him as he was of her.

In the area of corporate-domestic relationships there are some basic guidelines regarding the relative compatibility or non-compatibility of particular types of people—enough, at any rate, to justify a few fundamental suggestions for specific types of corporate bigamists.

For the monster type, today's culture makes things easier than ever in history. There is no longer any need for him to subject himself to a series of marriages and divorce-mill sessions. There is no reason why he should ever make an emotional commitment. The modern monster has what we call *zeitgeist* (the spirit of the age) going for him; he will not be a social outcast if he remains a bachelor with female companions.

I make that suggestion with some hesitancy, because I am fully aware that, where the monster is concerned, if you tell him what to do he will almost certainly do the exact opposite. Tell him what *not* to do and he will surely do just that. Whenever the odds are heavily weighted against something, the monster loves to tackle it. It becomes a challenge and he is compulsive about challenges. So, assuming that a few up-and-coming young empire-builders may read this and now insist on getting married, there are a few recommendations to help increase their chances for success.

Like my friend who runs that international conglomerate, the monster type should be extremely careful in the choice of a wife if he expects any kind of successful partnership. He definitely should not pick a woman who is competitive with him, who is extremely bright or interesting all the time. She'll destroy him.

He should not pick a woman who is inclined to one-upmanship. When asked why he was divorcing his first wife, one corporate empire-builder told me: "She's getting out of hand. She was embarrassing me in public." A wife who constantly attempts to upstage a monster-type personality by clever little devices eventually will drive him to a divorce solution.

The monster type would do well to choose a seriously religious woman (her reward will come later!). Rose Kennedy had her love story in the care of her home and children, and the support of her church. They were her moral fulfillment. There is one exception to this recommendation. A monster type with liberal leanings—and there are some today—will not be able gracefully to accommodate a partner imbued with the dogma and esoteric disciplines promulgated by the church.

For the need-achiever, things are not quite so black and white. Most of these fellows are predisposed to devote specific allocations of time to the family, as indicated in many of the examples already cited. Paradoxically, however, since the men in this category have a genuine warmth and sense of responsibility toward the family, they usually have no feelings of guilt about stepping out of the domestic role after their big bath in it. They do not feel compelled to pursue the paternal role indefinitely, and may decide to go the distance in business after the children are grown and on their way. When these men come to us for advice, we tell them: "You have options. You can be a business buff, a family father, or a little of both. And you will do well at whichever you choose."

Why are these men so family-oriented? If you ask them directly they usually will tell you something like: "I came from a divorced family, and I don't want that to happen to my kids"; or, like Robert Sweeney, "When I was a kid I learned the value of the warmth and satisfaction that comes from a close family life, and I want that for my kids."

Generally speaking, need-achievers should choose women who crave the role of being the power behind the throne. Many of the most successful do. Whether these women seek personal power in such a marriage or their choice of mate simply reflects the way they are, we do not yet know. What is most interesting is the fact that need-achievers appear to stay married to women of this type, who are distinguished by their quiet strength. The wife in these marriages often has been perceived by us as the glue that keeps her marriage together and her husband from going off the deep end in his business activities.

Most need-achievers do best when they select an industry—or

business of their own—that is seasonal. A cyclical operation on the job front gives the family a chance to plan around father's commitments. In large organizations need-achievers seem to achieve a higher degree of personal satisfaction if they can avoid contending for top-echelon positions—without jeopardizing their career potential—during the "growing family" phase of their careers. This is not always possible in the people-grinding mills of today's giant corporations, where an opportunity offered and turned down often is an opportunity forever lost. But, given a sympathetic, understanding management team, it can work. One young executive I know turned down a senior partnership when it was offered, because he knew it would mean virtual desertion of his family. He is still with the outfit in a lesser capacity without the relentless demands on his time. But he has every assurance that when the family pressures let up he is still in line for a front-line slot.

Executive jobs that call for a lot of travel should be avoided by the need-achiever if at all possible, for obvious reasons. Most of them know this instinctively, but occasionally there is no way around it. In such cases, you often will find them making special arrangements, like Alan Alda, to bring the family along occasionally and to make sure that some time can be spent at home each week.

Recently I had an opportunity to talk with Jesse Jackson, the inspiring black leader, about the problems of public figures caught up in the corporate-bigamy conflict. He made the point that it was vitally important for executives to take their wives with them on their travels whenever possible. He told me how he had just taken his wife to a carefully planned rally, where widely divergent points of view threatened to turn the high-principled event into a semiriot. The effort failed, due to the courage and loyalty of a dedicated group. "It was," he said, "an inspiring experience.

"If I had left my wife home," he added, "and tried to call her that evening to tell her what had happened, it would not have had the impact and excitement she got seeing it for herself. She may even have said, on the phone, 'Don't bother me with all your problems—you should see the problems I've had around here today.' When exciting moments are shared at the scene of action, they acquire an entirely different significance for both participants."

So take your wife on trips whenever she wants to go, no matter what kind of corporate bigamist you may happen to be. You're bound to win.

Finally, we have the Janus type, who loves to believe that he manipulates people, and good ones do. But just as the best salesmen (many of whom are Janus types) could, if required, sell air conditioners to Eskimos in Nome, Alaska, at winter's height and are also the world's most gullible sales targets, so the Janus loves to be manipulated. By all odds, any man who suspects himself of possessing the characteristics of a Janus-type corporate bigamist should marry a woman who knows how to manipulate him; a woman who, one way or another, continuously tells him and everyone else how wonderful he is ("Everyone loves you, dear—how do you do it?"). A perfect example of such a woman was the wife of the eighteenth-century British poet-painter William Blake. When someone observed to her that her husband's face was dirty, she replied: "Mr. Blake's face don't dirt."

Catherine Blake did, in fact, go down in history as "the perfect wife," for whatever that may have meant during the century from 1750 to 1850. Today, we know that she was a highly manipulative woman who applied techniques that worked for her particular situation: Blake adored her. It may be significant that they were childless and that she devoted her life to him and his career. She even learned to paint so that *she could help him*— she did *not* paint for her own satisfaction as an artist.

We do know that Catherine Boucher Blake was a perfect wife for a Janus-type personality. She would hardly have suited a monster or need-achiever, either of whom would have been on to her devices in short order and probably machoed her out of operation. She flattered her husband to his face and to all their friends consistently. She was a wife rather than a mother, or, if you will, a mother only to him. She seldom, if ever, questioned his judgment. At least, if she did, it was never recorded anywhere. She fed, fanned, pampered, and petted him. She was, in fact, both wife and geisha girl.

Curiously, or perhaps understandably, Blake never influenced any of his contemporaries, nor was he influenced by them. Nor did he ever achieve real stature in the eyes of his peers. It is interesting to speculate what might have happened if William Blake's wife had been more candid and self-serving.

Manipulation is more often a device of wives than husbands, and will have further consideration as such. But it also has a role in the behavior of the executive husband, and can be used to good effect if properly applied at appropriate times. It should not be considered a solution to deep-seated problems, or used as a long-term behavioral technique.

Praise is something that is often used manipulatively. Every executive knows, of course, that praise does not always pay off. For instance, insincere praise will kick back every time if used on intelligent, knowledgeable people—as most wives and children of executive families must be considered. Recently researchers have been conducting studies with classroom populations to determine when, how, and to what kind of persons praise can and should be meted out to produce positive effects. Most of what they have learned to date applies purely to classroom and educational situations, but a number of interesting phenomena have turned up that are applicable to husband-wife and intra-family relationships.

The researchers found that the timing and frequency of praise made a big difference in its effectiveness. Praise for things well done spurred the subject's performance when it was first made. Later, after the same people had been praised a number of times, it had almost no effect on performance, and reactions indicated boredom and indifference. The conclusion of the testers was that there's a point of diminishing returns. Too much praise becomes suspect and leads to staleness on the part of the subject and distrust of its significance.

When people were praised in front of others, it had a much greater effect than when they were praised in private. The obvious significance is that if you are going to praise your wife, you may achieve immeasurable good if you do it in front of the whole family. "That was a great job you did handling the cub scout group last week, dear. The kids all loved it and everyone in the neighborhood is talking about what a good time they had." Mom's stock will soar in the eyes of the kids, and her authority will be reinforced. For the same reason, in family arguments, the wife should be supported in front of the children: "Your mother is right, Steve, and I think all of you should know why. When she makes a rule about . . ." etc.

Generalized praise, such as simple exclamations: "Nice going!" "Great!" or "Good show!" are valueless compared with kudos for specific things: "That trade-in deal you made on Gordon's bike was a terrific piece of horse-trading. You've got a good business head."

Praise rendered too quickly on the heels of an event or observation is not as effective as expressions of approval made five seconds or more following it. A few seconds of silence seem to indicate that thoughtful consideration is being accorded the action, the information imparted, or the ideas expressed. This would be especially applicable in praising children.

Along the same lines, an astute observation by a child can be given dignity and importance among other siblings if father or mother ask the child to repeat it: "That was very well put, Joe. Say it again, so we're sure to get the details straight."; or "I hope you all heard Joe's idea, because it's very important. Would you mind repeating it for us, Joe?"

One of the problems faced by many executives on the home front is an image of spinelessness that they sometimes generate in the family because of their dedication to business responsibilities. On the one hand, father is the assertive man of the house when it comes to making budget decisions and family policies regarding discipline and rules for the children. On the other hand, when the boss calls on Saturday, he acts like a Milquetoast. The telephone business discussion goes on and on, while junior stamps around in his baseball uniform, slapping his catcher's mitt on the tabletop because the Little Leaguers have been on the ballfield for half an hour already. You can hear the little gears grinding: "Dad never tells the boss that he has important things to do today. Too chicken. Scared he'll get fired." And so on. Sometimes, if there is an emasculatory wife, such opinions are subtly encouraged in the children.

Part of the problem is the same old communication gap. But what can you tell the family so they understand?

There are several ways it can be handled. One is the old "macho" way. Father impresses on the family his "golden rule"—

the guy who supplies the gold establishes the rules, and if he decides that a piece of business is more important on a Saturday morning than batting a ball around the village diamond, that's the way it's going to be.

Perhaps more effective and less abrasive would be a family conference, in which dad explains to his wife and son that this is the way life is, that, indirectly, the boss is the guy who puts bread on the table "for all of us." An explanation of why the man who pays father is paying him for "thinking time," and why some of that thinking occurs on weekends or at other family moments, usually will be accepted.

Most effective of all, depending on the personalities in the family, is to cope with the problem creatively—make fun of it: "Sorry the president interrupted our fun. That's the way business is. But when I get up there, I'll call all the fellows under me and make them work weekends." Or point out to your detractors how important you are to the company: "He may be president, but he can't make a decision on Saturday morning without calling me to see if I think it will track. That's what happens when you're a key man."

The fact remains, however, that there are times when the Saturday telephoning is *not* all that vital to the survival of the company; when a conscientious executive father might even gain the respect of his chief executive officer with a candid explanation: "I was just on my way out the door when you called, C.J. My son and I had an important date on the Little League ballfield. If it isn't too urgent, can I get back to you in a couple of hours on this matter?" Most "C.J.'s" will honor that approach and will either make the conference brief or postpone it.

A major hazard to many executive marriages is a tendency to confrontation by one or another spouse—or sometimes both. And when two facile minds leap into the fray, the psychological blood-letting can be impressive. Adult-to-adult relationships go out the window, and the rapier tips slash with abandon. Most often, the method used in creating total disintegration of rational adult discussion and destroying any possible resolution of differences, is a process known in psychology as "discounting."

This phenomenon, investigated and described in fascinating detail by two psychologists, Aaron and Jacqui Schiff, is basically a put-down. You come home tired and your wife pirouettes with a coy smile as you shed your coat. "I just bought this new dress today. How do you like it?" You reply irritably: "Didn't they have your size?" You are discounting your wife and asking for trouble.

Psychologist Abe Wagner, a Denver, Colorado, expert on Transactional Analysis, has a graphic lecture on this subject that puts the whole business in a nutshell. "You ask me a question," he explains, "and in the middle of it I interrupt you. That's discounting you. You congratulate me on a talk I made by saying, 'You did a nice job on that, Al.' But my name is Abe. You are discounting me. If you are asked a question and deliberately do not answer it, you are discounting the questioner. If your wife feels strongly about something she really needs, but the 'parent' in her tells her—without good reason—that she shouldn't ask you for it, she is discounting herself."

Wagner points out the Schiffs have isolated four basic kinds of discounting that people use to demean each other and/or themselves. In family conflicts, the psychologists discovered that three of every four fights ended in at least one of these types of discounting. You straighten out relationships, they point out, *not* by discounting but by learning to deal with problems head-on —adult to adult. In "symbiotic" relationships, where adults revert to children versus parent versus adult roles in a conflict, the adversaries will usually employ one of the following techniques.

They discount the problem. Mom hears the baby cry and turns on the radio to drown the noise. She is discounting the problem.

They discount reasons for, or significance of, a problem. You are late for a meeting and blame it on the weather—which is sunny and fair. Actually, you left too late. You are discounting the reason for the problem. There's a little-remembered story about the day Harold Ross hired Dorothy Parker at the infant, poverty-pinched *New Yorker* magazine. The offices were in a decrepit loft building under New York's Third Avenue elevated train. Ross came back from lunch and saw his new employee through the glass in a street-level bar with her foot on the rail chatting with Thurber, Gibbs, Woolcott, and others. When she got upstairs, he called her in and roasted her. "I hired you to write, not to shoot the breeze in bars," he growled. Parker replied: "I came up here after lunch and tried to write but somebody else was using the pencil." She was discounting the reason for the problem. Nicely. But in a family situation, it might not be all that funny.

A husband comes home from the club depressed and his wife greets him with: "I can tell you've been gambling again, and you said you wouldn't. I've had it up to here and I'm thinking seriously of leaving you for good." The husband replies: "That's no big deal." He is discounting the significance of the problem. This happens regularly between husbands and wives and leads, eventually, to the pits.

They discount the solution to a problem. There has been a problem about a possible move from New York to Detroit, and the wife has been upset because junior will have to leave his private day school. The husband comes home all cheery and announces that he talked with George today, and George revealed that one of the best day schools in the country is only three blocks from the neighborhood where he is negotiating for a house. The wife's reaction is: "George is a total jerk and always was." She has discounted the solution. Negating the obvious solution is a common form of discounting: "I can't talk to my boss." Period. "I can't talk to my wife." Period. "I can't do" this, that, or the other thing. Period. That is discounting the solution. It is the height of defeatism, and a cause of much domestic grief.

They discount themselves or someone else. Somebody elbows in front of me in a line, and I say nothing and do nothing. I am discounting myself. And we have already provided abundant examples of how people discount each other.

There's one other technique used by feuding marriage partners that deserves attention here, since it serves only to irritate and solves nothing. It's known as "redefining" (the issue). Kids are good at it. What it involves is, simply, answering something other than the question asked. You ask your son, "Who did that?" and he replies, "I wasn't there." You ask somebody, "Who?" and they answer with a "what," "when," or "how." What's bad is when you do nothing about it but seethe. You are then discounting yourself. Make sure that the question you ask is the one that is answered, or know the reason why.

According to Dr. Wagner, it takes two discounters to play a game in any family, and a game is a destructive way of relating. If two people are aware of the danger in this phenomenon, and do not discount, there is no game.

Avoidance of fruitless confrontation is vital to the maintenance of decent family relationships, and it isn't all that impossible if certain rules are recognized and adhered to.

Never try to discuss anything important with your wife at night. Defenses are brittle, and results disastrously predictable. You come home figuratively bleeding and your wife asks you, "What's the trouble, dear?" You've had a couple of martinis in the bar car, and you unburden yourself: "You know what that SOB of a president said to me? He said I was sloppy!"

She thinks for a minute, then says: "Well, you know, he may be right."

And you've got a bloody confrontation. Never at night. Darkness and troubled noise make a poor combination.

Never try to be funny or smart in a name-calling contest with your wife—or anyone else for that matter. Besides being the worst kind of discounting, it is too often taken for sarcasm. Not long ago, as Chairman of the Department of Psychology at Baruch College, I had to check some papers on student evaluations of our professors. In one paper the student wrote about a certain professor: "Every time he opens his mouth he subtracts from the sum of human knowledge." That may have been pretty funny, even if it wasn't original, but it didn't help the evaluator.

And once, when Eli Culbertson was watching a woman play a good bridge hand badly in a tournament, she looked up at him after losing the game and said, "Mr. Culbertson, how would you have played that hand?" Culbertson replied, "My dear, I'd have played it under an assumed name." Pretty clever, but if he'd said it to a wife, he'd have had his head handed to him. And I somehow doubt that it helped the lady's bridge game.

Sometimes it is necessary to criticize. You might be discounting yourself if you do not, and an injustice let slide will be repeated. But it is vitally important to criticize with dignity and fairness— not with hostility or resentment. Good criticism calls for careful self-evaluation. Furthermore, you don't approach criticism by trying to soften up the subject with a lot of half-baked praise, and then yank the rug out: "I'll admit you're a great mother, and one of the best, most loving people one could hope for with the kids—*but* . . ."

Prepare your subject for what's coming with a straightforward statement of your dissatisfaction, followed by the factual reasons for it. *Then* say something positive so that your target isn't hopelessly demoralized, and the whole constructive purpose of criticism lost. No one likes to be taken by surprise. But lay it on the line without fudging, after a hint at what's on your mind—a criticism.

One of the best examples of constructive criticism was a letter written by Abraham Lincoln to General Joseph Hooker, after the general had played some slick tricks to further his self-interest at the expense of another flag officer. Lincoln wrote:

Dear General Hooker,

I am placing you in charge of the Army of the Potomac. However, Hooker, there are things in your performance with which I am totally dissatisfied. Hooker, you have been too ambitious for command. In this fashion you have done a great disservice to a brother fellow officer and to the US Army. You are brave, you are skillful, you do not mix politics with your profession as a soldier—for which I admire you. Now, Hooker, beware of unbridled ambition. But with sleepless vigilance and eternal fortitude, go forward and give America its much needed victory.

Sincerely,
Abraham Lincoln

Lincoln did not leave Hooker not knowing where he stood. Never at night. Never with humor. Criticize with dignity.

14

Survival for Corporate Wives

☞ An acquaintance of mine who heads an international corporation told me of an occasion when he and his wife, in a London hotel suite, were dressing for dinner. They were to fly on to Moscow next day for what promised to be an interesting combination business-holiday tour. Both had been looking forward to the trip. The phone rang. It was an overseas call from corporate headquarters in New York. The executive vice-president was on the line. He advised his chief that a prominent Wall Street magazine had just published an extremely unfavorable article about the company's economic future. It was imperative that the head man come home to handle the situation, which was threatening some touchy business negotiations.

After promising to get back to him in a few minutes, my friend hung up, turned to his wife, and gave her the bad news. She could go on to Russia, but he'd have to go home. Her response was immediate: "You see about the tickets," she said. "I'll pack."

A lot of verbal tears have sprinkled the literary landscape over the years to water the theory that the role of the corporate wife is a sorry, miserable, unjust, and totally abused one. Usually, she is pictured as a forgotten citizen whose needs and personal life rank second, third, or fourth to her husband's; an unpaid maid of all work whose sense of accomplishment and contentment must come from red-carpeting her spouse's pathway to riches, success, and fame, while she stifles her own potentials to raise the kids, keep the books, manage the household, act as family travel agent for vacations, transportation and real estate agent when the corporation moves them from Biloxi to Bimidji, social secretary and corporate Elsa Maxwell on the entertainment front. She must, the articles tell us, cultivate friendships with people she may despise and turn her back on friends she prefers as her man moves up the corporate ladder. With stoic bravery, she struggles in obedient silence to fight off deep pangs of loneliness, fear, depression, and complete loss of identity.

As in most such generalizations, there is some basis in fact for a few such impositions that a corporate wife may be called upon to endure on occasion. However, the implication that all or most corporate wives live in a constant state of misery, sorrow, fear, depression, and ongoing exploitation by spouse and company is far from true—at least for women married to *top* corporate executives. And that is according to the wives themselves.

In a 1978 survey of the *Fortune 500* chief executive officers and their wives, Maryanne Vandervelde, a practicing psychotherapist, turned up some surprising facts about such ladies and their attitudes toward their domestic and corporate relationships. The results are published in detail in Ms. Vandervelde's recent book *The Changing Life of the Corporate Wife.* Among her most interesting findings was a list of characteristics that these women deemed most essential, in order of importance, to the successful execution of their role as lifetime partners to corporate chieftains.

A vast majority of the wives considered "concern about my own identity" as the characteristic of the least importance to their role. "Adaptability" was most highly valued. In between came "intelligence," near the top of the list, and "independence" next to the bottom.

In human relationships, these ladies were "extremely moralistic, especially in sexual matters. Sexual conservatism is the norm." They are "overwhelmingly against open marriages, homosexuality or bisexuality, and extramarital affairs for themselves and others."

Maryanne Vandervelde was astonished to find that most of the women surveyed had experienced little change in attitude even "with the rapidly changing consciousness about women and women's roles"—a fact which she interpreted as indicating "a very unaware and/or unmoved group."

She shouldn't have been so surprised. Most surveys of corporate wives, including those that we have conducted, have shown them to be totally aware of, and basically satisfied with, their role. Most of those whose husbands have achieved the top spot will readily acknowledge that they knew what they were getting into. They confess that material success was important to them, and that the sacrifices they make are part of the price they expect to pay. Frequently, however, they reserve the right to complain about some of those sacrifices. The biggest complaint, as previously indicated, usually is the scarcity of time that they get to spend with their husbands. But their role as executive wives is approached with what can only be described as genuine maturity, and a realistic understanding of the overall goals they seek in life. One must add the caveat, however, that most of these women surveyed were born and raised in more traditional times. It is anyone's guess whether wives of chief executives surveyed in 1998 will reflect similar attitudes.

In her book *The Executive Wife* Ninki Hart Burger described the role of the corporate wife as follows:

"To help ease, perhaps even erase, some of the pressures on your husband, exposed each working day to the . . . intense experiences of executive life.

"To control a home environment—a small revolving world within a great world—that allows your family and you to grow inwardly and yet share with each other.

"To view, not with alarm, but with understanding, the demands essential to your role as the wife of today's executive, and to perform with patience and with sensitivity.

"To work to discover fuller, deeper enjoyment of your own life."

While Maryanne Vandervelde found nothing wrong with the objectives expressed in that quote, which she noted in her book, she stated that their priorities did not make sense for any woman concerned about her own identity. According to Ms. Vandervelde's own survey, as well as many others, however, the vast majority of wives of successful top executives are *not* concerned about their own identities. Identity as such is no problem for most top-ranking executive wives (as Rosalynn Carter exemplified).

In a survey we conducted of wives of executives in a large glass conglomerate most said quite emphatically that the wife of an executive didn't have such a bad life, as long as her husband was reasonably content with the progress of the children—even though he didn't necessarily participate in it. As one wife put it, "We have the money we want, and I have the time to spend it because he is seldom home!"

One of the most frequently heard complaints from wives of young executives on the way up is that their share in the marriage partnership represents all the drudgery, while the husband's features glamour and excitement. Occasionally perhaps; usually not. It's difficult for a wife, who has never seen the front lines of big business in action and who is trapped at home with babies and domestic problems, to comprehend fully the vicious politics, business crises, incessant and frustrating interruptions, the often-bloody and ruthless struggles for power and control that permeate the fabric of routine operations in a large corporation. The potential for defeat lies behind every move up the ladder.

More often than not, a high-powered career man will arrive home mute with fatigue, struggling with a genuine "reentry" problem. He is trying to "change compartments." His wife, who also may have had a frustrating and tiring day of crises, wants to unburden herself for any of several reasons: she may hope to elicit sympathy or understanding for her unrewarding efforts; to get him a little involved with his family; to seek revenge for his isolation from the domestic problems.

Should she bottle up her anger and frustration? Not at all. But a canny and insightful wife will exercise careful judgment and timing before dumping her day's grief on her husband. If it isn't appropriate over coffee at dinner, hold it for morning. One wife I know makes "business breakfast" dates with her husband, which she takes pains to make pleasant. Some couples, as indicated earlier, arrange luncheon dates downtown to discuss their domestic affairs and, sometimes, just to enjoy each other's company.

Every corporate wife who has never had a chance to see how

the office functions, should make every effort to have her husband invite her for a look, and lunch. She should arrive half an hour or more early, sit—anonymously if possible—in his reception room, and observe what goes on. She'll hear the continuous incoming calls being shuttled or parried by his secretary (whom she will discover is a *secretary*—period). She'll have a glimpse of her man in his business context, hear some of the background noises of the corporate playing field, and see the parade of people trooping in and out of the front ·office singly, in pairs, and in whispering groups like the characters in some Gilbert and Sullivan operetta. If she can talk him into taking her to a local restaurant patronized by the company's executives, she'll see them discussing their business affairs. She'll be exposed to some of the forced joviality, sense some of the tensions, and gain some insight into the non-glamour of the real "working lunch." A few such office visits have given a number of executive wives I know a whole new point of view, and tempered some resentments—to the distinct advantage of their relationships with their husbands.

Another complaint I often hear from wives of top executives is that they are not putting to use their (frequently) extensive education and fulfilling themselves intellectually. It certainly is true that there are no liberal arts degrees for pregnancy problems, tantrum analysis, leaky plumbing, furnace failure, or the hammer-forging of "unfinished little people." My wife once remarked that she was thinking of hanging her Phi Beta Kappa key over the sink to remind her that at one time she had stretched her mind further.

No one can deny that a career devoted entirely to grubby domesticity may not contribute much to intellectual satisfaction. But my reaction to the relatively few executive wives who constantly dwell on what they might have done with their lives ("If only . . .") is *Baloney!* Our consulting operation has brought us into contact with too many executive wives who have organized their domestic lives, and time, so they *could* keep their minds working. Many have professional careers; some are executives in their own right. One executive wife who came to us for testing scored in the top 1 percent of the population and was advised to start a business of her own. She did, and today operates a highly successful travel business. Probably most wives of corporate executives busy themselves with community and civic volunteer work—certainly not stultifying for those caught up in the maelstroms of local politics.

I once brought down on my head the wrath of feminine hordes by stating in an article for *Family Health* magazine, "The real problem is that most women who end up complaining about all they have sacrificed for marriage never should have gone to college in the first place, let alone gotten married.

"Society turns out holders of master's and bachelor's degrees who would have been better off taking a year of home economics. The BA-MA business also supplies many insensitive women with a carping leitmotiv that only damages their relationship with husband and children, and psychologically un-fits them for marriage. If a wife really feels like thinking, why doesn't she get a job? Even part-time services are much in demand and rewards are enormous. She will have . . . a deeper understanding of the frustrations and joys that people like her husband encounter every day." It is still true, whether or not the chronic complainers want to believe it. The wife of a corporate president we know got herself involved with the League of Women Voters for exactly the reasons mentioned. "When I first joined, many eons ago, with two preschoolers," she recalls, "I was fond of saying that the brain, without regular exercise, would shrivel up and die like any other muscle. The League provided my brain with that much needed exercise." Today, three leagues later, she is president of a county league group in Pennsylvania, and actively involved in behind-the-scenes local and state politics.

In probing the problem areas of the executive's wife, many other things she can do to improve her lot and her state of mind become clear. An ignored or badly used corporate wife should take her complaints directly to her husband, who is usually the only person who can do something about them. Studies by sociologists have demonstrated that many wives are more likely to spend hours on the telephone discussing the husband's short-comings with friends and confidantes. Usually it goes something like this: "The miserable creature is hardly home before he's up at that desk with his damned papers. Not even a 'How was *your* day?' or 'Where are the kids?' It's always, 'How much time before dinner? I have to work on that report. Call me when it's on.' He even brings his briefcase into the bedroom. If I want to talk to him I practically have to arrange it with his secretary." And so forth.

Unfortunately, the sociologists have learned that such a wife will confide the "miserable creature" story not only to her own relatives but also to her miserable creature's relatives, in an effort to solicit sympathy from both camps. Besides being a highly hazardous practice that will backfire if reported to the husband, it in no way helps to deal with the problem. The most she can hope for is a shoulder to weep on—not solutions. In the interests of preserving family peace, we have often advised husbands not to "blow" when they hear about such complaints secondhand. It should indicate to a man that his spouse loves him enough to talk about him behind his back. But how much better it would be if she were to confront *him* with her justifiable anger over his apparent neglect.

Among the things wives of high-pressure career men often overlook, and thus pave the way for senseless arguments, is that there are times when a man would rather be with members of his own sex. Women sometimes forget that a reasonable amount of their own free time is spent voluntarily with female friends, neighbors, and relatives. They assume that their husbands are largely in the company of men all day, and shouldn't need more of the same companionship after working hours. The key word here is "companionship." Most of the relationships among men in business is adversary in nature; companionship is what they seek when the day's or week's battles are over.

Any male golfer will tell you that the friendly, good-humored competition of the foursome develops a feeling of relaxed fellowship in the group, and that the nineteenth-hole session at the clubhouse, which provides the casual atmosphere of masculine cohesion in which .important business may be conducted, is one of the appeals of the game for most men. So, when a husband announces that he is spending Sunday on the golf course, or an evening at the club with friends, a smart wife will not raise the roof and make him feel guilty about it. Only a stupid wife will try deliberately to manipulate her husband's guilt to achieve her own ends. She will succeed only in turning her home into an emotion-fraught field of battle, which even the best-adjusted husband will avoid like the plague. Many a wife I know has tried to badger her executive husband into staying home on a sunny Saturday, when he has planned a fishing or golfing day with his friends. Some women, when they are unable to sell "father" on staying home with the children, insist on going with him, even though the wives of other men in the party are not going. When he refuses her, he gets a hurt look and a pouty: "All *right!* Go *ahead!* I suppose I'll find *something* to do . . ." as he slams out the door in a fit of angry frustration and guilt. The wife who does that has succeeded in two things: she has ruined her husband's day, and boiled up a resentment in him that will not simmer down for a long time.

All of this is not to say that fights should be avoided at all costs. Some things need to be fought for with firmness and determination in any marriage. But "if you must fight, fight fairly." That was the appeal of Dr. M. O. Vincent of Guelph, Canada, a psychiatrist who told a recent medical congress that couples often pull the behavioral trigger that turns an inconsequential incident into an opportunity for full-scale war. If any of the techniques described below sound familiar, the chances are you're not looking for a solution but a brawl! The comments would apply equally to wife or husband in a combative situation.

> *Temporal expansion.* Throwing in superlatives like "always," and "all" and "never," as in the expression "That's *all* you've *ever* talked about for months." This usually will be taken as an attack and can become a self-fulfilling prophecy.
>
> *Disparaging the other person.* Attacking almost anything important to the opponent—appearance, maturity, intelligence, identity, family, sex, national origins. If a husband has little admiration for his father it would be devastatingly effective to say: "You're even worse than your father." To which he is likely to reply: "Your whole damn family is even worse than that!" And away they go.
>
> *Crucializing.* Shifting focus from a particular problem to a test of love. Many embattled wives (particularly) introduce it with the statement: "If you really loved me you would . . ."

Steamrollering. Overwhelming the spouse with a generalized attack: "You bring up every good thing you have ever done, and everything bad the other person has ever done, completely clouding the issue."

Issue diffusion. To maintain conflict avoid focusing on the core problem. Focus identifies and sticks to the issue for possible solutions with logic, facts, openness, persuasion, and efforts to compromise. To perpetuate conflict, one needs to keep the issue confused, ill-defined, and avoid stating it. This helps prevent each partner from knowing what the other is talking about. An unfair fighter will focus on areas that threaten the self-esteem or status of the other, and imply a change in power. "You're so stupid you can't even pay bills correctly; from now on I'll handle the money."

Humor. As already indicated, for husbands, when used in a cavalier manner, especially maliciously, it can plunge a hurt wife into tears. Similarly, it may send a husband storming out of the house in a cold fury.

Mrs. Felix Frankfurter, wife of the late Supreme Court Justice, was famous for her tendency to deflate her indulgent husband with a tart and sometimes oversharp wit. At one formal dinner where he was the principal speaker, she observed to the table in general as the Justice returned to his seat, "There are only two things wrong with Felix's speeches: He digresses and returns to the subject." The smart crack did little to improve the relationship that one biographer graciously called "not one of easy stereotyping."

All these approaches are aimed at arousing anxiety and defensiveness, instead of calming with logic and reinforcing a partner's trust, autonomy, love, and power. They are most brutally effective, Dr. Vincent points out, "where basic trust or personal security is already tenuous."

In an effort to provide better guidelines for wives of corporate executives, I have tried to isolate some of the characteristics of women who I have observed are really destructive to a man and his career. Any corporate wife sincerely interested in preserving a tenuous union should, by all means, avoid these behaviors.

There is the "clothes horse." She is dressed to kill. She makes the president's wife look like Raggedy Ann.

Then there is the "teaser," forever making sexy remarks in front of the men at business functions. The men may seem to enjoy it, but their wives fume. The president of a steel company once asked me what he should do about the wife of a VP who kept telling off-color jokes that prompted angry complaints from the chairman, who felt the woman had exceeded the limits of good taste. He threatened to bypass her husband for promotion if she persisted. I had to advise the president to talk to his upwardly mobile VP and relay the chairman's threat, leaving it up the husband to handle his wife. Apparently he did, since he continues to progress in the company.

Another menace is the "Let's have another" girl, whose call for another drink triggers a disapproving frown on the boss's brow. Growing female enrollments in AA chapters in wealthy exurban communities indicate that more and more executive wives are becoming alcoholics. It reflects the problem of wives left alone too often.

A declining species, though still extant, is the Lady Macbeth of the executive arena, constantly pushing her husband to become king—this type usually ends up doing her husband much more harm than good.

And not to be taken lightly is the wife who fights her husband's career with endless medical misfortunes, draining him dry in the process, and then outlives him for thirty years.

Those are the obvious examples of destructive behavior in a wife bent on doing her husband no favors. There are a dozen or more "don'ts" for wives who really want their marriage to provide an oasis in a turbulent world for both partners.

Don't be an armchair generalist. No wife who wants a happy home should chastise her husband with statements such as, "I told you so." Help him absorb failures by sharing some of the responsibility, or by letting him know that your acceptance and love are based not on his material success but on his human value.

Stop "antiquing." Some wives I know have an unfortunate tendency during an argument to bring up some old grievance: "What you've just done reminds me of the time you called mother's cousin an ugly old sow." Never mind that it was twenty-five years ago and has nothing to do with the present argument.

Or that she probably *was* an old sow. Keep all discussions current and centered around today's challenges. Forget the negative nostalgia.

Don't demand more of your husband than he can afford to give you during the years of career growth. Most of the executive types I know have a genuine natural urge to make a go of their marriage and their family. "The affection of my wife and the respect of my children are on another plane of my existence, the one where I *really* live!" one executive expert in finance told me.

The fact is that when a top executive fails to resolve the conflict between his dedication to job and to family, the wife often is partly to blame. When she makes too many demands on his time, he is apt to turn away in self-defense. If she responds hysterically with more and more demands, in the mistaken belief that by having her husband at home more often her problems will vanish, she is sadly mistaken. Any man who senses that he is being "captured" by his family will almost invariably rebel. Successful executives are aggressive and ambitious men. Chained to a family, they become frustrated, angry and resentful of a partner who tries to keep them there. What, then, can a frustrated corporate wife do to involve such a husband in family affairs even a little?

Encourage him to spend time with the children. But remember that most successful executives—even the Janus and need-achiever types—have great trouble talking to children. They find small children inarticulate, unable to make their kind of pragmatic sense. It is hard for these men to crawl on the floor with their infant offspring. Their minds are on other things. They would *like* to spend more time with the children, especially as the youngsters grow, but often they don't know how. A genuinely concerned wife can—like Rose Kennedy—help by providing her husband with a list of questions he can ask the children when they go off on an afternoon together. I call them "talking points." Give him tips on what he might discuss with his son or daughter. You are familiar with their daily problems and growing pains. He's not. At least help him to get the conversation going because this is not the area of his greatest strength.

Most important, be patient. The pressures won't always be so great. Psychologists know that in most cases, when a man has achieved his ultimate corporate goals, he lets up a little. It is then that he may find the time to look homeward, with tokens of appreciation for your help and understanding during the tough years.

Meantime, don't shrivel up inside your domestic shell and brood over your misfortunes. Complaining is about as feckless as wishing you'd been born Grace Kelly. Get out and do some volunteer work for Meals on Wheels, the hospital, local charities, the League of Women Voters. Hire sitters if necessary; your husband can afford it. If you can spare the time, by all means get a job. Many corporate wives today are going back to school for graduate studies, to pursue careers of their own. Getting back into the real world, at least part of the time, can do wonders for "cabin fever."

Don't turn down anything your husband offers you—no matter how little or poorly considered it may seem to be. This is vital. If it's a gift, and it's the wrong color or style, take it and use it. He thought of you, and picked it out for you. It's great. It means that he took some time and made an effort to try to please you. It means he cares. Take it as a compliment.

Don't worry about arguments. They are going to continue. Most people after twenty years of marriage argue about the same things they started arguing about during the first week of their marriage. It may be golf, it may be the time he spends on the job, or it may be a mother-in-law. It merely gets more sophisticated twenty years later. Conflict is not the end of the world, but if you make an effort to keep cool and objective, and hew to the guidelines suggested, it will be much less painful.

Encourage your husband to take a vacation. Many men never will take one without a push from their wives. It is necessary for a couple to vacation together now and then, and to enjoy adult privacy away from the children. Even one day in the country or an evening together can be beneficial, for the reasons already discussed.

A concerned wife can help a workaholic husband achieve an awareness of the difference between "being" and "doing." Most of a top executive's life is spent in doing, achieving, evaluating, and creating. Hence, he finds it difficult to sense, feel, and just to "be." The latter are essential to a balanced existence. Most executives I know are fine for the first few days of a vacation, but after that are driven by their tensions and compulsions to "do" things.

A forty-five-year-old corporate officer I knew was eliminated in a power struggle and given a settlement of over a million dollars. With all that, plus his previous holdings, he refused to take even a few days off before plunging into an intensive hunt for another job, until I insisted that in the interest of his own mental health, he take a few weeks to try "being" somebody instead of just "doing something" that was not at all essential.

Watch your communication channels. Almost all marital impasses are blamed on the inability of the participants to "communicate." What is often forgotten is that communication is a two-way street. Samuel Butler, the English scholar, once observed that "It takes two people to say a thing—a sayer and a sayee. The one is just as essential to any true saying as the other."

The problem is that few of us want to be the "sayee" in any dispute. The sayee is the listener, and too often we confuse hearing with listening. "Hearing" is simply a sensory function. But "Listening," says communication expert Dr. Harry T. Allen, "is hard work and requires increased energy—your heart speeds up, your blood circulates faster, your temperature goes up." It can only be achieved by applying the power of the mind.

Most ordinary humans tend to apply that power only to hearing what pleases them. Their minds automatically reject ideas they find disagreeable. Such "communication" goes in one ear and out the other. It is a message transmitted to the airwaves with no receiver tuned in. The trick in listening, as one astute observer has pointed out, is to guard against our natural tendency to exercise "emotional censorship" of the "sayer's" message. And this, of course, goes as well for husbands as for wives.

So, be a good listener. Psychologists recommend some techniques which will help you to communicate to your partner that you are really listening. Here are a few:

Maintain eye contact.

Lean forward.

Repeat what he said, now and then, with the same emotional flavor.

The "echo technique" can be carried too far, so don't overdo it. The story goes that a young man said to his analyst, "I hate my mother." The analyst repeated, "You hate your mother." He said, "I hate myself." The analyst reflected, "You hate yourself."

Finally, after several minutes of this the patient jumped off the couch and said, "Heck, Doc, what's wrong with the way *I* have been saying it?"

On this subject of communication, it is essential for you to insist that your husband set aside at least one hour every week for "family conference time." This is the time everyone should be encouraged to bring up personal problems for discussion—a sort of family Town Hall meeting. It doesn't mean that problems will always be solved or disputes settled. But complaints *will* be aired—which is the first necessary step toward resolution.

Encourage him to share his emotional pressures. Let him be irritable, moody, tired, even angry. A good marriage can take this in its stride.

Don't belittle him when he is away, especially to the children. You are his gatekeeper. When the little boy says, "Where is daddy?" and mother replies, "How do I know? He's out somewhere doing his thing, I suppose," she has made father a self-serving egocentric in the eyes of his child. On the other hand, if she says, "He's out helping our country solve its inflation problems so we can all enjoy things," a totally different image emerges.

Wives can criticize constructively, as well as husbands—and the same rules we have already detailed apply. Act to spur him on, not to cut him down. It is important to believe that you are married to a man worthy of respect and affection, and by acting in a constructive way you can serve his purposes and your own as well.

Learn to use praise as has been recommended. But remember that, like seasoning, a little bit is a lot better than a lot. Praise him behind his back to friends and relatives. If he hears it from a third party it adds another dimension. And it is always better to praise a man in the areas of his anxiety. Arturo Toscanini told me about a compliment he treasured from Marian Anderson. At the end of a concert instead of rushing up to tell him he had conducted brilliantly (by the time he was seventy with thining hair, he noted, he knew he was a brilliant conductor), she said, "Arturo, you looked handsome up there tonight!" To Toscanini at seventy, it was more important to be perceived as handsome than as a great conductor.

That kind of thing is, admittedly, manipulative. In effect it is role playing, and you can't role-play forever. But attitudes may change as behavior changes. And such devices sometimes can serve a purpose if applied with discretion.

Some time ago, Garry Moore contrived a brainstorming session on one of his morning shows, posing the question: "What can wives do to help their husbands live longer?" The brainstormers, some half-dozen wives of executive and professional men, came up with a surprising list of recommendations, many of which are worth noting here. But remember, most are purely manipulative. They can be tried on appropriate occasions. If they fit, it may mean they are things you always wanted to do. But if you are hostile to the idea, or get a hostile reaction, drop it right away. And don't try to do all of them. No one wants to live with a saint.

Personal ideas for wife
1. Pretend you like your mother-in-law.
2. Sneak a love note into his pocket in the morning.
3. Flatter him—compliment him on his appearance . . . his thoughtfulness . . . integrity . . . once a day.
4. Do his shopping for him so as to eliminate nasty little errands he may not like to do.
5. Like his friends. Even if you don't, pretend you do.
6. Compliment and complement him. Be a complement to him.
7. Keep a special surprise savings account he doesn't know about. Then spend it on things your husband likes, but thinks he can't afford.
8. Have something interesting and amusing to say to him when he comes home at night even if you do have to look it up in a book.
9. Don't get annoyed at those little things that annoy him.
10. Have an "unbirthday" day. Give him a gift or celebrate on one day a year that's not his birthday.
11. Don't be envious of your neighbors. Don't push him to keep up with the Joneses.
12. Don't be jealous of his secretary or women associates.
13. Don't remind him of what he might do with his life that he hasn't done, but tell him how proud you are of what he has done.

14. Make a list of the things you'd have to do yourself if your husband died, and you will want to do more things to help him live longer.
15. Never let him worry about past, present or future . . . live every day as it comes.
16. Convince him if he is "chewed out" by someone, that person may have been chewed out by someone else, and is taking it out on him.

Husband and wife relations
1. Don't nag your husband.
2. Be a wife rather than a mother.
3. Don't discuss troubles before dinner.
4. Let him win every third fight.
5. Encourage him to tell his favorite jokes in public—don't try to shut him up.
6. Compliment him in front of friends and build up his ego.
7. Learn to do new things together.
8. Never have an argument after 9 PM.

Family life in home
1. Have the children out of the way when he comes home at night.
2. Set the clock ahead so he will get up early, and not have to run for the train without breakfast.
3. Have a special "quiet room" for dad.
4. Solve family problems by brainstorming with the family.
5. Don't threaten the children with dad's name for postponed punishment. Don't say, "Dad will take care of you when he gets home." Punish children right away and don't save it for your husband to carry out when he gets home from work.
6. Encourage him to be interested in the children's hobbies.

Physical
1. Put a scale right next to his closet, so he can weigh himself every morning. This will help him keep his weight down.

2. Take walks together.
3. When he is tired, give him a rubdown at night to relax him before he goes to sleep.
4. Slow him down occasionally. Get him to sleep late, take an afternoon off, or spend a Saturday in bed.

Eating and sleeping
1. Feed your husband a *good* breakfast in the morning, with a cheery smile.
2. Have a drink ready for him when he comes home at night.
3. Don't bring problems to meals.
4. Study your husband's sleep habits to be sure he gets a good night's sleep. See if he sleeps better in a night shirt. Serve him hot soup before he retires. Get him an electric blanket and a new mattress which just suits him.
5. No matter how loudly he snores, don't abandon the double bed.

Vacation and recreation
1. Plan vacations to suit his needs.
2. Every so often insist he go on a vacation alone, or with some other men. For example: an all-male hunting or fishing trip.
3. Every so often, give him a stag party at home.
4. Give him a surprise "Father's Day" not on Father's Day.
5. Don't make him go out evenings when he doesn't want to.

Church and community activities
1. Spend more time with the "old man."
2. Get your husband to attend church regularly with you. Statistics show that people who go to church regularly live longer because they are better adjusted to life.
3. If you are going to volunteer to work on community projects, get him to work on the same ones so you can spend more time together.
4. Get him to teach Sunday School. It will take his mind off his own troubles. Teaching young people will make him feel younger, and act younger.

Husband's work
1. Never press him about his problems at work. If he wants to talk about them, okay, but don't ask about them.
2. Help him to think creatively. Help him to develop ideas about his job, or new solutions to his problems.
3. Save his time by reading the trade papers and clipping items of interest to him.

Hobbies and outside-of-work activities
1. Encourage your husband to have a hobby.
2. Help him plan for his retirement.
3. Stir up new interests so he doesn't get in a rut.
4. Make a list of things you will do together when he retires.

So much for making executive husbands happy so that corporate wives can survive more pleasantly. In all fairness, it must be added that after the article for *Family Health* magazine was published, one irate executive wife and mother wrote a long, critical letter of noteworthy significance. Here are some of the points she made:

"Most women, too, want to make a 'go' of marriage. What does 'go' mean? Cars, for example, run with varying degrees of efficiency. In how good repair are *both* partners willing to keep their marriage?

"The husband comes home so tired he is 'mute,' you say. You acknowledged a full day of minor crises for the wife. Could she also be *bone weary*?

"When does the man become emotionally healed from a day's work? Late in the evening my husband is too tired to tackle problems, and problems do arise. In the morning he wants a pleasant head start on the day.

"Why doesn't the wife get a job? Child care, conflicting school schedules, low wages, and—often most compelling—*the husband's nonnegotiable objection.*

"I don't know of any women who have complained of their husbands' being away in a crisis—if they were working. I have heard complaints from wives whose husbands weren't home because they stopped for a few drinks . . . that became *quite* a few. You seem to see the husband as hard-working, long-suffering, never at fault, and the wife as an overeducated chronic complainer.

"When the poor woman with a complaint has shown that all other answers to her complaint are fallacious, she is told that her husband is *paying the bills* and thus is not to be disturbed. In other words 'might makes right' . . . at least financial might.

"Half of the bills are his—rent, clothes, food. He brings home the bacon; but his wife cooks it. That, in my estimation, makes the husband and wife *even*. They can begin negotiations from there.

"I do wish an 'ambitious' man could be just as 'ambitious' for a loving, giving, communicative family life.

"I wish a happy home were 'admired' by more husbands. Many just take the wife's opportunity for self-fulfillment for granted.

"But it's a two-way street. The husband must do some 'creating' too. A man can give all to his job and save the emotional leavings for his home. But he'll get what he is asking for . . . success, and an unhappy home. If husbands acted around the office the way they do at home, we would lose a lot of executives. And if husbands were as demanding of their secretaries as they are of their wives, they would soon run out of office help. . . . I don't think it is too much for a wife to ask to be treated with the same respect as her husband's worthy colleagues.

"Complaining wives are told that:

"They've had more education than was good for them. (True, unaware women *are* less of a threat.)

"They should keep their problems to themselves. (Shut up.)

"They should be grateful to have breadwinners. (But we are taking about husbands, not paychecks.)

"It is their own stupid fault anyway; they probably married the first guy to come along—and married too young and for the wrong reasons."

This letter was written in 1970. A lot has happened since then to the attitudes of society toward women and the resources available to women. But the letter expresses a side of the problem that still exists in many executive "castles" and will never go away by itself. The points made should not be overlooked by any corporate executive who expects to achieve anything approaching success on the home front.

15

The Children of "God"

Under the shadow of a great oak tree the small sapling does
not perhaps receive enough sunshine.

RANDOLPH CHURCHILL

☞ "There are some extraordinary fathers," the French essay-
ist Jean de La Bruyère observed some 300 years ago, "who seem,
during the whole course of their lives, to be giving their children
reasons for being consoled by their death."

He wasn't exaggerating. Ernest Hemingway may have been
"Papa" to his outdoorsmen friends and literary fans. But the
youngest of his three sons, Gregory, who is a physician today, has
recalled in a recent biography of his awesome sire a feeling of
"relief when they lowered my father's body into the ground and
I realized that he was really dead, that I couldn't disappoint
him, couldn't hurt him any more."

Thomas Alva Edison, probably America's greatest inventor,
may have brought incandescent light to the world, and made
significant contributions to the development of some thousand

other wonders of the day—including the phonograph, the storage battery, the mimeograph, motion pictures, and the telephone. As an inventor he was unquestionably a genius. In business he was ruthless and predatory. As a husband and father, he was a total disaster, a prime example of a monster-type corporate bigamist. Edison almost totally ignored his two successive wives (the first died young, and vastly overweight; the second referred to the disappointing relationship as devoid of any "great love").

According to Robert Conot, whose recent book *American Odyssey* is one of the most revealing biographies of Edison ever written, the towering inventor-genius spoke of his children (three by wife number one; two by number two) as "unsuccessful experiments." Even Charles, who managed to survive the paternal ordeal and serve as governor of New Jersey and, for a time, chief executive of the Edison Company, once wrote to his father: "There were times when I felt you had struck the spurs in so deep that I would surely bleed to death."

Many corporate bigamists—monster types in particular—tend to make excessively heavy demands on their children. They see no reason why their progeny should not be perfect in every respect (like them). For years, the late Supreme Court Justice Hugo Black—an arch perfectionist—made life next to impossible for his young son who reveals some of the hell he went through in a recently published book entitled *My Father*. At the time of his appointment to the court in 1937, Black was senator from Alabama, a self-made man steeped in the Puritan ethic. He disapproved and was highly critical of everything about his son—school grades, work habits, his penchant for the funny papers, and even the fifteen-year-old boy's acne: "Can't see how you can have it, son. I never did."

Fathers like Black, if their youngsters are not super beings, take it as a reflection of some imperfection in themselves—a totally unacceptable concept. It becomes a disapprobation of their superiority and is not to be tolerated. During the brief time they spend with their kids, whether it's playing softball, a game of chess, or bridge, their technique for "teaching" and "improving" the youngsters' performance usually takes the form of stinging criticism of everything they do and the way they do it: "You're standing too close in—no wonder you're missing.

Throw it harder! It's too high!"; "You leave your knights wide open! Pay attention to the openings in those pawns!"; "Why *can't* you remember what's trump—you *heard* the bidding!"

Needless to say, such a running commentary—delivered in an irritated tone—is counterproductive. Kids consider it crass, grueling pressure to "win" with no enjoyment of the game or pastime —anything but fun. "My dad keeps telling me what to do and how to do it, and it's a drag. So I avoid him whenever he's around— which luckily isn't often," the ten-year-old son of a corporate chairman told me when I asked him why he'd turned down an offer by his father to take him deep-sea fishing.

When you see some of these fathers in action, it's easy to understand why their kids are completely turned off by them. An international tycoon I know had a son who had just started working for the company when he had a near-fatal car accident one evening. His father was alerted at home and he asked to be connected to the young man immediately. He was told that his son had just come out of coma and should not be subjected to lengthy or stressful conversation. The father's first words when the injured lad came on the line were: "Hi! That shipping contract you negotiated yesterday: what have you done on it?"

In another case, a steel company executive acquaintance of mine had an active, competent son—himself the father of two youngsters. The son, in his early twenties, was a promising young stockbroker who had decided to take flying lessons so that he could fly himself around to see important clients. He happened to mention this to his father on the phone one day. "A good idea, don't you think?" he asked.

"No!" barked his father. "What about your family?"

The younger man revealed that he had sufficient insurance to cover them.

"What about my grandchildren?" the tycoon asked.

His son said he'd had himself covered for them, too.

"And what about yourself," his father pressed. The young man replied that should anything happen to him ("God forbid!") his clients would get another broker.

"So will I," growled old dad. "Right now!" and hung up.

That same steel executive, when a young member of his firm came to him for financing to support his penchant for sports car racing, was thoroughly compassionate and called on a number of his personal friends to help the fellow.

Problems with children often are exacerbated by the failure of autocratic types of successful executives to remember that their offspring are not employees. Some of them tend to confuse their cold, impersonal office attitudes with the way they react in family situations—often absurdly.

When the wife of one top executive I know was hospitalized for about three months, her husband put their son in a clerical job at the company office and brought him to work each morning in the company limousine. When the father visited his wife at the hospital one evening, she asked him, "Do you ever have lunch with Junior?" He replied, tersely, "You know I never eat with the help."

The pressures executive parents put on their own children, and the discipline they try to impose, may even be vicious in their rigidity. Some years ago, a Florida executive (and former swimming champion) decided that his subteen daughter, who had shown some talent as a diver, could be molded into Olympic material. He drove her through a daily regimen that was actually pitiless. Often there were tears, but the father's only reaction was a cold, grim insistence on obedience to the training schedule. One afternoon after school, the youngster—then nine—pleaded for a break. She'd had an hour or so of harsh criticism for endless mistakes. She wasn't feeling well and her timing was off. Father would brook no interference with the program and insisted she "perfect" her back jacknife, which she had been doing badly. When neither pleading nor copious tears would move the man, she climbed the ladder, jumped, clipped the front end of the board with her head as she passed it on the way down, and broke her neck. She was killed instantly.

The effect on the children of these driven high achievers is appalling, even at best. Few of their offspring are able to handle the resentments with the emotional maturity of one of former President Lyndon Johnson's daughters, who admitted that: "My anger was aimed at him because he seemed to be always taking my mother away. . . . Even when my father was around, I'm afraid I didn't do much to help our relationship. So eventually he stopped trying, too. This bothered Mama a great deal. . . .

So I stopped thinking of him as a father and started thinking of him as a friend. Eventually, I learned to love him as a person, not as a father, because he seldom had time to be a father."

Retaliation of offspring against an overbearing or indifferent parent can take many forms. Randolph Churchill was often belittled by his overpowering father, and managed to get back at him in curious ways. One reporter told how, at a black-tie dinner for Sir Winston, the British leader rose and delivered a remarkable impromptu speech on the then-current state of world affairs. The writer, seated beside Randolph, was unable to hear enough of the talk to take proper notes because the Prime Minister's son spent the entire time exclaiming over, and playing with, a cheap cigarette lighter that the host, Bernard Baruch, had provided each guest.

The motive in such behavior, of course, is derogation of the offending parent. It is behavior intended to hurt him, damage him at any cost. Such children tend to try to "kill" him—at least figuratively—sometimes by noncompeting (which usually disturbs aggressive sires) or battling them for control of the corporation or family fame. The extent to which some noncompetitive offspring of high achievers will go to avenge real or imagined hurts may involve anything from total surrender to self-destruction of one sort or another. Charlie Chaplin's son Sidney, had absolutely no intention of trying to rival his famous comedian father. "I don't know why everyone compares me to my father," he said. "He is truly incomparable." While he did follow a theatrical career, Sidney refused any and all comedy roles.

The really tragic cases of "revenge" are reflected in the frightening growth of the number of teenage suicides. A June 1979 report in the *Journal of the American Medical Association* revealed an increase in the rate of self-destruction among fifteen to twenty year olds of 124 percent since 1961, making it the third-ranking cause of death in that age group. Recently, Dr. Frank E. Crumley, a Dallas, Texas, child psychiatrist, probed forty adolescent attempts at suicide in an effort to determine motivations.

The typical patient was described as "a girl drug abuser of upper middle class, with a major depressive disorder." Personality characteristics included "a tendency to react severely to a loss, poorly controlled rage, and impulsivity." All the youngsters were psychiatrically ill before the attempt, Dr. Crumley reported. The most common problems were drug abuse, depression, and borderline personality disorder. All except three of the twenty-nine females and eleven males were average or above in intellectual ability. Their ages varied from twelve to nineteen.

It should come as no great surprise that most of these young people are from executives' families. A truck driver's children are streetwise and can control their environment. Sons and daughters of high achievers are given little opportunity to do so.

In most cases where children (particularly sons) of high achievers refuse to become students of their fathers, it is either because they don't think they can make it, or because they think it makes them infantile.

Arndt Krupp, heir to the German Krupp empire, was expected to prepare himself, as his father Alfried had done, to take over the reins of the giant company. Instead, he devastated Alfried by dropping out of university after two semesters and—by his own account—committing himself to a "life of pleasure." In an interview some years ago, he told a reporter that he had renounced his right to inherit the Krupp fortune. "I am not like my father," he said, "who sacrifices his whole life for something, not knowing whether it is really worth it in our time."

Perhaps the all-time classic tragedy in this context was that of William James Sidis, a startlingly brilliant child prodigy. William, the son of a pair of self-made Russian immigrant academicians, Boris and Sarah, was taught by his parents to spell and read before age three. By five, he could read Russian, German, French, and Hebrew as well. The boy was accepted as a special student at Harvard in 1909, when he was eleven years old. Within his first year he had delivered a lecture on higher mathematics before the Harvard Mathematical Club, bringing himself national acclaim. But he was so exploited and driven by his father's efforts to make him "the perfect man" that, after graduating, he defied the elder Sidis and dropped out of academics entirely. He died an emotionally disturbed, reclusive, and obscure clerk.

Boris has been pictured by psychologists who have studied the case as a vicious, driving fanatic who used his brilliant son to promote his own theories on education and child-rearing which, many conclude, were the whole cause of his son's sorry end.

The father, it has been pointed out, was totally devoid of any deep paternal feeling. Intellectually, he could drill and educate a bright child, but he was completely incapable of conveying even the rudiments of emotional security to his son. He was, in short, an archetypal corporate bigamist, monster style.

For *all* types of high achievers, however, the demands that many of them make at home for the same prompt, unquestioning responses that they get from business or professional subordinates undoubtedly produce many disastrous behavioral problems in today's children. If I were to check all of the board members I know, I would estimate that at least 70 percent of them have serious problems at home—children running away to join the "Moonies," communes of one sort or another, and drug cults; the "loners" are apt to be suicide prone. These are the very problems that the fathers who precipitate them usually complain about most bitterly.

A few years ago, Drs. Alan Sostek and Stanley Sherman, a Boston psychology team, published the results of an eight-year study of executives' children, probing their attitudes toward parents, their behavior and the reasons behind it.

The reaction of most of these kids to their super-successful parents, and to parental authority, was resentment—often bitter. The self-confidence, achievement orientation, and pride of workmanship in this group was significantly lower than in control groups of young students with less affluent or "important" parents. Biggest complaint of the study group was the nonnegotiable parental demand for compliance with their own point of view, and no interest in, or effort to understand, the views or rationale of the children. In most cases, the response of these young people was to "opt for failure rather than aggressive, socially acceptable goal-seeking behavior." Their reaction was to look elsewhere for acceptance, finding it most often and easily among nonachieving peers who "understood" them. The more intelligent ones admitted to becoming bored with these dullards, however, and eventually sought their stimulation and gratification in alcohol and/or drugs.

According to the researchers, more than half of today's progeny in upper-middle-class families demonstrate the symptoms described, whether or not they leave home. "The same factors," they point out, "which helped the executive to achieve monetary success [also, ironically, help to] create a nonacademic, suffering child who may go through life with a fear-of-failure, nothing-ventured-nothing-lost behavior pattern." The products of such a life-style, they note, enter adulthood with no goals or aspirations and without motivation to assume even the least pressing of adult responsibilities. Not surprisingly, many of these are the "children of affluence" who, to their privileged parents' horror and disbelief, often join and are exploited by exotic and erotic cults and causes. Depending on whose research you read, they make up about one-quarter to one-half of the estimated one million runaways who inhabit the hippie warrens of most major cities in this country, at any given time. New York City's East village was one such mecca where one could see messages scrawled in chalk on dirty brick walls: "Janie, we were wrong. Please come home. Mom and Dad," or "$1000 reward for any information about Alan Dyson, missing since January."

In the late sixties, when Linda Rea Fitzpatrick, the teenage daughter of a wealthy importer whose home was a rambling estate in Greenwich, Connecticut, was found murdered in an East Village boiler room, I was interviewed by *Dun's Review*. The editors wanted to know why children of top executives, pampered with all of life's goodies and endowed with what Harvard psychologist Robert Coles has called built-in "entitlement," should want to run away. In the course of our own research, we have had occasion to talk with a great many such young people. Their reasons for escaping the shelter of the family manse are remarkably similar, and much of what they revealed is worthy of the attention of success-oriented parents.

The first thing to recognize is that today's kids are under tremendous pressure to be a credit to their successful parents—to do well scholastically, athletically, and socially. Mother grooms her daughters for one of the Seven Sister schools that still bear the subtle stamp of quiet wealth and quality. Father covets the status symbol of a son attending an Eastern Ivy League school. Few top corporate officials want to admit that a son goes to Skunk Holler U. and is majoring in wrought-iron crafts. From a generation to which so much has been given, a lot is also expected!

Usually at the high school or prep-school level, the kids become fully aware that they are being aimed at these targets, and thoughts about the consequences of failure dance in their heads: "They'll hate me if I don't make good; I'll be a total disgrace." Many can't take that pressure, and make the decision to run away from home and its threats. They cop out, wear long unwashed hair, get dirty, and abandon the race.

This sense of futility is something fairly recent in our society. Our parents' assumption that a big home on parklike grounds in exurbia, a holiday haven in "the islands," a car for each family member, a live-in maid, and private schools for the kids would solve all the problems on the home front, belongs to a former age. Children today are not so easily fooled. They look at their folks and tell themselves, "My parents are not happy; they don't even talk to each other when they're together, except maybe to fight. What right have they got to criticize me if I want to smoke a few joints and socialize with my friends?"

One of the things that bothers these dissatisfied youngsters is the belief that their big shot fathers know the price of everything, but the value of nothing. Make no mistake. The kids like and want that fat allowance, their Swiss ski vacations, their Mercedes SL coupe or horse, and all the privileges dad's money permits them. But they suddenly have become concerned about Vietnam, Kent State, the urban crisis, and starving people. Many of them want to know what father is doing to meet these social challenges. When they discover that he's leaving most of it to the federal government, which "taxes us plenty for it," they are not satisfied that he's doing anything at all. To show him up, they may bite the bullet and throw away all their material goodies. They reject the country club, expensive clothes, care, and the whole upper-middle-class morality because it is simply the most devastating way they can rebel against their parents. It's a brutally effective way to *hurt* them.

What they are trying to sell themselves, and say to their folks, is that a well-to-do suburban life is not enough, that they must have a mission, must have ideas, must be more honest with each other, that what they see as the "Great Society" is not going to be based just upon economic security. There's nothing wrong with all that. What *is* wrong, of course, is their belief that to achieve those goals they have to run away from home in a near-psychotic frame of mind and live in a ghetto, instead of facing up to the problems and fighting them out with their parents on their own home front.

They probably don't know what they are looking for in the East Villages of the world. They usually say they want to identify with honesty, poverty, and a "meaningful" life. They claim to achieve this with things like Zen Buddhism, or with pseudo-philosophies, but this is highly doubtful. Most adolescents are confused people. They used to have heroes, like poet Allen Ginsberg, but they seem not to anymore. Their attitude is nihilistic. Nobody matters; nobody is honest. Their new companions are, for the most part, stupid and uninteresting. So they cop out. Drugs are available, forbidden, and provide another dimension. They try marijuana and move on to methedrine, LSD, and the opiates. It's an adventure and they just don't care any longer. By the time a kid is on LSD he or she is in bad shape in terms of any awareness or self-fulfillment. But marijuana still is the really big problem, despite all the mindless efforts to prove it harmless. Sometimes, it is the first stepping stone to the catastrophic progression that leads to self-destruction.

It must be emphasized that what we have been talking about so far on this subject deals almost entirely with the families of real monster-type "Caesars" and, perhaps, unreconstructed Januses— not the need-achiever and the more family-oriented Janus-types who make sincere efforts to relate to their wives and children. Not that these parents are completely without offspring problems, however.

In 1977, a survey of top and upper-middle management families of major US corporations turned up a number of interesting facts about the young people involved. Some seventy of the children in those families were in the seventeen to twenty-four-year age group, and all were either attending or had graduated from college. But only nine of them planned a corporate or business career. The remainder already had opted for what one of them described as "people careers, jobs where we can see the results of our efforts." The careers they specified were in fields such as psychology, sociology, environmental work, medicine, law, social work, and special education for youngsters with learning problems. The wife of a large service industry executive observed:

"[Our son] plans to work in prison reform after college. But I'm afraid his altruism isn't going to keep him in the style to which he has grown accustomed."

Even more significant, perhaps, was the fact that of the nine families in which children had opted for a business future, five had never experienced a transfer and in several of the nine, the excitement of the business world and the father's job satisfactions were actively communicated to the children. In some cases, the youngsters were encouraged to participate in problem solving and decision making. The children of one banking executive were introduced to the stock market via their mother's investment club activities. Her trading maneuvers were discussed every evening at the dinner table when the two oldest sons were still high school students. The father would expand on the more intricate details of the fast moving pace of money markets and how they functioned. Today, both of the older boys plan banking careers, and the youngest son, still in grade school, started reading the *Wall Street Journal* when he was eight.

According to Ms. Patricia Brooks, who conducted the survey for one of the top *Fortune 500* companies, "my observations . . . seem to confirm that a man's job satisfactions were not being adequately communicated to his children [in most of the cases], even in families with close rapport."

Brooks's findings, interestingly enough, dovetailed with some of our own in a survey of thirty-six sons and daughters of Young Presidents Organization parents, at a seminar in the Soviet Union half a dozen years ago. These were children of parents who *do* communicate their career satisfactions. By and large, the fathers are need-achievers who *are* family oriented, or they wouldn't have brought the kids along on such a trip. I asked each of the young people, mostly teenagers, the same question: "Would you want to work for your father and eventually take over his business?"

Here they were in a country where there is no profit motive or proprietary value, and they were quick to recognize the significance of the question. The great majority said they *would* like to get into their father's business or would, at least, like an opportunity to make the decision. The few who thought they would not had highly rational reasons, but did not opt against business careers of their own. One was concerned that fellow employees wouldn't know how to treat the president's son; that he would be overpraised or overcriticized. Another was afraid he'd be used as a tool by ambitious employees trying to get to his father. A third said: "I would never really know if I could have done it on my own."

But the great majority of these youngsters were quite willing to move into the company of which dad was president or chairman. The difference between the attitude of young people in such groups and the children of affluent parents who have little or no time to devote to them and their problems, seems worthy of something far more than just passing interest. It also indicates that there are specific things that can be done by parents of executive families to help ensure the kind of life they desire for their heirs.

Perhaps the first thing to recognize is that children of affluence *are* different, and they seem instinctively to know it. As Harvard's child psychiatrist Robert Coles has pointed out, they are kids for whom life is made up of a vast array of options, chosen against a backdrop of servant-staffed mansions set in acres of manicured parklands. They can take for granted private instruction in all of the fashionable sports and social graces such as golf, tennis, swimming, dancing, entertaining, riding to the hounds—which they learn to slip into or out of with the same casual ease that they change clothing. Theirs is a special world of ample surroundings, with which they must come to terms, each in his or her own way. They must learn to master their special, complex circumstances and to become a functioning part of them. All of the overwhelming privilege and wealth at their beck and call tends to give such youngsters an awareness of their uniqueness, Dr. Cole points out—an identity that is communicated to them with additional reinforcement by their families. This message from the parents, an expression of the prerogatives of money and power, embodies the concept of entitlement as Dr. Coles has explained it.

It is this world that the less affluent eye with envy, awe, and often with bitter resentment. But it is a far from easy world for children to live in and adjust to. Even those who have made it to adulthood with apparent ease and grace testify to some of the problems such a life entails.

"The advantages in being the child of a multimillionaire chief executive of a gigantic food supply corporation are pretty much counterbalanced by the disadvantages," the daughter of one such tycoon told me. "Such fathers usually are tight with money for the family. And I can't brag about who I am, because nobody ever heard of my father's corporation, anyway. And if they did, they'd probably try to kidnap my son."

In a similar vein, Susan Newman, the daughter of actor Paul Newman, told an interviewer, "The blessings in being the child of a famous, successful person are obvious. The liabilities are less apparent. You have to work twice as hard to prove you're not just another spoiled brat kid. You have to establish a 'self' for yourself. When I walk into a room everyone in that room already knows a dozen things about me, right off the bat. And I don't know a thing about them."

It's all very well, of course, to point out pitfalls and disasters that may befall the top executive's family, but it is quite another to suggest ways to avoid them. However, there are a number of possible approaches that should suggest themselves in light of what has already been discussed.

Earlier, we pointed out the potential hazards of hammering at kids to win at any cost, driving them relentlessly until there is no fun left in the pastime. All of that is not to say that spending time with your kids, playing games with them, and even coaching a little to improve their performances, isn't a good idea. It can be the best thing going, if done in good humor, with a light touch, and if the games are played for enjoyment of the sport or the mental exercise rather than just to win! The hard-driving male parent must learn to control his achievement orientation if he hopes to hold the respect of his children and not alienate them. Any child, constantly driven to win at any cost (unless so oriented himself), is a candidate for antiauthority and antiestablishment attitudes.

Something we have discovered in our studies may come as a rude shock to the sort of fathers we have been discussing here. In the eyes of the children themselves, "father" is not the most important factor in their lives. I tell executives who think they are: "You're chasing butterflies. You are no great shakes to your kids —in their view. You *are* important to your wife, however; she *knows* you are important to her, and needs your continuing co-operation and support in her management, training, and disciplining of the children. She is the one who lives with them day after day—and she is the parent most children consider the important one in their lives."

A friend recalls witnessing a bitter discussion between a top NBC executive and his wife over cocktails one summer evening. The husband dismissed his wife's nasty comments with a sharp, biting criticism, at which point their little five-year-old daughter marched up to her daddy, shook a finger at him, and said: "How *dare* you talk to my mother like that!"

She broke up the party. But there was no question about who was important to the child in that house.

Even among young adults "mother" is the key factor in their emotional requirement; the healing balm in time of trouble. On the battlefields of World War II and Korea, the only cries on the lips of the severely wounded were: "mother" and "medic"— usually in that order. This from brave men.

During our session with the wives of executives of a large glass corporation, this whole subject of parental influence and involvement prompted a wide range of comment and inquiry among the mothers present. Here are some of the more significant questions and answers:

> CORPORATE MOTHER (with a British accent): Isn't it a fact that, if it's a serious drug or liquor problem, a boy would relate better to the father as a model? I think I would just buzz off on holiday and let them have at it.
>
> FEINBERG: Sometimes it may be better for the mother to handle the problem rather than to call the father and have him come screaming home for a shoot-out at high noon. He might well make things worse. Some years ago, the wife of an Oklahoma executive I know found several pounds of marijuana in her son's dresser drawer when she was replacing his laundry. She was beside herself, but knew that if she told her husband, he would come charging home from the office and a violent family crisis would erupt. When her son arrived for lunch, she took him by the hand to the office of her husband's brother, who happened to be a lawyer. The boy's uncle calmly spelled out the legal consequences of

marijuana pushing, and the youth decided on his own to get rid of the grass by burning it in the fireplace. That evening, when the father was told what had happened, he angrily accused his wife of having exposed the family's soiled linen to outsiders. She was able, however, to report that, "Your brother was very helpful, and the episode had a happy ending." It did. The lad straightened out and now is a Phi Beta Kappa graduate of a leading university law school. He later told his mother that had it not been for the way she handled the situation he probably would have continued hobnobbing with the drug crowd to spite his father, even though he disliked it.

CORPORATE MOTHER: Most articles I've read on the subject stress the importance of the father's influence with the sons. Are you saying that it isn't possible for a man on his way up the corporate ladder to become involved? And that he's unimportant to the children?

FEINBERG: No. What I have said is that it is difficult, but possible—if an executive father faces the issue. And I didn't say that the father is unimportant. What I tried to convey was that the mother is *more* important to the children. It's a matter of emphasis. The father becomes important when, first, he takes the pressure off the mother and, second, when he reinforces her role. If the father and mother are constantly at each other regarding family matters, the children will be poisoned by the atmosphere they create. In most cases, if the executive father and his wife will solve their differences, other domestic problems will tend to resolve themselves.

CORPORATE MOTHER: I know a number of mothers who will not let their husbands get involved. These women want to keep their husbands out, where the kids are concerned. It's an area they want to monopolize. Father is written off, whether or not he may want to be involved. What happens to such children?

FEINBERG: According to most studies I've seen, when you have a strong, overbearing mother and an indifferent, unconcerned, weak father, the children are apt to be average, routine adults. It's "regression in the service of normality," as one authority has put it.

CORPORATE MOTHER: Writing off father isn't necessarily a matter of upstaging him. Year after year, you get the phone call: "Sorry, I know I said I'd be home for the birhday party, but I can't make it." So you learn to move in and take charge to shield the child from hurts. With trick-or-treating at Hallowe'en, the youngster says: "I want to wait. Daddy promised he'd take me." Then you hear the phone ring, and you know it's not going to happen as promised. So, you're not really pushing him out. You're protecting the child from constant disappointment. You're not just doing it for the kids, of course. You're also doing it to protect yourself. If you don't count on father you're not going to be disappointed, either.

CORPORATE MOTHER: Wouldn't some of these problems be solved if father made himself more important when the children are two, three, or four years of age? Their involvement should be less vital as the kids grow older.

FEINBERG: That may be true. But the children's early years usually span the period when the father is under most pressure in business. It is the period when he is being watched by his bosses and sized up for his future business potentials. It's a tough time. It would be great if he could get involved then. What I object to is the idea that mothers can't raise happy or successful children if father is not always at hand.

The fact is, of course, that fathers *should* make themselves available to the children whenever it is at all possible—but with tact and understanding. No husband should delude himself into believing that he can recover for lost time by stepping up the tempo of family affairs and disrupting plans already made by the children and their mother. To some extent, he may be able to "make up" to an extremely understanding wife. With children, however, this is difficult if not impossible.

Above all, affluent fathers who are tempted to buy performance from their youngsters with gifts of money or things should lie down and close their eyes until the idea passes. This was mentioned earlier in another context, but it can't be overemphasized.

One top executive I know had a "deal" with his prep school and college-age children. Whenever one of them got an "A" average, he'd get twice his tuition. A "B" student got one-and-a-half times the tab. Anyone with a "C" for the semester got his tuition paid and that's all. A "D" would not get his tuition paid, and an "F" meant that the child paid his own tuition and owed father the amount of the tuition besides. This put the grades on an economic basis, and youngsters do not like to feel that economics is the way in which their performance is evaluated. Such a scheme can cause problems for the losers, who become highly confused regarding the dichotomy between the absurd generosity lavished on some of their siblings and the insinuation that "money doesn't grow on trees" for them.

Fathers should try more often to discover what their youngsters are like—to listen to them as though they were important customers, to take their problems seriously. Snap decisions and fast disposal have no place in dealing with kids' troubles. The youngsters need evidence of dad's concern and involvement. Without it, they can be expected to slip away and seek it elsewhere.

There are specific signs that a teenager is on his way down the hippie trail. Psychologists and psychiatrists look for:

- Violent and extreme changes of mood and personality.
- Vagueness about appointments and itinerary.
- A suddenly heightened level of irresponsibility.
- Noticeable switching of friends.
- A sudden exaggerated interest in mystical symbols and books on cults.
- Intense and surreptitious reading on drugs.
- Open rebelliousness toward family.

If such indications appear, a busy executive father may find himself hard pressed to control the relationship, but there are steps that should be taken promptly. First, it's important not to be oversensitive or overcritical, and not to crack down on every rebellious act. Second, don't make a big issue of small things such as a scraggly beard and long hair, or short dresses and sneakers. On the other hand, if the youngster checks out to "stay with a friend" for a few days, use any excuse you can think of to check up on the friend and the setup. You are entitled to be a little paranoid. The child may act hostile because you "meddled," but will learn that you cared enough to become involved. The point I want to make is: don't trust today's youngsters. They aren't trustworthy and they know it.

Realize that children are almost invariably hostile to parents at some stage during adolescence. One young daughter of a psychiatrist I know told him: "I am going through a difficult time, so let's shake hands and have no hard feelings when it's all over." These youngsters cannot afford to be less hostile until they have matured enough to stand on their own feet and function successfully. Until then, most kids expect and need limits—if they are reasonable, appropriate, and applied discriminately but firmly by a respected authority figure.

Try applying principles of delegation on something like use of the car. Never mind the time sharing and limits. Stress responsibility: "Drive carefully, be back on time, be sure you leave it with a full tank and as clean as you found it." As the responsibilities are assumed add more, as you might with a new man in the office. Try to remember that the hair and the tight, faded denim shorts with ragged bottoms are not nearly as important as school attendance, achievement goals, and self-identification. Those are the things that justify a busy executive's time and attention. And he can't handle them by coming home briefly one evening and saying to a kid, "Tell me your problems and I'll have my secretary take care of them for you."

And don't make the mistake of trying to be a "friend." As one youngster I know said to his dad: "I have all the friends I need. I don't want another friend. I want a father." And who said children were friends anyway? Friends don't come home at the age of eighteen arrogantly pregnant and unmarried. And friends don't wake you in the middle of the night to let them in with a bunch of scruffy characters who want to sleep on the living-room floor and smell up the house with pot. Kids like that are not friends. They are enemies. Since the beginning of time adolescents have been the arch enemies of their parents because they are dependent on them and hate it. The flip side of dependency is hostility.

If distinct signs of a break from the family become apparent, thoughtful but decisive action is strongly recommended.

- Recognize the problem.
- Recognize the need for understanding and loving the child on his or her own level. When one youngster I knew told his corporate chairman dad that he wanted to be a Rabbi, the old man actually replied, "What the hell kind of job is *that* for a smart Jewish boy?"
- For indecisive youngsters with confused orientation, good psychological testing can often provide them with acceptable direction. It has saved innumerable young people from years of unsettled and disturbed floundering.
- If they do decide to go into business, let them assume their own responsibility rapidly. There may, indeed, be some costly errors, but they must learn from their own mistakes. Your wisdom, regardless of how sound, will usually have a reverse effect unless specifically requested.

Whatever else you do, try to keep the communication lines open. Kids are always communicating. The messages may not be vocal, but they're there, all right. It may be some new piece of hideous wearing apparel or a newly acquired irritating mannerism. But it is saying something and it's important to stay tuned in. On the rare occasions when they do talk, it probably will bug you, because it's meant to. Be bugged, but listen and respond as well.

In order to respond constructively, it's recommended that you keep up to date with developments in the teen field. That briefcase you trot home with you every night is filled with stuff that you read to keep up with the trade so that you'll know what you're talking about in the office. The same principle should apply to the home front. There are plenty of magazines that will update you on the drug scene, the school scene, and all that. And often there are usable quotes in the tabloid-type personality stories that you skip past in the paper every morning. One that I remember well was a statement by a teenage girl who ran away to the East Village and came home sadder but wiser. "It's very lonely there," she reported when interviewed. "And it's filled with hate—not love or peace. It's full of jerks who live in a dream world."

As long as a child is not smoking pot, parents perhaps have

little to be greatly concerned about. They can start worrying when they find soft-cover books about LSD jammed under the mattress at the head of the bed, or when the kid starts bringing home friends who wear sunglasses at night to protect their dilated pupils from the glare of forty-watt bulbs.

The most important thing for an executive father with problem teens to remember is to keep his cool. He remains unflappable in the face of skittery million-dollar office negotiations, and there's no reason why any attempts to manage his kids should throw him. While it is true that a teenage son sometimes may stir his competitiveness, and a daughter who attempts a close relationship may alarm him with her—and his—sexuality, such responses are familiar to psychologists as natural and normal. But an effective manager will not allow emotional reactions to interfere with his objectivity. And an effective father must not, either.

The whole point is that if an executive father is to provide a warm, personal image to match his more easily communicated image of strength and success, he must *work* at being a father. If he can do so with the same skill and intelligence that he takes to his job, he may well find it the most rewarding and fulfilling thing he has ever done.

16

The Two-Career Marriage

☞ The two-career marriage, with its dual paycheck and its dramatic impact on the kind of nostalgic family life, depicted in reminiscences like the television series *I Remember Mama*, has been variously and antithetically described as: the single most outstanding social phenomenon of the century; a death knell for the family unit; a ray of hope for marriage on the rocks; the coup de grace for marriages that might otherwise have worked; the only hope for congenial cohabitation of men and women; the end of lasting human relationships; the best way to improve a couple's sex life; the formula for creating a whole new world of bed-hoppers. And so on.

Regardless of what people may think and say about it, the working wife/mother, for better or worse, is a fact of life here to stay for the foreseeable future.

Judging from endless studies that have been made, and volumes of reports that have been written on the subject, it has thus far proven to be all of the things mentioned above, depending on the personality, motive, and desire-to-make-things-work of each individual involved.

Most drastically affected, understandably, have been conventional lower- and middle-income families in which father and mother previously have played sharply defined traditional roles. When a homemaker-mother in such a household moves out to a full-time job, there can be hell to pay. In most cases, her husband feels threatened, her in-laws are indignant at what they consider an implied insult to their son, and her own guilt may drive her to continue trying to be a homemaker-mother while assuming additional responsibilities to an outside employer. The strains in such situations can build to the breaking point. Sometimes the only solution is divorce. The sharp increase in broken families —which have doubled since 1970—is attributed in large part, by marriage counselors and psychologists, to the stresses that working wives have imposed on their marriages.

Besides setting up the ingredients for an explosive situation in a marriage that might be tenuous anyway, a wife who goes to work can find herself not only abundantly appreciated outside the family, but also with an independent income—making divorce more readily affordable for an unhappy husband and more plausible for an emancipated mother. As one exwife put it, "Without my job I probably wouldn't have gotten a divorce." Her annual salary of nearly $12,000, supplemented by a modest $4,000 in child support from a husband who she claimed was a workaholic with no time for anything but his job, made divorce the practical "out."

Psychologists admit, however, that when families are able to accommodate the dramatic role reversals and stresses implicit in a two-career marriage, benefits can be impressive. The sense of fulfillment and self-confidence communicated to her family by a working wife and mother can bring a whole new perspective to the household. And the added income can provide a margin to relieve the grim financial struggle many young families must face just to stay even.

Psychologists know, too, that almost any marriage in which both partners work will be hectic, subject to tensions, and fraught with problems. Where children are involved, the difficulties will be magnified. According to Dr. Jeff Bryson and his wife Rebecca, a husband-wife psychology team who have conducted a number of studies on dual-career marriages at San Diego State University, one of the biggest problems is the sharing of domestic responsibility and labor.

"The women in our surveys generally considered their jobs to be secondary in the household—and said so," the Brysons observe. Most working wives carry a burden of guilt about their deviation from the traditional wifely role. The upshot is that they try to be "supermom" to make up for it, working all day for the company, then coming home and being housewife and mother at night. In most cases where the husband participated in the housework, wives said the work was shared about fifty-fifty; husbands generally said they did less than half the work. Most surveys indicate that the wife handles about 65 percent; hubby 35 percent. The cold, hard truth is that in most two-career households, if a child is sick it's the wife who stays home to take care of the problem. If there's a car pool arrangement, mom is the one who usually does the chauffeuring. The consequence is that many working wives put in an 80- to 100-hour week. Hence, two-career marriages, the Brysons conclude, involve three careers—two of them pursued by the wife.

The guilt, Dr. Bryson points out, is less for women who are forced to work because they need the money than for those who take up a career for their own self-fulfillment. And it is particularly poignant for working women with children. It springs, inevitably, from the employment of child care and the limited contact that a working wife has with her own children. At some point, a child will want its mother, and she won't be there.

The lady director of a large national advertising agency recalls telephoning home during a recent business trip. The baby-sitter put her two-year-old son on the wire, and she heard him say, plaintively, "Mommy, I miss you."

"You can't imagine," she said, "how I felt, sitting on the edge of that hotel bed, the tears streaming down my face."

There is little question that a working mother commits herself to a substantial trade-off. Depending on the woman and her goal orientation, the sacrifice she must make can be critical or otherwise. Most executive mothers will never enjoy many of the warm pleasures of parenthood—hearing the first spoken "mommy," watching the first tottering step, enjoying the often-hilarious blossoming of spoken words and sentences. Unfortunately, the step-by-step development of a child can't be run through for a second showing.

Few knowledgeable career women try to kid themselves into believing that their two-paycheck marriage is a glamorous, idyllic fifty-fifty proposition which allows each partner to come and go at will. The career-wife of the president and chief executive of a large New England insurance company put it concisely when she observed in a recent interview, "Marriage is not a matter of you do your thing and I'll do mine. . . . My goal is to keep intellectually alive . . . and I will."

For most working couples, life is a continuing struggle with schedules and obligations that get in the way: a matter more often than not of tense, hectic arranging and sharing of time for household chores, dealing with inevitable domestic problems, and caring for the children. In cases where two-career marriages don't work, frequently it is because the husband has made little or no effort at role-changing trade-offs—usually in all honesty—to the very real pressures of his own work. In a typical instance, the president of a successful business that he himself founded had a wife who, when the kids reached school age, went to work teaching full time, and also assumed outside club and political activities at night. In this particular case, neither partner was willing to assume the new role of sharing necessary responsibilities to make things work. The wife wanted it both ways: a career with no responsibility at home. The husband was tolerant of her working as long as his role as "king of the cave" wasn't altered.

"My attitude was," the husband told an interviewer recently, "I work like a bastard all day and I'm not coming home to more work." In this same partnership, when the husband's business ran into financial problems at one point, and he asked his wife for an assist with the house bills (the only time he had ever suggested that her money be used for anything other than herself), her answer was: "Nothing doing. My money is my own." Needless to say, the upshot of this marriage was divorce.

Successful two-career marriages—and there are many—even in top-echelon executive families where servants may handle most of the routine household chores, nearly always feature a reasonably fair division between the partners of such domestic duties as may be required of them personally.

American Can Corporation's President, William S. Woodside, whose income considerably exceeds $300,000 a year, has a lively high-achiever wife named Miga who manages a full-time consulting career for the United States Senate subcommittee on juvenile delinquency. They have, according to Mrs. Woodside, a kind of contract agreement. "We said, Okay," she recently revealed, "if I handle this part, you have to help me handle that. I insist on having my own itinerary and schedule." Mr. Woodside went along. Their partnership, he observes "involves a lot of give-and-take." He does all their weekend shopping and other agreed-upon chores. She, in return, becomes a corporate wife when occasions demand. Recently, she took time off to attend an industry convention with him, where she acted as hostess at business soirees for his associates. She also maintains correspondence and social contacts with her husband's business friends. "It's all part of our contract," she explains. Apparently it works, though she admits that it sometimes takes fancy head work to switch from a report on heroin traffic in Afghanistan to discussions of profit and loss in the canning industry. Contrast this approach with that of a psychiatrist's wife who once told a patient who called, "I do not take messages for him. I am not a secretary." Apparently her status as vice-president of a travel agency was threatened by doing her spouse a simple favor.

Organization of time and duty appears to be a key factor in the successful survival of any dual-career partnership. A recent survey of some 200 husbands of working wives by Suzanne McCall, Associate Professor of Marketing and Management at East Texas State University, revealed that more than a quarter of the men shared in the housework; nearly as many in child care duties; and almost half took their turn at shopping for food and housewares.

In emergencies, one or the other partner may take over the domestic duties completely. One young California architect, whose wife works full time as a designer and editor, handles all the household chores, chauffeurs their subteen son to scheduled functions, and otherwise operates as "househusband" when his wife has a deadline to meet. If she drums away at the typewriter until nearly dawn, he reads until the typing stops. Then he's up at seven, throws breakfast together, and drives their son to school. When he has office problems, the roles are reversed and she climbs into harness. When everything runs normally, they share the work.

It has been emphasized in dozens of studies that our cultural heritage is responsible for much of the lack of real sharing in many two-career marriages. As Dr. Jeff Bryson points out, "When a man performs even the smallest domestic chore he thinks he should get a medal for it. A woman, on the other hand, feels guilty if she fails to perform the least important household function." How many husbands, Bryson asks, are ever aware when they've used the last tube of toothpaste, that the dishwasher detergent needs restocking, or that the family is down to its last roll of toilet paper? And who's to blame if a mother-in-law comes to visit and finds the house a mess? Is the husband the guilty party? No way!

Many of the traditionally assumed "psychological differences" between men and women are, under serious investigation today. Some years ago, a popular national magazine ran a lighthearted survey of those differences. For one phase of the study, interviewers were instructed to get themselves invited to dinner by friends. They were to ask the person who did the food shopping in the host family a simple question: "Where did you get this meat?" In every family where the husband did the shopping, the reply was invariably: "At the so-and-so market." In families where the wife did the shopping the reply without exception was: "Why? What's the matter with it?"

Whether the differences—including the guilt complex—that plague women have been deeply ingrained via cultural tradition (as most psychologists today believe), or are female characteristics imparted by genes or hormones, as the popular magazine study tried to imply, is beside the point. The significant fact is that differences do exist. What's more, they involve characteristics that create a considerable hurdle for women trying to make the transition from housewife to "workwife." Some of these differences, and the problems they impose, have already been closely examined by Drs. Margaret Hennig and Anne Jardim, codirectors of Simmons College's graduate school management program.

Their findings, spelled out in detail in their now-famous book *The Managerial Woman,* are the result of a study involving more than 5,000 men and women executives in a wide variety of corporate enterprises. Their findings have exploded many myths and provided new and not particularly painless insights into the often-prejudiced assumption that men and women have been making about each other for years. Some of the things that came out of that survey:

• Women see themselves in the position of waiting to be discovered, then chosen, for desired jobs or responsibilities; men see themselves as competent in a given area and move out aggressively to get themselves picked by cultivating the right people and lobbying among them.

• Women see their work as an endless stream of endeavor, requiring them to work hard in all areas in order to do everything well, and they admit to feelings of confusion about ultimate goals; men see themselves as planners, who give projects priorities and deal with one thing at a time, in series, to achieve a specific result about which they are usually very clear—rightly or wrongly.

• Women see themselves as uncomfortable about moving with positive force and direction in important matters until they are told what to do; men see themselves as decision makers who establish the important goals and set out to achieve them.

• Women see themselves as tending to play things conservatively and safe; men see themselves as ready and willing to take substantial risks to achieve success.

• Women see themselves as carrying a burden of guilt about having an outside career, for which they compensate by attempting to be the perfect mother, wife, and business woman at one and the same time; men see themselves as guiltless if business keeps them away from the family for extended periods, or if there's no food in the house, or the beds aren't made.

Although Drs. Hennig and Jardim were more concerned with the executive woman's performance on the job front, their findings have important implications for the domestic scene as well.

As Dr. Hennig points out, "The difference between us and the women's movement is that they say women have to make men change and we say we women have to change first."

Many (if not most) two-career marriages that founder on the shoals of divorce do so because the wife, driven by guilt, tries to be both career woman and supermom as well. In consequence, she wastes energy with her anxiety over not neglecting her family and trying to handle both jobs to perfection. Most wife-executives who successfully rise to top management, and stay married to boot, Dr. Hennig found, are those who risk being themselves, have firm arrangements with their husbands about sharing domestic responsibilities, and/or use some of their income to hire domestic help and child care. Detailed planning worked out with the husband, say the authors, is the key. Women who try to do everything and make all the decisions alone, are the ones who have trouble.

The few wife-and-mother executives who do swing it both ways are exceptional. And they admit to excessive tensions. One young full-time lady commerical artist in Minneapolis, whose husband holds down two jobs in order to "put it all together" for the two of them and their six year old, is frank to acknowledge the hazards:

"With the situation we're in, I have to work and do the housework, too," she reports. "That load—job, housework, and child care—can really drain you, but you learn to cope with it." She admits that her husband does a little to help by sweeping up and occasionally making beds and so on, but points out that with two jobs, his time is limited. "I wouldn't pretend to say we divide the housework evenly," she says. Her husband agrees, and reveals that "We have to be careful that we don't get snippy with each other when we're tired in the evening."

For executive mothers (who represent a quarter of all mothers who work today) the problem of proper child care is a far greater obstacle to their dual-career marriages than it is for clerical and labor-class couples. A secretary, retail clerk, or manufacturing plant worker is through at 4:30 or 5 PM and can count on spelling-off the baby-sitter or picking up the kids at the day-care center. A marketing director, or vice-president for corporate public relations, on the other hand, has no such privilege. Corporate planning sessions often continue until eight or nine at night.

Consequently, corporate mothers who can't afford full-time housekeepers usually depend on many part-time helpers. "In addition to paid child care," *Business Week* magazine observed in a recent report on the subject, "daily or part-time housekeepers, baby-sitters, neighbors who serve as surrogate mothers, and private schools with afterschool activities—all of which cost an estimated 24 percent of her take-home pay—the executive mother must depend on the volunteer help of husband, friends, relatives, and neighbors."

The outside help is essential, according to these women executives, in order to avoid any suspicion on the part of their employers that they will put their youngsters ahead of the company in a crisis.

As for the question of whether substitute parents, or heavy father-daughter relationships, are good or bad for the offspring of career-bound mothers and dads, "the vote is still out," according to the Brysons, who even now are gathering data on that matter. "Obviously," says Jeff Bryson, "kids who are virtually abandoned so both parents can work don't flourish. The big variable," he adds, "is the quality, not quantity of care the child gets —both from its own parents and the day-care center. For the children who attend good day-care centers or good schools, there is so far no evidence of any adverse effect. The need today is for good quality day care." The pros and cons on this subject are under emotional debate today, and no one will have definitive answers until today's infants have become adults.

Despite surrogate mothers and housefraus, however, marriage counselors stress that for a two-career marriage to succeed it is really essential for the husband to abandon any semblance of the old tiger-of-the-house role and do more pitching in around the place. In case after case where a wife tries to do it all, they point out, the result is divorce.

The Victorian tradition that it is "unmanly" to have a wife who works is vanishing, particularly among younger people, due in large part to our runaway economy. Curious side effects of the dominant male tradition may linger on, however. Alice Rossi, Professor of Sociology at the University of Massachusetts, has suggested that working wives hesitate to move up to higher positions or salaries than their husbands for fear of jeopardizing their marriage. Whether this is an honest reason for such reluctance, or perhaps an excuse, is probably unprovable. While the masculine ego unquestionably is under strain in the present trend to sexual equality, psychologists differ widely in their analyses of the movement's effects. Suzanne McCall's previously mentioned survey of husbands of working wives also turned up the information that the more income a wife produced, the more pleased her husband was about her outside job. "If she contributed 40 percent or more to the family income, regardless of the amount," Mrs. McCall reported, "he is extremely happy she's working." So you pick your source and take your choice.

According to Jeff Bryson, for instance, "for a lot of people the biggest problem [in the two-paycheck family] is just the threat to the male ego. We've seen in some areas where people overwhelmingly adopt the traditional ideology that the husband supports the family and when he can't or doesn't for some reason, it means he has failed and it's a threat to his masculinity."

Dr. Barbara Butek, Assistant Professor of Psychology at the University of California L.A., modifies this view with the observation that the male-ego syndrome in two-career marriages usually is confined to blue-collar families. More significant, perhaps, is the question of whose job will come first in the pinches—when one or the other of the working pair is offered a promotion requiring transfer. Until now, the husband's career has taken precedence in most dual-career marriages. But what will happen if the wife's job becomes the bigger money-maker for the family remains to be seen. Unless there is a mutual agreement with full understanding on both sides, there are almost certain to be many more family blow-ups.

Frequently overlooked as a serious hazard to the success of a dual-career match are in-laws. "The folks" on both sides often create unneeded problems for the working couple, especially if there are grandchildren. Usually it's the husband's parents who resent it if their son's wife takes on a job—firmly convinced that she is neglecting their boy and "his" children. A brilliant woman we know who is general counsel for a well-known national corporation, told us the other day that her exmother-in-law had a particularly sly way of needling her. "She'd call me early in the morning or late in the evening," the lady lawyer recalls, "and, when I answered, she'd say something like: 'Oh, it *is* you. I didn't think you'd be home!'" The intensity of this problem undoubtedly depends on whether the in-laws live on the next block or the other coast.

Recently, a brand-new problem for two-paycheck families has surfaced: galloping alcoholism among the working wives. According to a study performed by Paul B. Johnson for the University of California L.A. and the Rand Corporation, "Married women who are employed have significantly higher rates of both problem and heavier drinking than either single working women or housewives."

The researchers were aware that alcoholism among women in general is on the rise (currently up to an estimated 2 million female problem drinkers). But they had assumed that the increase would be found in low socioeconomic-level groups. "To our surprise," reports Mr. Johnson, "the relationship is even stronger for women at middle and higher socioeconomic levels, while it disappears for women at the lowest levels. No similar relationship occurs for men, raising the distinct possibility that this type of nontraditional role for women leads to an increased risk of alcoholism."

The UCLA report indicated that possible causes for the phenomenon were, first, the working wife's role-model conflict and resultant psychological stress brought on by the demands of being both a wife and an employee. And, second, her attempts to emulate what she may consider to be men's traditional behavior, in this case, one's drinking pattern.

A third possibility, not touched upon by this study, may well be brought on by the tensions incurred when a woman enters a masculine domain where, for the first time, she faces a kind of competitive world that may be frightening and stressful for her. Those women who have a competitive spirit of their own, and are able to cope with that environment, are the ones who often make it to the top. In such cases, however, many of them tend to overcompensate. When that happens, and if a husband is also highly competitive, the domestic situation is apt to hit the fan.

Two power-driven people with competitive spirit can manufacture problems for a dual-career marriage that, most psychologists agree, will almost surely cause it to fail unless there is a determined effort by one partner or both to make the marriage work. The Brysons cite one case in which both husband and wife were biophysicists working in the same area, and competing wildly for attention at scientific meetings and in the journals. A breakup was inevitable, until the wife changed her field entirely in order to salvage the marriage.

A happier solution to a similar conflict involved a young California couple, Richard and Helen Allen, recently cited as a unique working couple. Their courtship had been spent largely in competitive boat racing, as a team—"to win!" Once married and parents of a son, Michael, the need to win for each of them continued apace. Mrs. Allen wanted a business of her own, and decided to open a cheese shop over her stockbroker husband's objections and constant criticism of her methods. Without his help, she got financing, struggled with building permits and service people. Somehow in the course of their bickering, they began to revert to their competitive team spirit. Today, the Allens are partners in the successful cheese business. They still compete strenuously but "not to the point of dangerous rivalry. To the extent that we challenge each other, it's good," Mrs. Allen told *New West* magazine recently. "We don't try to get the upper hand with one another. If we have a problem we both attack it with tremendous energy."

Her husband agrees. "We pretend we are riding tandem on a bicycle," he explains. "If one lets down, the other can't make it alone." Both admit that neither can stand to fail in front of the other. An interesting sidelight to their accommodation is their casual but effective division of domestic labor. When Mrs. Allen chauffeurs their son to various activities, Mr. Allen cooks dinner, and vice versa. Both deplore housework, so meals usually are prepared at home, and the funds thus saved by not dining out are applied to a housemaid who comes three days a week. Everything else is similarly shared. Dick Allen pays the business bills; Helen the house bills. "He takes our stuff to the Chinese laundry because he wears cotton underwear," says Helen. "I take it to the cleaners because if I don't get my wool slacks cleaned I have nothing to wear. After that, we just wait to see who will give in first."

One more disruptive problem for working couples is "the jealous husband." Occasionally, a possessive male partner has trouble adjusting to his wife spending her days in the company of attractive and successful men. Actually, as has been pointed out by Dr. Ruth Moulton, Assistant Professor of Clinical Psychology at Columbia University, the attitude is illogical "since the husband does not have any more control over his wife when she stays home than he does when she's at work." The fact remains, however, that some husbands can drum up enough of an imagined cause célèbre to run a marriage onto the rocks. An extreme case in our files involved a brilliant lady editor of an international publishing company who found it necessary to "retire" in the interest of saving her marriage. On one occasion, after a visiting male superior from the home office bussed her affectionately on the cheek at the airport, her husband flew into a rage so violent that the nonplussed visitor was sure it would precipitate a divorce on the spot.

Suspicions about a working wife's (or husband's) behavior in the office are not *always* unjustified, naturally. Reports from a number of psychologists specializing in marriage counseling reveal that in dual-career marriages outside affairs by both partners are much more prevalent than in traditional family groups. When both partners are preoccupied with career advancement, says Margaret Bufkin, an Atlanta, Georgia, marriage counselor who has studied the problem at some length, they put in long hours and often come home exhausted, late—or not at all. The result is a cooling off of the marriage relationship, and a tendency on the part of both to seek romantic attachments outside.

Despite all the problems that the two-career marriage poses for contemporary families-in-transition, however, all the signs indicate that the trend will continue at an accelerated rate. Most working couples who have managed to keep both marriage and careers intact, however, are quick to point out a number of advantages in their way of life. In a vast majority of such cases, both partners are convinced that the wife's job has made the match a better one. The wives believe firmly that they contribute far more to the husband's career than if they were just home managers and business hostesses. The full-time lawyer-wife of a Chicago corporate vice-president insists that her work experience makes her far more knowledgeable about business matters and better able to carry on intelligent and interesting conversations with her husband and his business associates. Her husband agrees, and adds: "She understands the occasional late night, the extended business trip, or the general bad humor after a particularly tough week, since she has them herself."

Most husbands of successful working couples say that the confidence and spirit of independence, previously mentioned, that the women acquire through their work makes them better, more understanding and interesting partners. The wives think so, too. In one of the UCLA surveys they were almost unanimous in stating that the work experience improved the marital relationship in several ways:

It provides more money for buying houses, for luxury purchases and investments, family trips, and fun; they had more interest in the things they discussed with their husbands; the new closeness even improved the sexual relationship in some cases.

Solving family problems and making family decisions, according to many working couples, becomes a joint venture, relieving the often-harried husband of the sole responsibility and (often) worry.

A working wife also can provide a measure of independence, they point out, for a husband who must sometimes put his job on the block in the rough game of office politics. He can, as one sociologist has expressed it "quit the job or simply tell his boss to go to hell."

A surprising number of dual-career families insist that their children are much better off, too. "They are more independent and self-sufficient since they must make their own decisions more often than the sheltered offspring of traditional families," says one career wife. She points out further that the kids are really proud of their parents, and are far more interesting than most of their friends, due to the broad spectrum of their parents' combined interests, and the independent thinking they must do for themselves.

What it boils down to, according to William F. May, Chairman and chief executive officer of American Can Company, is that "She [the working wife] isn't just the sweet little thing at cocktail parties, making sure all the social amenities are taken care of, anymore. Today, the wives aren't just talking about children and the latest movie; they're talking about cash flow."

While the two-career marriage still is relatively new as a standard life-style in America, some guidelines can be drawn to help facilitate sensible planning in approaching such an arrangement, and in making it work with the least possible trauma.

• Where possible, a woman would do well to try and plan her married life so that during the period when she is having and raising children, she will be home with them at least before they leave for school in the morning, and when they return in late afternoon. The difficulty in trying to swing a full-time business career along with motherhood is the most frequent cause of broken marriages in two-paycheck families.

• A woman's first job should not be looked upon as the first step in a long, unbroken business career, but rather a place where she can polish and develop skills that can be carried further after the children are old enough to permit her daily absence without jeopardizing their healthy development.

• When the children are still too young to be left full time, there is no reason why, with planning and time-sharing with her husband—or by rotating with baby-sitters—a wife can't work out a reasonable part-time schedule at a job in which she will keep her skills and talents honed for more intensive use after the children are sufficiently on their way.

• The greatest impact on family life will come in the second full-time work period. As of right now, social scientists and psychiatrists do not know how children—across the board—will manage without the full attention of a mother. A lot more research is needed to get answers. Our own tentative exploratory research indicates that working mothers may create problems for some adolescents. Certainly for the extremely sensitive child, mother may have to stay home until the child's emotional stability is assured. To do otherwise possibly is to court tragedy.

• Bring your children into your work by talking about it. Don't isolate yourself in the job because you think they won't understand it. Most jobs can be made understandable. One thing psychologists do know is that kids tend to be proud of the work their parents do, and a mother's outside interests are bound to broaden them and expand their own interests. When a child is old enough to be properly impressionable, an occasional visit to the office can be a great idea. We tend to isolate children from our world of work and deprive them of a great introduction to the realities they will face. When I was about ten my father had me working with him and his brother after school, shipping garments from a Seventh Avenue establishment in New York. I shared the excitement of filling a large order, and the anxiety of misplaced shipments. I remember telling my son when he was about ten, "When I was your age I was much older."

• Spend time with the children and use it effectively. It's not how much time you spend with them but how you use it that matters. Some parents can spend a lot of time with the kids and provide no impact; others, in a short period, can really help a child grow. Games, sports, planning ahead for weekends and holidays, based on a child's needs, will help enrich the lives of all.

• It is important for the children that a mother give daddy his due, and not lose her own femininity. Whatever dad's areas of control in the family, he should always "wear the pants" in those areas, not for his sake but for the children's. I believe, in the final analysis, that this is really what most women want. Even those who work want father to act the masculine role, to be the control, the support, and the head of the house in ultimate responsibility and decision making, after due consideration of everyone's desires.

Couples who have made two-career marriages work have occasionally suggested hints and tips for helping to smooth the rough road. Here are a few:

• Keep your sense of humor. If you can joke about something, it becomes less of a problem.

• Learn to give and take on all negotiable issues so that there will be less reason for antagonism on tough decisions.

• Accept the fact that there will be problems—money, division of responsibilities, imposition on each other, etc. If you are aware that these difficulties exist and have to be tackled, you'll cope with them more easily. Verbalize them and talk them out together.

• Don't take the plunge until there is a reasonable attitude of acceptance on all sides. In those marriages where both couples are in favor of the wife working, there is a much greater record of success and marital satisfaction.

• Both partners must maintain a commitment to the maintenance of the marriage and protection of the family unit, or they may as well throw in the sponge at the outset.

The future may not be easy. If the times call for it, then by all means let's modify the traditional role models of men and women. But let's never lose the essentials of nature's differences or, as Shakespeare put it, "the country's done for."

17

Corporate Bigamy Female Style

☛ The Chairman of the National Broadcasting Company takes off at seven every morning in the company limousine from an impressive estate in a fashionable section of Greenwich, Connecticut, spends the day working on all aspects of corporate activity, and usually is able to leave the office at about eight-thirty in the evening for the forty-five minute ride back to Greenwich. On normal days, that is. The schedule can be destroyed by extra meetings when you also happen to be a trustee of the Rockefeller Foundation, Kettering Foundation, The University of Notre Dame, and a director of J. C. Penney Company, the Bache Group, International Paper Company, and Chesebrough Ponds, Inc.

But that's about the kind of work schedule you'd expect for a corporate chief married to a heavyweight business career in New York as well as to a loved and respected spouse in Connecticut. What's different about this particular case is that the corporate chairman is Mrs. Jane Cahill Pfeiffer, a handsome, personable, and brilliant lady.

For women like Mrs. Pfeiffer, who aspire to the top of the heap, it is almost essential that they be "married" or dedicated to their business career or there's little chance they'll ever make it. In short, to get there they pretty well have to be corporate bigamists, by definition, and most of the really good ones are. But for reasons probably peculiar to our battered cultural role model for the American woman, remnants of which still remain despite ardent and for the most part well-meaning feminist efforts to wipe it out, relatively few of these top-echelon women fall into the monster or Janus categories. Most would, however, fit the need-achiever description—highly motivated to succeed and lead, tenacious, and dedicated not just to the job, but to their marriage and family as well. Jane Pfeiffer once turned down an offer to become the United States Secretary of Commerce because, as she told a *New York Times* reporter, "My marriage is my first priority. . . . I could not take on the responsibility of an assignment in Washington without my husband with me, and that just wasn't possible." She and her husband—a vice-president of IBM and father of ten by a former marriage—apparently are crystal clear about just what it is they're working for, and are in an excellent position to know exactly what "priorities" are all about.

Whether the mothering and domestic orientation of Mrs. Pfeiffer and many other top women executives is, as many psychologists insist, prompted by "guilt," or is perhaps a perfectly normal biological behavior due to the genetic programming of the female of practically every species of living fauna on earth, constitutes a question that isn't going to be resolved in a hurry. I happen to believe that most women basically want to be mothers, and that a few are gifted enough to achieve other goals as well—without subjecting themselves to undue frustration in either role.

As with men, many women corporate bigamists find it difficult to perform with complete success in both business and familial contexts. As one promising young lady executive puts it: "My priorities are very clear. If a child's health or happiness or sense of security is involved, that has got to have priority over everything else. But on a day-to-day basis, the job comes first."

Another high-level woman executive, the editorial director of a large reserach organization, who has been through the death of one husband, divorce from another, and has put two sons through school, is emphatic on this subject. "The role of wife, mother, and top executive," she says, "is virtually impossible to bring off if one comes from a generation raised in the years between 1920 and 1970. I quickly discovered that being top banana in an office was exciting for me; there is exhilaration in giving commands and having them carried out. Then I would go home and find a husband who expected to have dinner served up. I wanted to go out to a restaurant. He wanted the traditional family scene, which was impossible for me to provide."

This marriage, not surprisingly, broke up. When a woman is a strong personality and makes substantially more money than her husband, she is apt—as happened here—to dictate family policy on things such as whether they go out to eat, stay home so many nights a week, or whether the children get cars at seventeen, and so on. Given such authority, however, it doesn't necessarily follow that the career-oriented woman will opt for a warm "motherly" attitude with her offspring. She may like the authority, but not the broody role. The same lady we've been discussing also observes: "It is tough for a woman with a top job, who has gained the respect of many associates in business, to come home to demanding adolescent children. It takes a lot of control to keep one's cool."

Although this lady did carry out basic parental responsibilities, there is little question about where her primary interest lies. Had it not been for a deep-seated maternal instinct it is unlikely that her behavior would have been much different from that of the typical male corporate bigamists we have described. The characteristic maternal conflict is one reason why it is so much harder for a woman to reach the top slot in a large corporate enterprise. In our society men traditionally have been the breadwinners. And for high achievers among them the job must come first. There is no other way for them to succeed. A woman on the other hand may achieve success both in motherhood *and* in business. As the lady editorial director puts it: "She is torn in ways to which a man has no clues."

There are, of course, some women in business who are not "torn" at all, but who know exactly what comes first for them: career! They have managed to sever the traditional (and/or inherent) navel cord to motherhood. Or, perhaps, their X and Y genetic constitution makes them more competitive and masculine in their approach to career. Such women are no eye-batting, honey-throated damsels. They are literal-minded, ambitious, and as well equipped to draw blood in the corporate corridors as any of their male peers.

One young woman executive on her way up the corporate ladder of a book publishing empire admits having given up long since any ideas of children. "Friends would have these cramped apartments with the dining room converted to the baby's room," she says. "The whole thing was depressing." Soon after her introduction to the executive suite, her marriage broke up. She has decided to forego any remarriage for the present in order to concentrate on work and social life. "My work," she adds, "has become almost a lover to me. When I say my career comes very high in my life, it's because it *is* my life."

Just as families and wives of male corporate bigamists must, as Consolidated Edison's Mr. Luce put it, "adapt as a man climbs up the ladder . . . and find a life of their own," so families of female corporate bigamists apparently have to do the same thing. Recently Billie Jean King acknowledged that she has had to sacrifice domesticity to her tennis game and fame. Mr. King has admitted that he's "sick and tired of sharing her with the world." Billie Jean has described their lives as "intersecting circles," adding, "marriage isn't fifty-fifty—it's more like a hundred to zero one minute and zero to a hundred the next."

Corporate-bigamist women, like their male counterparts, generally assign second place to the family when the chips are down. One up-and-coming lady executive with a large communications concern insisted that the family move from their spacious suburban house to a small condominium to simplify the housekeeping. Short-order cooking via microwave replaced more elaborate culinary efforts. There was no time for family meals, she points out. The family had to accommodate itself to her career.

There is, usually, one modifying element when the lady of the house is a corporate bigamist. Most husbands of such women have careers of their own to offset the kind of stresses imposed on marriages where the man is the corporate bigamist and the woman is a housewife with no outside power base to bolster her ego. Hence, husbands are less inclined to get uptight about taking a back seat on their wives' turf.

Bella Abzug's husband Martin, who seldom gets to see his bustling political spouse, continually assures people that his ego is intact. "I'm not neglected; I'm not in the background. I do my own thing," he told a badgering *Time* magazine reporter when Bella was busy as a Congresswoman commuting between New York and Washington.

An interesting by-product of the increasing number of female corporate bigamists is a phenomenon known as the "long-distance," "weekend," or "commuter" marriage. It's the kind of partnership that develops when a high-status career-oriented corporate-bigamist wife is offered a job "too attractive to turn down" in another state, and when her corporate-bigamist husband's job is "too attractive to leave." A Kent State University study of 160 married couples living separately revealed that there is an accelerating trend in this direction. Although evidence to date does not indicate that such arrangements result in a higher rate of divorce, some psychologists believe that they may have that effect. A greater concern is that they will influence couples to avoid having children at all, precipitating drastic changes in the nation's economy and life-style.

Costs involved in commuter marriage—air fares, phone calls back and forth, separate establishments, and so on—can make a substantial dent in any additional income a wife may acquire in the move. So far, however, the most notable cases of long-distance partnerships seem to be surviving. One of the toughest commutes was the one taken on by Mrs. Adriana Saltonstall, when she accepted the directorship of California's Transportation Department at $37,000 a year. Her husband John is an outstanding lawyer with an important commitment in Boston. He says that he and his wife get together every few weeks "for a long weekend. We also vacation together."

The Saltonstalls, in their middle years, have a marriage uncomplicated by children. But kids don't necessarily hinder parents from parting, congenially, when the stakes are right for them. After a decade of marriage and raising two sons, Mrs. Harriet Michel took on an assistant directorship in the US Department of Labor's Employment and Training Administration in Washington, D.C. Her husband Yves holds the fort with the boys in their home on New York City's West Side—some 200 miles away. "I've questioned if I'm placing my own needs and career ambitions before the needs of my marriage and family," says Mrs. Michel. "But in the end, I believe it will have been a good move for us all."

In spite of this apparent ability of some career-oriented women to shut the door for brief periods on the domestic sector of their lives, most female corporate bigamists admittedly find it hard, or impossible, to separate their lives into business and family compartments—divorcing all domestic concerns from their career world, and vice versa. This, as indicated earlier, is something monster-type men profess to do regularly. Although the males' compartment reserved for family is pretty limited in monster types, such executives certainly do manage to put the blocks to any family concerns infringing on their business time, as has been pointed out. For *most* women executives, the family—at least the children—nearly always are a hovering concern. And frequently the career is a hovering concern at home. The workaholic syndrome in corporate bigamy is in no way limited to men. When Helen Gurley Brown, Editor of *Cosmopolitan*, was invited by a top officer of the Hearst Corporation to spend a weekend with his family in their Pocono Mountain retreat, she showed up with a suitcase full of letters and manuscripts which she worked at on and off throughout the entire holiday.

For mothers who lean to corporate bigamy, that kind of dedication to career can take a considerable toll. The thirty-one-year-old branch manager of Chicago's Continental Bank, a mother of two, admitted to the *Wall Street Journal* recently that the price she pays for her career includes a twelve-hour work day at the office plus a briefcase full of work to be done when she gets home after 7 P.M. She's also working toward an MBA degree one day a week, and gets up at 4 A.M. to study if she has a lot of homework. Her husband openly resents her extended absences and the domestic responsibilities that have shifted to him due to his wife's career.

Her lack of leisure, tensions of the job, and guilt about being away from the children so much of the time, also have brought this lady stomachaches and colitis flare-ups. Despite the problems, she says emphatically that she wouldn't dream of giving up her management job. It gives her, she says, "a deep sense of fulfillment and accomplishment" that she wasn't finding as just a housewife and mother. What's more, like many other women executives, her sights are aimed well beyond her present second vice-presidency. But, she admits, her conflicting loyalties make her unsure about the president's chair.

"The road to the top," she notes, "is filled with more and more commitment to the job, and less and less family time. If I spend more hours away from home, I may not have a family."

This lady's conflicting desire for the best of both worlds also exacts a price both mentally and physically, as she and many other female corporate bigamists are discovering.

Medical records today already indicate that women executives are falling prey to heart attacks, ulcers, high blood pressure, and other stress-induced ailments traditionally associated with pressured male executive types. Dr. Ray Roseman, Associate Director of San Francisco's Brunn Institute for Cardiovascular Disease, recently noted that as more and more women move into managerial ranks "we will see an increase in coronary heart disease" among younger and younger women.

In addition to the ordinary stresses of the executive suite, however, many women corporate bigamists are victims of special stress-induced afflictions unique to their breed. The three most common and painful are chronic depression, confusion in female identity, and the "supermom syndrome" already described.

At Karen Horney clinic in New York City, analysts have long specialized in problems of successful professional women. Dr. Horney herself, the noted psychoanalyst for whom the center was named, classified women into three specific character types: expansive, detached, and dependent. The first is, of course, the characteristic associated with the aggressive, driving, achievement-oriented type most apt to fit into our corporate categories. These ladies, according to the Karen Horney experts, are the ones who "often avoid tender feelings, and have a taboo against being dependent. They may exploit and triumph over others. For them, the appeal of life lies in its mastery."

Those same executive types are just the ones who may develop problems due to the fact that in early childhood they spurned girl things, and the feminine role in general, to avoid emulating mothers whom they considered passive and dominated. Instead, they strove mightily to reflect traits of courage, strength, self-sufficiency, and achievement. Such rejection of the mother, say Karen Horney Clinic experts, brings on neurotic reactions—a pervading sense of emotional deprivation and depression that is there throughout their lives. Even total absorption with work and career never is able to provide a real sense of fulfillment.

In addition, the aforementioned confusion in their female identity can actually terrify such women if they have—as many do—a deepseated need for dependency which they have tried to smother over the years. One eminently successful career woman who came to the clinic concerned about her constant depressions, described to a therapist a dream in which she was dangling from a window ledge by her fingertips. She knew that her husband was inside and tried to call out to him, but when she did all that came out was an inaudible whisper. She was unable to ask her own husband for help, except in a voice he couldn't hear.

The inability to acknowledge dependency when it is justified, and share real trouble, can result in a variety of unpleasant symptoms, including stifled rage, depression, insomnia, and sexual problems. The only recourse for afflicted high-achiever women usually is lengthy therapy that can provide real insight into their emotional hang-ups. Usually, dedicated success-oriented women are completely unaware of their unresolved needs and are inclined to believe they can cure their symptoms with practical concrete action, such as finding the right job or husband. It isn't the answer. According to the Horney analysts, "They have to face up to their own inner feelings before they'll start to feel better. A lot of these women don't want to look into their childhood and recognize the negative factors there."

In short, it is not a simple cut-and-dried matter for a woman to "be more like a man" in business without—as Drs. Hennig and Jardim indicated—careful self-examination and a change in basic deepseated attitudes. Among other things they must learn, say these researchers, are to accept leadership; to delegate authority; to work with people whether they like them or not; to develop and carry out planned strategies and tactics; to anticipate road blocks and develop contingency plans as alternatives; to take substantial risks when results may justify them; to avoid taking criticism personally; to refrain from showing emotion in any crises; to seek help when needed from superiors regardless of sex; to learn how to make trade-offs and negotiate conflicts between career life and personal life.

Women executives who are able to do all those things and maintain a good self-image, are the ones who really make it to the top. R.H. Macy's Vice-President for Labor Relations, and board member of General Electric, G. G. Michelson, is a shining example of the kind of personable, cool, objective, competent female personality it takes to achieve complete success on both fronts—career and family.

Though she denies being "an achiever," Mrs. Michelson, who is fifty-four years old and has been with Macy's for thirty-two years, does consider herself "highly motivated." Actually, she finished college at eighteen, and went to law school because "I needed some growing up." Her father, "a dynamic man," neither encouraged nor discouraged her (her mother died when she was eleven). In law school she met her husband—"a humanist way ahead of his time, who believes everyone has a right to personal fulfillment." He encouraged her to take maternity leave during her pregnancies with two daughters and return to her job, rather than drop her career and devote herself solely to rearing a family. "He knew that staying home was not my thing," she says.

The dual role was managed, according to Mrs. Michelson, thanks to "expensive, competent, live-in help, in whom I had complete trust." She did not, however, use the domestic assistance to escape family responsibility. Her priorities, she insists, always have been family first, career second, social activities with friends third. In her first job—a high-pressure stint for NBC— a male boss taught her that it was vital to "turn it off" at quitting time. She learned to do just that. On evenings and weekends she was able, thanks to the domestic help, to devote herself solely to the family—and did. "I attended all of the children's school functions," she reveals. "I was a class mother, a den mother, and all of those things." She and her husband took an annual month of vacation together and, when school was out, they had a family vacation, visited national parks, and journeyed to other interesting places. "I was never," she says, "unable to attend a school function or go on vacation because of the job."

Like Jane Pfeiffer, G. G. Michelson has been offered tempting, prestigious labor relations jobs in Washington, but turned them down. Her husband had no objections if it was what she wanted. But she couldn't see uprooting the family, having her husband find another job, or trying to maintain two houses and commute.

The upshot of it all was well expressed recently by Pamela Loren, founder and President of Loren Communications International, Ltd. "I am,'" she said, "thrilled to have achieved . . . success . . . but am much more thrilled by my ability to handle a multifaceted three-dimensional life involving not only the corporation . . . but a wonderful marriage to a man I married before I was twenty, and three exquisite and well-adjusted little children. . . . If indeed it is said that one's career has to be one's own favorite child, then I would be in a mess. . . . I love 'having made it' but not for one moment would I ever give up or could I put into words the wonder of a hug from my six-year-old. . . . In order to manage it all I had to be more meticulous, alert, organized, informed, resilient and less moody, sensitive, tumultuous than some others. . . . But none of it overshadowed my pride in also raising children who are going to be positive contributors to the next generation."

18

The Company's Role—Today and Tomorrow

🖝 For years, corporate bigamy actually has been encouraged and even nurtured in this country by company policies deliberately aimed at tethering a man totally to his job. There aren't many top slots in major corporations that do not require an executive to be out of town at least a quarter of his working time. Dr. Robert Seidenberg calls such globe-trotting company bosses "elite hoboes."

An executive's domestic affairs have not, until now, been of much concern to companies. When someone asked screenwriter Collier Young what story conferences were like at the Goldwyn studios, he replied: "Long. Sam held a lot of them on weekends. He didn't do anything for the institution of marriage."

More than a few large corporations still go so far as to assume that wives and families of their top executives are, or should be, corporate appendages to whom the company has no obligation— two employees for the price of one, as it were. When Charles Revson was alive, wives of Revlon executives were expected to attend a special "wives clinic" where they were advised among other things, says Andrew Tobias in his book *Fire and Ice*: "If he [your husband] doesn't feel like playing bridge or is too tired to go to the movies, you get your bridge-playing and movie-seeing in during the afternoons. If he gets home most nights too late to see the children, let them stay up now and then and make it up with longer naps in the afternoon. It won't kill them. If he has a lot of paperwork to do, learn to type if you don't know how, and then give him a hand with the reports if he wants the help."

Many companies fully expect wives of their top executives to put themselves at the disposal of their husbands and the corporation whenever a business occasion calls for it. It isn't necessarily spelled out, but the clues are highly visible. A recent survey of winners of American Cyanamid's "Golden Oval" sales award revealed that not one of the wives of the company's top sales executives worked at outside paying jobs or professions. A top Ford Motor Company executive is on record as having told a meeting of corporate wives: "An executive's wife should watch her figure and not nag!"

Perhaps the most significant factor in the business of fostering corporate bigamy, however, is the still-prevalent tendency of some companies to discount executives who have a more than casual concern for their wives and families. Recently the president of a large corporation cabled to inform me that he had to choose among his vice-presidents for someone suitable to replace him when he retired. He had three possible candidates but disqualified one instantly when the man said he wanted to check with his wife first.

Executive recruitment organizations frequently are asked to fill particularly tough jobs with men who are not apt to be diverted by their families. One chairman recently told a recruiting firm to get a man "as unhappily married as I am, so he'll devote full time to the job."

Along the same line, a significant new trend that has begun to gather momentum is the practice of corporate boards to look for divorced executives—who now total 10 percent of all executives, as against 2 percent a decade ago. The divorced single suddenly has become a coveted prize to capture, since he or she will devote nearly every waking moment to the job, undiverted by family problems or interests. The chairman of one Midwestern corporation went so far as to encourage the marital breakup of an applicant for a top executive marketing position in the company. When the marketing expert revealed that his wife would sue for divorce if he took the job, and he'd need time to see it through, the chairman replied: "Go ahead . . . just raise our sales 30 percent." The man got the divorce and took the job.

According to executive recruiters, more and more companies are specifying a preference for divorced or single people particularly among women executive candidates. The reason is interesting: a married woman's career, as has been pointed out, usually is considered second in importance to her husband's. If the husband's company moves him, the wife usually has to go with him. That means her employer has a replacement problem. Furthermore, according to the personnel director of one large company, "single people are easier to move."

The business of relocation is, in fact, a primary cause of domestic strife in the modern business world. Each year hundreds of thousands of top- and middle-management employees are transferred by the corporations they work for. All but a handful, according to the Employee Relocation Council in Washington, D.C., are males, half of them thirty-to-forty-year-old family men the majority of whom have school-age children. Nearly half of all these relocated people have experienced four moves and anticipate many more. One IBM excutive, with a wife and two teenagers, has survived nine transfers in his twenty years with the company. He admits that his family bears the scars. "There's a loss," he told the *Wall Street Journal* recently. "I can't measure it."

The fact is, however, that most of the corporate practices—past and present—that mitigate against the family, and the domestic scene in general, are wearing thin. Even the trend to divorced people and singles isn't working everywhere. Recently one international corporation instituted a "married managers only" policy when their singles in top management positions overseas began chasing the wives of married executives and making off with the company jet every weekend to live it up in European capitals.

Enlightened managements are beginning to realize that the total-dedication-to-the-job approach simply will not work anymore. Too many developments run counter to it. Wives are no longer willing to wait for the few emotional crumbs that the job pressures permit their husbands to bestow on them. A generation of children of corporate biagamists has grown up to hate the entire business community, and industry no longer is able to draw at will on a reservoir of gung-ho young talent. The talent isn't that gung-ho anymore about the autocratic posture of big business. Those who *are* willing to enter the business world are beginning to insist on doing it on their own terms. In short, they have no intention of marrying themselves to the job irrevocably. More and more executives are refusing relocation opportunities if they will disrupt the family. One vice-president turned down a transfer that would have added $50,000 to his $75,000 salary, because his wife had a nursing job she liked and didn't want to leave it. Many executives refuse transfers when they discover that schools in the new location are no good for their children.

Actually, the ability of the average corporate bigamist to do his undiluted superlative best for his organization has come under serious question. Full-scale dedication to the job is not everything. Companies need people who are emotionally healthy and not subject to the constant stress of trying to balance job against family. Many companies are beginning to recognize this. And it is becoming increasingly clear to managements that the organization can no longer require destructive personal sacrifice as a condition for advancement; that even the most dedicated employee must be allowed to exist in the family dimension without strain or guilt. This awareness has been enhanced as more and more women move up the corporate ladder. Should business fail voluntarily to adopt more humanistic policies, indications are that it may be compelled to do so. Recently several states have approved legislation mandating sick leave for pregnant mothers, and there is talk about mandatory paternity leave for men who want it. Recently, New York State's Disability Benefit Law was revised to require companies to pay benefits for pregnancy-related disabilities.

It's doubtful, however, that extensive legislation will be required to bring industry to heel. Already, many forward-looking companies have taken dramatic steps to solve some of the major corporate-bigamy problems they helped to create, and measures that should be taken by corporations are no real mystery. The best recommendations already can be based on a background of proven experience in many cases. In order to establish healthier and more productive company-employee relationships, there are specific things corporations can do. The following recommendations deal with the most important of these:

• The company must, first of all, recognize that there is a corporate-bigamy problem, and publicize a policy statement to let everyone know exactly where it stands on this issue. It should be made clear that the company believes in the concept of "the balanced man" for its entire management team; that it does not believe it should own all of a man's time.

• Seminars and counseling should be provided for both husbands and wives to help resolve the myriad job-versus-home problems that arise with high-achiever executives and their families. The Aluminum Company of America and the Ford Motor Company both have consulting psychiatrists on staff. Kennicott Copper Corporation has instituted a dial-a-consultant program called "Insight." All such services are strictly confidential and conducted by top-drawer professionals.

• More and more corporations are coming to an awareness of the conflict between job and home for a variety of reasons. Joseph McCullen, Jr., Vice-President for Personnel at New England Mutual Life Insurance Company, was alerted to the problem when a relative of his went back to work after a maternity leave and was berated by neighbors and family for repudiating her family responsibilities. As a result, he had a firm of psychology consultants run a series of ten confidential lunch-hour seminars for company parents, from executives to clerks, on coping with the pressures of home and career. It was a huge success and follow-ups are planned. I am called in more and more to give seminars for corporations. In some, managers and wives are present. In others this popular subject is discussed with wives only. It is fast becoming a frequent topic for convention planners.

• Even municipalities are being awakened to the problem of job-home conflict among city employees. In Lockport, New York, the Police Department faced a rising number of divorce cases involving a fifth of a fifty-man force, due to unhappy and suspicious wives of overworked husbands who came home to sleep and little else. They met the problem with an innovative experimental "ride-along" program for wives. On designated nights, the women were invited to ride the patrol cars with their husbands, on active duty. The idea was to open their eyes to the pressures of the job and give them a picture of a duty tour devoid of glamour. "It helped wives understand their husbands' jobs better," according to Lockport's Police Captain Norman Tiplady. Results of the program have still to be evaluated against the future divorce rate. Wives who agreed to take the rides had mixed reactions—some were impressed; others bored or a little frightened. Most agreed, however, that they had a clearer picture of their husbands' problems.

• A whole new approach to personnel transfers and corporate relocation is clearly indicated. In 1978, a Merrill-Lynch survey of some 250,000 executives in 686 major corporations included a question regarding their willingness to relocate with promotion and a raise. Nearly half said they would refuse to go. Why? Most said the move would be too upsetting for their wives and families. Nothing gives wife and family more trouble than moving. When the corporation says "We need you in Los Angeles (or Boston, or Albany)," domestic tranquility and what little loyalty modern families may feel for a company hits the fan. Studies have shown that relocation problems for a wife include stress, loneliness, identification difficulties, and problems with the children. The wife has to make a whole new world of social contacts to establish her family in the new community, while her husband is away more frequently adjusting to his new responsibilities.

At a dinner in San Francisco recently I sat beside a woman who began, for no apparent reason, to cry. When I passed her my handkerchief, she related all the traumas she was enduring because the company had forced them to move. Her daughter is now in a mental hospital because, she is sure, the child was uprooted from friends and security at a critical time during her impressionable years. You don't have to believe that. But *she* believes it.

• Before a corporation moves an individual it is important that all possible candidates know about the opening. Who knows? Maybe some qualified manager *wants* to go to Kamloops, British Columbia. The company should by all means assist in the sale of the present home and purchase of the new one. Employee and spouse should be encouraged to visit (more than once, and for more than a few days or even a week if necessary) the new community at company expense so they can check housing, schools, shopping, etc., and see what living there will be like. It is also vital to provide the wife with what I call a "transfer of credentials"—an introduction to the director of the Theater Guild, the Historic Society, Garden Club, League of Women Voters—depending on her interests. Maybe she's a decorator, a church devotee, a golf or tennis buff. A simple questionnaire from the personnel office can solicit that information. If the company will open doors that give her an opportunity to pick up the threads of a life torn from her, she may well be eternally grateful rather than forever bitter.

• Then there is the considerate gesture so important to almost any woman. One company president told me that when he was young and was asked to make his first move, his wife had a fit. She said the drapes wouldn't fit and the rugs wouldn't be right in the new home. She had just painted the kitchen cabinets all by herself. All her sweat and toil had gone into *this* house. He decided, then, to make certain that when he became top dog, whenever he asked a male executive to move, he would send the man's wife a check in her name with a note, such as: "Dear Jane, I know that your drapes won't fit and the rugs may not be right, so here is $500 [sometimes more]. Do what you want with it to make things a little more pleasant and comfortable, with the company's gratitude and best wishes."

• Today, most large corporations are beginning to change their transfer practices to alleviate the hardships imposed. Many provide liberal time and allowances for house-hunting, including meals, motel costs, car rentals, and so forth. More than one company provides psychiatric consultation. International Business Machines now takes the relocating employee and spouse to the new town for a leisurely tour of the environs, to investigate the local schools and government (including the tax situation), and talk with the realtors and business people. The family can say "No thanks!" if they wish, without jeopardizing the executive's career.

When Alcoa moves an executive and his family nowadays, it provides interest-free loans for new home purchase, a differential allowance to cover increased mortgage interest rates, and money to cover virtually all moving costs. There's also an allowance for the increase in income tax incurred through receiving all the foregoing funds.

• The newest development in the transfer field are outside "relocation consultants" who, for a fee, will package relocations for individual executives or entire corporations. Such firms study all the angles of any move planned by the company or individual employees—housing costs and availability, schools, churches, transportation facilities, tax situations, etc., and produce a complete report. The company then studies the area analysis and can decide whether or not to proceed. If it's "go," they can hire the relocation company to package the transfer.

Recently, when the Union Carbide Corporation moved its headquarters from New York City to Danbury, Connecticut, Merrill-Lynch's "relocation management" subsidiary handled the entire switch for them. The program included employee counseling to determine what the person should pay for a home, recommended the neighborhood depending on the employee's pay and the family's interests, and arranged for the best available mortgage deal. They ran employee workshops on home-buying. Finally, they managed the entire move. Carbide, meanwhile, provided each employee with expenses for a week of house-hunting, including baby-sitters, car rental, meals, lodging—even driving lessons where necessary.

• It's time for business in general to encourage the model of the successful marriage instead of imposing strains on it—often to the breaking point. Companies can easily make it clear that an executive isn't required to be a monster-type corporate bigamist to be successful in the organization. As recently as the fifties and early sixties many companies actually endorsed the monster model. It was, in fact, about 1960 when Arthur Railton, a magazine editor we know (who later became a vice-president of Volkswagen International), was about to make an extended business trip to Europe and asked the company for a short-term insurance policy to cover his family. The executive vice-president of the giant publishing house he then worked for informed him: "Buy your own. This company is not in business to make rich widows."

That's not a very effective model. It would be hard to imagine a successful company damaging its dignity or financial position by humanizing its image a little with any of a dozen or more simple policy innovations. When a man has been traveling for more than two weeks, for instance, his boss might write a letter to the wife, acknowledging the company's appreciation for her forbearance and offering an extended weekend holiday when her husband returns. Some companies throw parties for the top executives and their wives on milestone wedding anniversaries, like the twentieth and fortieth. For executives who have pushed particularly hard and given much time, one company has special dinners hosted by the president or chairman, and the wife is presented with a diamond pin with a "number one" engraved on it as a token of thanks. Travelers Insurance Company presents "diplomas" to wives of executives, suitably worded to show appreciation.

• No company should ever interfere with an executive's holiday plans. Family time should be held sacred. Some companies insist that all executives take every day they have coming. One corporation we know pays for its managers to take spouses with them on one business trip each year. "When a wife goes along," says the president, "she sees that such trips involve work, not play, and is more understanding about them." Another company has a program in which wives are invited to a short annual working holiday at a villa in the south of France.

One of the most imaginative programs aimed at integrating the family with the company was instigated by Robert Coppenrath, President of Agfa Gevaert in Teterboro, New Jersey. Children of all employees on summer vacations and old enough to work are employed by the company, not in some menial sweep-up job, but right beside the parent, at a substantial salary. The tour involves five thirty-five-hour weeks which can be worked at any time, in any combination of hours, over an eight-week period. "We don't do enough for our youngsters," says Coppenrath. "I wanted to prove my theory that a child does want to know what his parents do. I believe they care very much." According to reports, the program, which began two summers ago at the suggestion of Coppenrath's oldest daughter, has been a resounding success.

• More consideration for mothers in two-career families is becoming vital for most companies, in order to avoid excessive turnover. Large corporations such as Gulf & Western Industries and New York Telephone have found that about half of their women employees who take maternity leave don't come back. Inducements to return are proliferating. In many of the big outfits mothers now get maternity disability payments for six weeks after the baby comes home, plus child-care leave and job insurance. At several companies the job is held open for them for six months.

Working mothers with growing families figure in a number of new plans. At the Commercial Savings Bank in New Haven, Connecticut, there's a shorter workday for mothers, with hours to match those of the children's school day. During school vacations, mothers are replaced with substitutes— for the whole summer if the kids are home. About a third of the mothers at the bank are in management and love the program which, after five years, has proven a success. "I felt that companies had to be more imaginative and less demanding," says President Paul H. Johnson, who devised the plan and set it in motion.

At Agfa Gevaert, Robert Coppenrath's "flexitime" schedule used in the summer-student program also is applied to working mothers. It allows them to set their own working hours, as long as they put in thirty-five hours a week, permitting a four-day-week for some, and special short days for others. It gives mothers leeway in scheduling doctors, dentists, school visits, and special events, the president points out.

For valued executive mothers, some companies are bending all kinds of rules. Several large banks allow mothers to take whatever time for the children is necessary, and make it up at will. The United Bank of Colorado went so far as to hold an annual convention a month early because their woman economist expected a baby. One company in Western Canada permits women executives to combine managerial careers and families by letting them take an "organizational leave" of up to eighteen months and return at the same salary.

• When top executives in two-career families are transferred, some companies today are bending over backward to keep them happy. Recently, Standard Brands promoted a New York executive to a managerial spot in its Iowa office. The man's wife had to quit her job with a New York law firm. So the company let the husband set up his office in Chicago—130 miles from his Iowa headquarters—to permit his wife to relocate with a top metropolitan law firm. Actually, Merrill-Lynch's previously mentioned survey revealed that nearly one-sixth of the 686 corporations questioned already have programs to help working spouses get a good comparable job wherever an executive is transferred. Both Eastman Kodak and Alcoa try to find a place in their own organization for such spouses

• Smart managements do not neglect the widows of ex-executives. Top brass should exercise the simple courtesy of inviting to company functions these women—particularly the widows of former presidents and chief executive officers who often feel resentful that they have been totally abandoned after years of self-sacrifice in the interests of the company. They should be at the head table at annual affairs and thus know they are not forgotten. Other wives at the dinner who see them will have a better feeling about the corporation, too. Today, most people are losing a sense of attachment to the organization, which is bad for both of them. People need to be attached to something. It gives them a feeling of permanence, a sense of belonging and continuity. Widows of the former executives of one large corporation, who live in Florida now, have formed a sort of alumnae club—which should say all that needs to be said on this subject. Remember that in colonial America the best seats in the church were reserved for the wife of the minister and the widow of the previous minister—an excellent model for industry.

And where do we go from here? What happens to our corporate bigamist of tomorrow? It's going to be a lot different, certainly. One hint has been dropped by Rosebeth Kanter, Professor of Sociology and Management at Yale University, in her book *Men and Women of the Corporation*: "A lot of things that the corporation has done socially," she wrote, "will be handled in a more humble way in the future. Out-of-town business meetings will be shorter and without spouses. Wives no longer will be relied upon for such tasks as picking up—and planting—corporate rumors at cocktail parties." And, she adds, it may "reduce the incidence of alcoholism and depression among executive wives."

But that's only the beginning. There are straws in the wind to suggest that we may even now be drifting toward the Japanese concept of the corporate umbrella.

We have nothing in our business world today that remotely resembles Japanese corporate life. Over there, as briefly mentioned earlier, especially in large organizations, employment is for life. Even among younger executives turnover is four times less than it is here, and most of it occurs in smaller companies. Every employee from top executive to lowliest worker is almost totally immersed in the corporate entity. The company—not the family center—is "home base," and the entire family lives for it. Managers and top executives are deeply concerned with the personal life of each employee responsible to them. All have a deep and abiding identification with the company, which often supplies housing and large bonus rewards in good years.

Most corporate leaders in Japan are convinced that the organization, as the central focus in an employee's life, solves the problem of corporate bigamy and may—with modifications—portend the wave of the future.

Recently, William G. Ouchi, Associate Professor of Organizational Behavior at Stanford University and Alfred Jaeger, industrial engineer and doctoral candidate, studied the implications of such a model in a paper entitled "The Corporation: Alternative to Village Life—Stability in the Midst of Mobility." The authors admit that Americans may take a dim view of the seeming paternalism of the Japanese corporation. They blame this on unpleasant memories of the totalitarianism once practiced in our mining communities and on plantations, and suggest that we have not followed the Japanese model because it encroaches on the individual freedom Americans consider a basic right. "What we must discover," they suggest, is "that unique American solution which allows individual freedom while using the work organization to support and encourage the stability of organizational ties."

But it wasn't just slave quarters and dingy mining company compounds that turned American workers against "organizational ties." The oppressive paternalism of corporate kingdoms like the one in Hershey, Pennsylvania, and in mill towns like Maryland's Dickeyville (both of which communities were products of reasonably benevolent companies, incidentally) finally had to give way to the American spirit of independence. So, despite the assumed benevolence of Japan's "broody-hen" corporations, it may perhaps prove impossible for Americans to feel "free" when they know they are captive workers. The Liberty Bell and the huge statue of Miss Liberty in New York's harbor may say more about the importance of individual freedom in America than the industrial engineers have reckoned with. Furthermore there appears to be a growing suspicion that, while the Japanese model may have proved acceptable in earlier times when more Japanese companies were family-owned and -operated—and may even be great today for top executives—the impact of the benevolent industrial complex on domesticity at lower-manager and -worker level isn't quite so rosy as has been implied. The fact is that while even the executive is patted and promoted and protected by the company, his family is virtually ignored and left to the wife to handle as best she can. We can't see that kind of operation working very smoothly under a simmering Equal Rights Amendment.

But, should the family be taken in under that corporate umbrella in a real sense—well, it's interesting to think about. And certainly some United States corporations are moving in that direction.

Meantime, plenty of other changes are imminent. The predilection of big corporations to move people around the country —and the world—like pawns on a chess board will diminish. Resistance to such practices by wives and families is growing. Industrial experts are beginning to ask hard questions about the economics involved. They no longer buy offhand the assumption that an individual who has been doing a good job in one locale will, perforce, do an equally good job when uprooted and planted elsewhere.

Recently I asked my psychologist son what he saw in the future for the business-family relationship. "Maybe I'll be bringing my children to work with me," he answered promptly.

Maybe he will, indeed. Maybe fathers and mothers will bring the kids to the office or the factory where big, efficient day-care centers are located. Or perhaps many of us will be working at home. Ed Uhl, chairman of Fairchild Industries, pointed out to me not long ago, when we were discussing the business of corporate bigamy, that within the foreseeable future satellite communications will be available everywhere. An executive could work at home and have at his disposal the ability to communicate in seconds with anyone at any point anywhere in the world. Phone-a-vision will flash people and things on a screen in front of him; conference calls will put people's faces and voices together without the necessity of battling traffic to a board room an hour away.

Maybe there will be nurseries at convention centers. The American Psychological Association every year sets up a child-care service for its annual convention so that each psychologist can bring his or her family and have baby-sitters. Who knows what dramatic changes are really in store for us?

Whatever happens, there is little doubt that the atmosphere that fosters corporate bigamy will diminish. But it is doubtful that the monsters, unlike the dinosaurs, will ever become extinct. There will always be some of them because I believe it is in their genes. For the same reason there will always be at least some of those other corporate-bigamist types—the Januses and need-achievers—in real life as well as in Feinberg's Wax Museum.

As for their spouses, forever trapped in a frustrating partial leave-taking; their children forever reaching out for a little more of them; and the corporations that helped to create them, I can only hope that some of the insights and suggestions provided by this book will help in some small way to bring more satisfaction and fulfillment to each of them.

Bibliography

Angrist, et al. "How Working Mothers Manage: Socio-Economic Differences in Work, Child Care and Household Tasks." *Social Science Quarterly*, Vol. 56 (1976).

APA Monitor, May 1977. "Mothering Figure and Good Child Relationship."

Argyris, Chris. *Personality and Organization: The Conflict Between System and Individual*. New York: Harper & Row, 1957.

Balswick, Jack. "The Effect of Spouse Companionship Support on Employment. Success." *Journal of Marriage and Family*, Vol. 32, No. 2 (1970), pp. 392–407.

Bane, Mary Jo. "Here to Stay: American Families in the 20th Century." *Across the Board*, March 1977.

Bartoleme, F. "Executives as Human Beings." *Harvard Business Review*, Vol. 50 (1972), pp. 62–69.

Bass, Bernard M. *Leadership, Psychology, and Organizational Behavior*. New York: Harper & Bros., 1960.

———. *Organizational Psychology*. Boston: Allyn & Bacon, 1965.

Battalia, O. William, and Tarrant, John J. *The Corporate Eunuch*. New York: New American Library, 1974.

Bell, C. "Ocupational Career, Family Cycle and Extended Family Relations." *Human Relations*, Vol. 24 (1971), pp. 463–475.

Bell, Joseph N. "Sucess Is a Family Matter." *Christian Science Monitor*, March 6, 1979.

Bendheim, Joanna. "What It Takes to Get to the Top." *Westchester Magazine*, September 1978.

Bird, Caroline. *The Two-Paycheck Marriage*. New York: Rawson Wade, 1979.

Black, Hugo, Jr. *My Father: A Remembrance*. New York: Random House, 1975.

Bradley, Nelson. "Are You a Work Addict?" *Across the Board*, October 1977.

Bray, D. W., Campbell, R. J., and Grant, D. L. *Formative Years in Business: A Long-term A T & T Study of Managerial Lives*. New York: John Wiley & Sons, 1974.

Brodlie, Jerome. "How Well Do You Relate to Your Children?" *Management Review*, AMA Forum, August 1978.

Bronfenbrenner, Urie. Papers, reports on child psychology. Cornell University, 1978–79.

Brooks, Patricia. "Whatever Happened to 'Following in Dad's Footsteps'?" *TWA Ambassador,* May 1977.

Bryson, Jeff and Rebecca. *Dual-Career Marriages.* Professional papers, 1977.

Burger, Ninki Hart. *The Executive's Wife.* New York: Macmillan, 1968.

Burke, R. J. "Relationship of Wives' Employment Status to Husband, Wife and Pair Satisfaction and Performance." *Journal of Marriage and Family,* Vol. 38, No. 2 (May 1976), pp. 279–287.

Burke, R. J., Firth, L., and McGrattan, C. "Husband-Wife Compatibility and the Management of Stress." *Journal of Social Psychology,* Vol. 94, No. 2 (December 1974), pp. 243–252.

Business Week, April 9, 1979. "The New Corporate Wife Goes to Work."

————. April 18, 1977. "When Mothers Are Also Managers."

Chenoweth, L. *The American Dream of Sucess.* North Scituate, Mass.: Duxbury Press, 1974.

Coles, Robert. "Children of Affluence." *Atlantic,* September, 1977.

Conot, Robert. *A Streak of Luck.* New York: Seaview Books, 1979.

Coser, R. L., and Rokoff, G. "Women in the Occupational World: Social Disruption and Conflict." *Social Problems,* Vol. 18 (1971), pp. 535–554.

Crumley, Frank (Dallas, Texas, child psychiatrist). Report on adolescent suicide attempts. 1979.

Culbert, S. A., and Renshaw, J. R. "Coping With the Stresses of Travel as an Opportunity for Improving the Quality of Work and Family Life." *Family Process,* Vol. 11, No. 3 (September 1972), pp. 321–337.

DiFiore, C. J. "Robert Coppenrath, Philosopher at The Helm." Bergen/Passaic (N.J.) *Record,* January 29, 1978.

Dorschner, John. "The Delicate Balance of Jack Nicklaus' Life." *Family Weekly,* March 27, 1977.

Duncan and Penucci. "Dual Occupation Family and Migration." *American Sociological Review,* Vol. 41, No. 2 (April 1976), pp. 252–261.

Easton, Carol. *The Search for Sam Goldwyn.* New York: William Morrow & Co., 1976.

Edmiston, Susan. "They Made it Work—Their Way." *New York* magazine, April 4, 1977.

Elder, Glen H., Jr. "Role Orientation, Marital Age and Life Patterns in Adulthood." *Merrill Palmer Quarterly*, Vol. 18, No. 1 (January 1972), pp. 3–24.

Evans, April. "Washington Life—A Life in Limbo." © *The New York Times*, March 31, 1977. Reprinted by permission.

Fasteau, M. F. *The Male Machine*. New York: McGraw-Hill, 1974.

Faunce, W. A. *Problems of an Industrial Society*. New York: McGraw-Hill, 1968.

Feinberg, M. R. "A Man on the Way Up Needs a Boost." *Family Health*, December 1969.

———. " 'Corporate Bigamy' examined by Mortimer R. Feinberg." *The Lasser Globe*, Summer 1976.

———. "Corporate Bigamy: How to Resolve the Conflict Between Job and Family." *Business Management*, 1975.

———. *Corporate Bigamy—Job/Family Conflict: Treat or Prevent?* New York: American Management, 1975.

———. *Effective Psychology for Managers*. New York: Prentice-Hall, Inc., 1965.

———. "How Not to Commit Corporate Bigamy." *Tempo*, Vol. 24, No. 1 (1978). (Touche Ross & Co., accountants, house organ)

———. *Leave Taking*. New York: Simon & Schuster, 1978.

———. "Seventeen Guidelines for Tension." Paper delivered at 28th Annual University for Presidents, 1978.

———. "The Corporate Bigamist." *The Conference Board Magazine*, Vol. 13, No. 11 (November 1976).

———. *What Is Corporate Bigamy?* New York: American Management, 1975.

———. "Why Do Executives' Children Run Away?" *Dun's Review*, January 1968.

———. "Women's Lib and the Executive Suite." *Business Management*, January 1971.

———. "YPO Kids." *Enterprise*, Winter 1972–'73.

Fendrock, J. *Goals in Conflict*. New York: American Management, 1970.

Ferretti, Fred. "New Experts Easing the Corporate Move." *New York Times*, March 20, 1979.

Foreman, Laura. "Spend More Time With the Family? Carter's Aides Find They Can't." *New York Times*, February 24, 1977.

————. "Washington Wife—a Life in Limbo." *New York Times,* March 31, 1977.

Foy, G. A. "Individual Growth in the Family." *Psychological Perspective,* Vol. 4, No. 1 (Spring 1973), pp. 44–59.

Freud, Martin. *Sigmund Freud: Man and Father.* New York: Vanguard Press, 1958.

Friedenberg, E. Z. *The Disposal of Liberty and Other Industrial Wastes.* New York: Doubleday & Co., 1975.

Fuchs, R. "Different Meanings of Employment for Women." *Human Relations,* Vol. 24 (1971), pp. 501–518.

Galvin, Ruth Mehrtens. "Goal Consciousness: You Have to Have a Strategy." *New York* magazine, April 4, 1977.

Ghiselli, E., and Brown, C. *Personnel and Industrial Psychology,* 2nd ed. New York: McGraw-Hill Co., 1955.

Goldman, Daniel R. "Managerial Mobility Motivators and Central Life Interests." *American Sociological Review,* Vol. 30, No. 1 (February, 1973), pp. 119–126.

Gooding, Judson. "MBA, Harvard, '78—Sweeney's Way." *Across the Board,* June 1978.

Gordon, Gene, M.D. (Children's Hospital of Washington, D.C.) "Maternal Identification in the Male Executive." Paper, AAAS Annual Meeting, 1978.

Gould, Roger L. "The Phases of Adult Life—A Study in Development." *American Journal of Psychiatry,* Vol. 129, No. 5 (1972), pp. 521–531.

Gove, W. R., James, W. G., Motz, S. C., and Thompson, J. D. "The Family Life Cycle—Internal Dynamics and Social Consequences." *Sociological and Social Research,* Vol. 57, No. 2 (1973), pp. 182–195.

Gronseth, E. "Work-Sharing Families: Adaptation of Pioneering Families With Husband and Wife in Part-time Employment." *Acta Sociologia,* Vol. 12, No. 2–3 (1975), pp. 220–221.

Hall, D. T. "Pressures From Work and Self and Home in the Life Stages of Married Women." *Journal of Vocational Behavior,* Vol. 61 (February 1975), pp. 121–132.

Haller, M., and Rosenmayr, L. "The Pluridimensionality of Work Commitment." *Human Relations,* Vol. 24 (1971), pp. 501–518.

Hennig, Margaret, and Jardim, Anne. *The Managerial Woman.* New York: Doubleday/Anchor Press, 1977.

————. "Superwoman." *Across the Board,* July 1977.

Henry, W. E. "Conflict, Age and the Executive." *Business Topics*, Vol. 9, No. 21 (1961), pp. 15–25.

Hirschowitz, R. G. "Family Coping Patterns in Times of Change." *International Journal of Social Psychiatry*, Vol. 21, No. 1 (Winter–Spring 1974–'75), pp. 37–43.

Horrel, L. E., and Ridley, C. A. "Substitute Child Care and Maternal Employment and the Quality of Mother-Child Interaction." *Journal of Marriage and Family*, August 7, 1975, pp. 556–564.

Hudis, Paula M. "Commitment to Work and Family—Marital Status Differences in Women's Earnings." *Journal of Marriage and Family*, May 1976, pp. 267–272.

Imundo, L. L. "Problems Associated with Managerial Mobility." *Personnel Journal*, Vol. 53, No. 12 (1974), pp. 910–914.

Irving, John. *The One Hundred and Fifty-Eight Pound Marriage.* New York: Random House, 1974.

Jay, Antony. *Management and Machiavelli: An Inquiry into the Politics of Corporate Life.* New York: Holt, Rinehart & Winston, 1968.

Jennings, Eugene Emerson. *The Executive in Crisis.* East Lansing, Mich.: Michigan State University Business Studies, 1965.

———. *The Mobile Manager.* Ann Arbor, Mich.: The University of Michigan, 1967.

Johnson, P. B. "Drinking Practices Among U.S. Adults Males and Females." Rand–U.C.L.A. report, 1975.

Kanter, Rosabeth M. *Men and Women of the Corporation.* New York: Basic Books, 1977.

Katelman and Barnett. "Work Orientation of Urban Middle-Class Married Women." *Journal of Marriage and Family*, Vol. 30 (1962), pp. 80–88.

Kazickas, Jerome. "Life in Washington Difficult, Politicos' Wives Agree." *Westchester Newspapers*, September 6, 1978.

Kearns, Doris. *Lyndon Johnson and the American Dream.* New York: Harper & Row, 1976.

Kieren, D., and Tallman, I. "Spousal Adaptability: An Assessment of Marital Competence." *Journal of Marriage and the Family*, Vol. 34 (1972), pp. 247–256.

Kirschner, E. F. Study on couples living separately. Kent State, 1977.

Klemesrud, Judy. "Helping Troubled Women in an Era of Change." *New York Times*, May 21, 1979.

————. "Policemen's Wives Go Along for the Ride to Save Marriages." *New York Times*, January 21, 1977.

————. "Women Executives: View from the Top." *New York Times*, March 11, 1979.

Knebel, Fletcher. *The Bottom Line*. New York: Doubleday, 1974; Pocket Books, 1975.

Koliwosky, Michael, and Taylor, Lawrence J. "The Importance of the Spouse in One's Work." *KT Notes*, Bulletin 152, March 1978.

Korman, A. K., and Tanofsky, R. "A Study of Alienation Among Middle-and-Upper Level Executives." In preparation. Baruch College, 1977.

Kraut, Grace. "She Watched Over a 'Lion Among Thinkers.'" *Rochester Democrat & Chronicle*, May 13, 1977.

Krupinski, J. E. Marshall, and Yule, V. "Patterns of Marital Problems in Marriage Guidance Clients." *Journal of Marriage and the Family*, Vol. 32 (1970), pp. 130–143.

Kundsin, Ruth B., ed. *Women and Success: The Anatomy of Achievement*. New York: William Morrow & Co., 1974.

Leider. "The Changing Success Ethic." *Personnel Administration*, 1974.

Leslie, Gerald R. "Life Cycle, Career Patterns and Decision to Move." *American Sociological Review*, Vol. 26 (1961).

Loeb, Marshall. "Millionaires: How They Do It." *Time*, December 3, 1965.

Lowry, Thomas and Thea (psychologists). "The Seven Danger Signals of Divorce." Professional paper, 1978.

MacArthur, General Douglas. *Reminiscences*. New York: Mc-Graw-Hill Book Co., 1964. All rights reserved.

McCarthy, Abigail. "Are Political Wives Getting Different?" *San Francisco Examiner and Chronicle*, December 8, 1974.

————. "Rosalynn Carter: Product of American Culture." *New York Times*, November 30, 1978.

McClelland, D. C., and Winter, D. G. *Motivating Economic Achievement*. New York: The Free Press, 1971; London: Collier-Macmillan Ltd., 1969.

McClendon, M. J. "The Occupational Status Attainment Process of Males and Females." *American Sociological Review*, Vol. 41, No. 2 (1976), pp. 52–64.

Maccoby, M. *The Gamesman*. New York: Simon & Schuster, 1976.

————. "The Corporate Climber." *Fortune,* December 1976, pp. 98–108.

Machlowitz, Marilyn. *Workaholics.* Addison-Wesley Publishing Co.

Mannila, E. H. "Satisfaction With Family, Work, Leisure and Life Among Men and Women." *Human Relations,* Vol. 24 (1971), pp. 585–601.

Martin, Berry, and Jacobsen. "The Impact of Dual Career Marriages on Female Professional Careers." *Journal of Marriage and Family,* November 1975, pp. 734–742.

Maslach, C. "Burn-out: The Loss of Human Caring." *Psychology and Life,* 9th ed. Glenview, Ill.: Scott, Foresman & Co., 1975.

Mayo, Elton. *The Social Problems of an Industrial Civilization.* Boston: Harvard Business School, 1945.

Miller, Gordon. "Decision Making for Spouses." Professional paper, 1978.

————. "The Working Mother—Issues and Implications for Family Counselors." *Journal of Family Counseling,* Vol. 4, No. 1 (Spring 1976), pp. 61–65.

Mittenthal, Sue. "After Baby, Whither the Career?" *New York Times,* February 14, 1979.

Montour, Kathleen. "William James Sidis, The Broken Twig." *American Psychologist,* April 1977.

Moore, Kristin A., and Sawhill, Isabel. "Implications of Women's Employment for Home and Family Life." *American Economy,* August 1975.

Mulligan, L. W. "Wives, Women and Wife Role Behavior: An Alternative Cross-Cultural Perspective." *International Journal of Comparative Sociology,* Vol. 13 (1972), pp. 36–47.

Murphy, Mary. "How Working Couples Work it Out." *New West,* February 14, 1977.

Nation's Business, November 1965. "Lessons of Leadership: Howard Johnson."

Nemy, Enid. "Is There Lunch After Marriage?" *New York Times,* January 21, 1979.

————. "Networks: New Concept for Top-Level Women." *New York Times,* April 29, 1979.

Newsweek, February 10, 1964. "Don't Fence Him In."

————. August 1, 1966. "The Ladies, God Bless 'Em, of the Executive Suite."

New York Times, June 11, 1975. Obit., Mrs. Felix Frankfurter.

————. December 13, 1977. Obit., Lady Spencer-Churchill.

————. June 7, 1968. Obit., Randolph Churchill.

————. January 14, 1979. "What's an Entrepreneur," essays by five men (Kroc, R., Honda, S., Little, R., Gordy, B., Olson, K.).

Noda, Mitz. "Business Management in Japan." *Technology Review*, June/July 1979, pp. 20–30.

Norton, A. L. "The Family Life Cycle Updated." *Selected Studies in Man and the Family*, March 1974.

Odlum, Dr. Doris. "Should Forrester Jeopardize His Job to Save His Marriage?" *International Management*, May 1977.

Orden, S. R., and Bradburn, N. M. "Working Wives and Marriage Happiness." *American Journal of Sociology*, Vol. 74, No. 4 (1969), pp. 392–407.

Packard, Vance. *The Sexual Wilderness*. New York: David McKay Co., 1968.

Papanek, H. "Men, Women and Work: Reflections on the Two-Person Career." *American Journal of Sociology*, Vol. 78, No. 4 (1973), pp. 852–872.

Pett, Saul. "Comments and Opinion" (President Carter profile). Associated Press in *Los Angeles Herald Examiner*, October 23, 1977.

Playboy magazine. December, 1977, interview with John Denver.

Poloma, M., and Garland, T. "The Married Professional Woman— A Study in Tolerance of Domestication." *Journal of Marriage and Family*, Vol. 33, No. 3 (1971), pp. 531–540.

————. "Toward a Theory of Career Development for Women." *Personnel & Guidance Journal*, Vol. 47, No. 7 (1969), pp. 660–664.

Ramey, J. W. "Communes, Group Marriages and the Upper Middle-Class." *Journal of Marriage and the Family*, Vol. 34 (1972), pp. 647–655.

Ramirez, Anthony. "A Manager's Transfers Impose a Heavy Burden on His Wife and Children." *Wall Street Journal*, February 28, 1979.

Rapoport, Rhona. "The Dual Career Family." *Human Relations*, Vol. 22 (1969), pp. 3–30.

————. "Further Consideration on the Dual Career Family." *Human Relations*, Vol. 24, No. 6 (1971), pp. 519–533.

Rapoport, Rhona and Robert. "Early and Later Experiences as Determinants of Adult Behavior: Women, Family and Career Patterns." *British Journal of Sociology*, Vol. 22, No. 1 (March 1971).

Ricklefs, Roger. "Firms Become Willing—or Eager—to Hire Divorced Executives." *Wall Street Journal*, May 18, 1978.

Ridley, C. A. "Exploring the Impact of Work Satisfaction and Involvement on Marital Interaction When Both Partners Are Employed." *Journal of Marriage and the Family*, Vol. 35, No. 2 (May 1973), pp. 229–237.

Riley, L. E., and Spreitzer, E. A. "A Model for the Analysis of Lifetime Marriage Patterns." *Journal of Marriage and the Family*, February 1974, pp. 64–70.

Roberts, W. R. "Executive Wives and Trouble." *Dun's Review*, January 1965, pp. 34–35, 75–76.

Robins, James. (Wall Street Journal-Ottaway News Service). "Sweetened Relocation Benefits Making Moving Easier." *Pocono Record*, May 8, 1977.

Roosevelt, James, with Libby, Bill. *My Parents: a Differing View*. New York: Playboy Press, 1976.

Rosen, B., Jerdee, T., and Prestwick, T. "Dual Career Marital Adjustment." *Journal of Marriage and the Family*, Vol. 37, No. 3 (August 1975), pp. 365–372.

Royal Bank of Canada, Monthly Letter, January 1979. "The Act of Listening."

Rule, Sheila. "Long Distance Marriage On the Rise." *New York Times*, October 29, 1978.

Russell, Bertrand. *Power*. London: Allen & Unwin, Ltd.; New York: Barnes & Noble, 1962.

Saikowski, Charlotte. "Cinderella Doesn't Live Here Anymore." *Christian Science Monitor*, October 17, 1978.

———. "Who Will Raise the Children?" *Christian Science Monitor*, October 18, 1978.

Saline, Carol. "A Marriage That Made It . . . and One That Didn't." *Working Woman*, February 1977.

Sawhill, Isabel V. Paper: "Are Homemakers an Endangered Species?" The Urban Institute, Washington, D.C., 1977.

Sawhill, Isabel, and Moore, Kristin A. "Implications of Women's Employment for Home and Family Life." Paper prepared for the American Assembly volume: *Women in the American Economy*. August 1975.

Schuyten, Peter J. "A Sure-Footed Climb to the Top." *New York Times*, December 10, 1978.

Sease, Douglas R. "Women at Work." *Wall Street Journal*, September 19, 1978.

Seidenberg, R. *Corporate Wives—Corporate Casualties?* New York: American Management, 1973.

Sennett, R., and Cobb, J. *The Hidden Injuries of Class.* New York: Alfred A. Knopf, Inc., 1972.

Sheehy, Gail. *Passages—Predictable Crises of Adult Life.* New York: E. P. Dutton & Co., 1976.

Silber, Dr. Mark B. "The Corporate Wife." *Agri Marketing,* May 1970.

Singh, K. P. "Career and Family." *Indian Journal of Social Work,* Vol. 33, No. 3 (October 1972), pp. 277–281.

Snyder, David P. "The Family in Post-Industrial America." Paper, February 16, 1978.

Sostek, A., and Sherman, S. "Report on children of executives." *Behavioral Sciences,* August 8, 1977.

Stackton, William. "Celebrating Einstein." *New York Times Magazine,* February 18, 1979.

Steiner, J. "What Price Sucess?" *Harvard Business Review,* Vol. 50, No. 2 (1972), pp. 69–74.

Sussman, M. B., and Cogswell, B. E. "Family Influences on Job Movement." *Human Relations,* Vol. 24 (1971), pp. 477–487.

Swanberg, W. A. *Luce and His Empire.* New York: Charles Scribner's Sons, 1972.

Thomas, Bob. *Walt Disney.* New York: Simon & Schuster, 1976.

Thompson, Barbara, and Finlayson, Angela. "Married Women Who Work in Early Motherhood." *British Journal of Sociology,* Vol. 14, pp. 15–168.

Time magazine, December 3, 1965. "Millionaires—How They Do It."

———, October 7, 1974. "The Relentless Ordeal of Political Wives" (cover story).

———, April 4, 1977. Article on James Schlesinger.

Tobias, Andrew. *Fire and Ice.* New York: William Morrow, 1976.

Tolchin, Martin. "Rosalynn Carter: An Advisor in Her Own Right." *New York Times,* May 30, 1979.

TWA Ambassdor magazine, May 1977. "Pursuing Dad's Career."

Tyler, Marianne. "Working Couples: A System of Checks and Balances." *Los Angeles Herald Examiner,* October 23, 1977.

Vandervelde, Maryanne. *The Changing Life of the Corporate Wife.* New York: Atheneum, 1979.

Wagner, Abe (Director, T.A.C., Denver, Colorado). "The Executive and His Wife—a Sound Partnership." Professional paper, 1978.

Waik, L. J. "Working Wives, 1940–1960." *American Sociological Review*, Vol. 41, No. 2 (1976), pp. 65–80.

Walker, E. J. "Till Business Us Do Part?" *Harvard Business Review*, Vol. 54, No. 1 (1976), pp. 94–101.

Whalen, Richard J. *The Founding Father—The Story of Joseph P. Kennedy*. New York: New American Library, 1964.

Whitney, General Courtney. *MacArthur: His Rendezvous with History*. New York: Alfred A. Knopf, 1956. © Time, Inc. All rights reserved.

Whyte, William H., Jr. *The Organization Man*. New York: Simon & Schuster, 1956.

Winter, David G. *The Power Motive*. New York: Free Press, 1973.

Yankelovich, Skelly & White, Inc. "Raising Children in a Changing Society." *The American Family Report*, General Mills, Inc., 1977.

Zemon-Gass, Gertrude, and Nichols, William. "Take Me Along—A Marital Syndrome." *Journal of Marriage & Family Counseling*, Vol. 1, No. 3 (July 1975), pp. 209–217.

Zytowski, Donald G. "Toward a Theory of Career Development for Women." *Personnel and Guidance Journal*, Vol. 47, No. 7 (1969), pp. 660–664.

Index